OFF THE RECORD

Caroline ADDERSON / Kristyn DUNNION / Cynthia FLOOD
Shaena LAMBERT / Elise LEVINE / Kathy PAGE

OFF THE RECORD

Edited by
JOHN
METCALF

BIBLIOASIS
Windsor,
Ontario

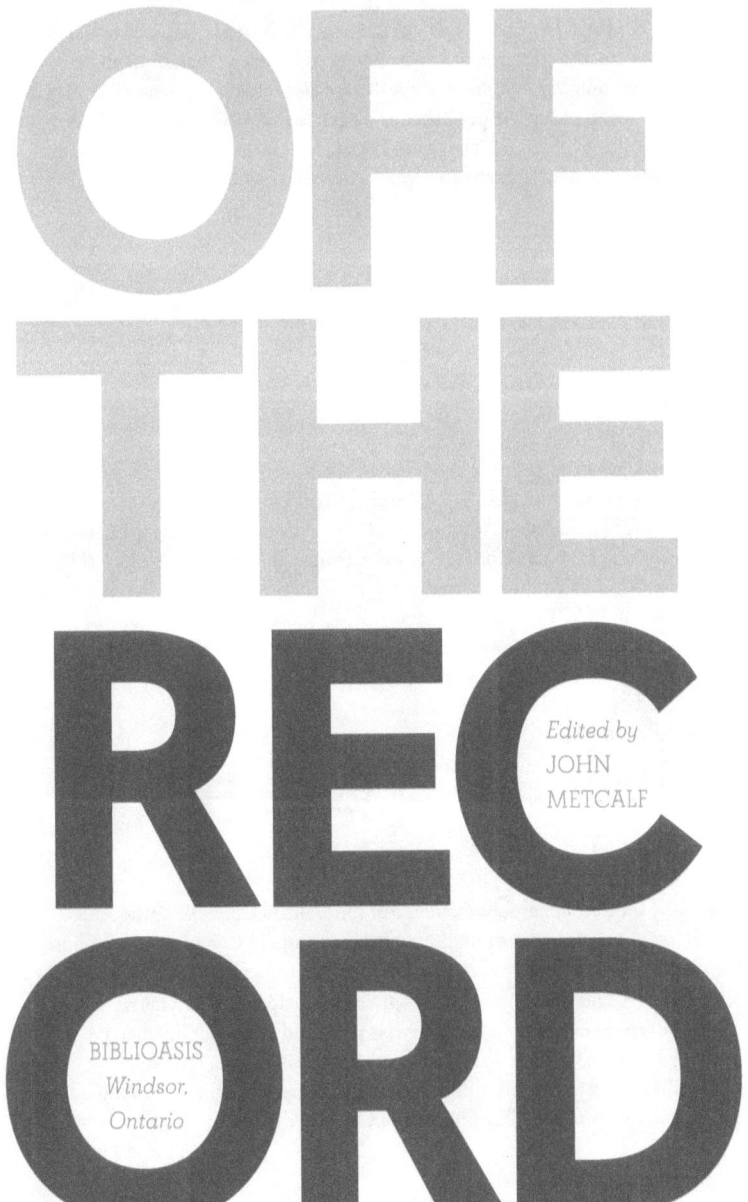

FIRST EDITION
10 9 8 7 6 5 4 3 2 1

Library and Archives Canada Cataloguing in Publication
Title: Off the record / Caroline Adderson, Kristyn Dunnion, Cynthia Flood,
Shaena Lambert, Elise Levine, Kathy Page ; edited by John Metcalf.
Other titles: Off the record (2023)
Names: Metcalf, John, 1938- editor.
Identifiers: Canadiana (print) 20230510345 | Canadiana (ebook) 20230510396 | ISBN
9781771965453 (softcover) | ISBN 9781771965460 (EPUB)
Subjects: LCSH: Fiction—Authorship. | CSH: Authors, Canadian (English)—
Interviews. | CSH: Short stories, Canadian (English)—21st century. | LCGFT:
Interviews. | LCGFT: Short stories.
Classification: LCC PN3355 .O34 2023 | DDC 808.3—dc23

Edited by John Metcalf
Copyedited by Emily Donaldson
Cover and text designed by Vanessa Stauffer

Published with the generous assistance of the Canada Council for the Arts, which last year invested $153 million to bring the arts to Canadians throughout the country, and the financial support of the Government of Canada. Biblioasis also acknowledges the support of the Ontario Arts Council (OAC), an agency of the Government of Ontario, which last year funded 1,709 individual artists and 1,078 organizations in 204 communities across Ontario, for a total of $52.1 million, and the contribution of the Government of Ontario through the Ontario Book Publishing Tax Credit and Ontario Creates.

PRINTED AND BOUND IN CANADA

CONTENTS

FOREWORD

JOHN METCALF, EDITOR

The listing of authors is alphabetical. The contributions were elicited in every case by continuing questions. To leave in the questions once they'd been answered seemed to me rather like leaving up unsightly scaffolding when the building was finished so I removed them all enabling the responses to flow as seemingly unprompted narrative.

My starting point with all six was to dig into what had lured them into this writing life. I wanted them to recall the books that had thrilled them, the vistas that painting and music had opened up for them, the time when language had first exploded upon them. I wanted them to reveal how, hoping against hope, they slowly became citizens in that other country, how, slowly, they learned its arcane laws and customs, and then learned enough to break them.

I'll let Elise Levine speak for all in this lovely excerpt in which she's recalling her fifteen-year-old self.

FIFTEEN!

I don't date during my high school years. Instead I have my other best friend.

Her father is the literature and film officer for the Ontario Arts Council, separated from her mother when my friend is maybe in third grade. By high school this friend and I are skipping classes to hang out downtown at the Royal Ontario Museum, the Art Gallery of Ontario. We peruse books at the grungy, dimly lit former Central Toronto Public Library on College Street—where late one winter afternoon I pull a copy of Samuel Beckett's prose trilogy off the shelf and read the first few pages of *Molloy*, skip to the opening of *Malone Dies* and the first page or so of *The Unnamable*. The top of my head catches fire and blows off.

I've already been reading George Orwell, Aldous Huxley, browsing the Penguin Classics at the Coles bookstore in my neighbourhood. I adore Mervyn Peake's *Gormenghast* gothic fantasy novels. At fourteen I'd read Tom Wolfe's performative, strutting *The Electric Kool-Aid Acid Test*, discovered it at another friend's house, something her older sister had to read for a class and hated and donated to me when I pawed the cover and admiringly scanned a few pages.

But oh, Beckett: I sign the book out and in its highly pressured, precise language, its elliptical, disintegrative approach to narrative, its treatment of character psychologically *in extremis* and ultra-compressed interiority, I truly uncover a path. Techniques, methods. I read his plays and attend productions of them by tiny Toronto theatre companies who offer student tickets for a song. In his works I find a means with which to capture the psychic and emotional states of betweenness, constraint, defiance, the craft involved in giving shape to the tension between the abjection of self-exile and the unyielding human voice. I grasp how what is not said on the page can speak volumes: how silence itself can render an eloquent and moving subtext, and wrenchingly convey the unspeakable. I locate the effects of a dark humour, with its underlying austere pathos and compassion. I discover a deeply immersive technique that functions as a possibility space.

Each time I crack the spine of his prose trilogy, especially, I feel I'm holding self-knowledge, an eerie sense of the future, in my hands. *This* is it. What I want to do.

CAROLINE ADDERSON

CAROLINE ADDERSON *is the author of five novels* (A History of Forgetting, Sitting Practice, The Sky Is Falling, Ellen in Pieces, A Russian Sister), *two collections of short stories* (Bad Imaginings, Pleased to Meet You) *as well as many books for young readers. She is also the editor and co-contributor of a non-fiction book of essays and photographs,* Vancouver Vanishes: Narratives of Demolition and Revival *and guest editor of* Best Canadian Stories 2019. *Her work has received numerous award nominations including the* Sunday Times EFG Private Bank Short Story Award, *the International* IMPAC Dublin Literary Award, *two Commonwealth Writers' Prizes, the Governor General's Literary Award, the Rogers' Trust Fiction Prize, and the Scotiabank Giller Prize longlist. In 2017, she was a* YWCA Women of Distinction Award for Arts, Culture and Design *nominee. Her awards include three* BC Book Prizes, *three* CBC Literary Awards, *the Marian Engel Award for mid-career achievement, and a National Magazine Award Gold Medal for Fiction. She teaches in the Writing and Publishing Program at* SFU *and is the Program Director of the Writing Studio at the Banff Centre for Arts and Creativity.*

TINKERING

My parents. My father was born in Birtle, Manitoba, in 1928. Apparently, his father was a "home child"—essentially an indentured child labourer brought to Canada to escape poverty in England. (I've only made a cursory effort to confirm this.) Whether he was or not, he died when my father was an infant, leaving my grandmother destitute. She later remarried and had several more children.

When I first learned that my father had had a stepfather (associating "step" with fairy tale nastiness), I asked if he'd been mistreated. He admitted that he had been. Maybe this was partly to blame for the bouts of severe depression he suffered all his life. During my childhood he was mainly in the background, brush-cut, hard-working, and fastidious, remote and slightly odd, but not unkind. He was very much of his generation, quiet about both his troubles and his achievements, which were significant on both counts. He could fix anything, and at the age of fourteen rigged up a wind generator to power the family's rural home. His various other adolescent jobs were general store clerk, stooker (I love this job! I love this *word*!), and butcher's delivery boy. He enrolled in a correspondence course in "electrical installations," became an electrician's helper at sixteen and later went on to earn a degree in electrical engineering from the University of Manitoba, then a master's of engineering from McGill University, in Montreal, which was where he met my mother. He worked for Dow Chemical for most of his professional life, first in Sarnia (where, coincidentally, my future father-in-law was also employed), then Fort Saskatchewan, Alberta. I know these early details about my father because he wrote out his life story a few years before he died in 2013. My mother predeceased him by four years. After her death, he had a breakdown and while hospitalized was diagnosed as being "on the autism spectrum," which explained a lot.

My mother was a much more forceful presence in my childhood, my whole life actually. I managed to dig up some notes I took in my twenties when I got her to sketch out her family tree. She was born in 1930 in Sioux Lookout, into a family that came from Co. Monaghan, Ireland and settled first in the Eastern Townships of Quebec. She left home at seventeen with a grade 12 education and some business courses under her belt, possibly because she hated her father. (She confided this to me once, also that she married my father because he was the opposite of hers.) She first worked for Hudson's Bay in Winnipeg for their unfortunately-named magazine, *The Beaver*, and later moved to Montreal, where she worked as a stenographer for the CNR.

I think those Montreal years were her best, when she was living her single independent life in a glamorous city. I have photographs of her standing on the steps of the apartment she shared with girlfriends in Westmount, looking stylish in a long coat, and another of a group of elegantly dressed women out for dinner at Au Lutin Qui Bouffe, where a piglet would be carried from table to table for diners to feed from a baby bottle. My mother met my father at a party in Montreal and thus, I fear, ended her happiness. They left Montreal for Edmonton, then Sarnia, then to a new housing development in Sherwood Park, Alberta—all a far cry from Montreal. She became a suburban housewife. Her first baby was stillborn. Then my sister was born. I came three years later.

When I think of what I know of her life, I see it as part Mavis Gallant, part Alice Munro (two writers she loved). First she was Gallant's stylish Berthe Carette, a career woman who puts on her earrings first thing upon waking, then takes out her curlers and passes them to her sister in the opposite bed. But after marriage she became one of Munro's stymied protagonists, intelligent and witty, held back by societal expectations of women in the fifties, and the fact that she could never have afforded a university education.

I certainly inherited my artistic streak from my mother, who dabbled in several artistic pastimes, among them painting, drawing, and that 1970s craze—*découpage*. She was an avid smoker and avid reader. But she was also frustrated and often angry, and no wonder, living with an emotionally remote man in a cultural backwater. There was also mental illness on her side of the family, which eventually led to our estrangement from all our relatives, a situation I knew nothing about until I was an adult.

In short, Tolstoy was right. But I was for a long time sheltered from, or oblivious to, the unhappiness. Sherwood Park, which could not technically be considered a town because it had no main street, was not so terrible to a child. For one thing, it was much more rural at that time. Farmland separated it from the refineries on the outskirts of Edmonton. Additionally, our housing development was surrounded by a golf course, which may as well have been a vast playground. Behind our fence were woods where we practically lived. They opened onto a fairway, which was thrilling to cross. Always the chance that we'd get brained by a golf ball! We could cross-country ski in the winter and there was a large pond in the middle, which was our outdoor skating rink. The golf course also offered an entrepreneurial opportunity; we would collect lost balls in the woods and sell them to golfers out of egg cartons. For quite a few years new houses were still being built in our development so we spent many wonderful hours monkeying around on construction sites where no child would be allowed to set foot today. But this was the seventies and we just walked out of the house in the morning and came home to eat and nobody cared.

As for what I was "intended to be," I have no idea beyond the fact that my father insisted my sister and I go to university, though this was not expressed until closer to the time. He also stressed that he didn't want us to be dependent on men, which was a surprisingly advanced idea for that period. He especially wanted us to do well at school; my sister, who is now a paediatric specialist in infectious diseases, complied. I couldn't have cared less.

While I enjoyed learning, I remember that the social aspect of school was the main draw for me in those early years. Generally, television made a bigger impact on me than reading, though I have memories of being read to by my mother and loving the physical closeness of it. We had the complete twelve-volume set of the 1950s edition of *My Book House*, with illustrations I pored over. I also loved *The Golden Treasury of Poetry*; again, the illustrations were as much a draw as the poems. *Winnie-the-Pooh*, *The Wind in the Willows*, *The Kingdom of Carbonel*, *Anne of Green Gables* (all the Anne books, actually), *The Black Stallion*, *Black Beauty*, Beverly Cleary, *Harriet the Spy*; in other words, the sort of books every girl in the 1970s read. I was completely ordinary.

Being hard-working and disciplined are, I think, character traits I got from my father. Or maybe I saw my mother's frustration at being purposeless. My sister was always thus, but it only kicked in for me when I was diagnosed with thyroid cancer at fifteen. I used to think it was the cancer that changed me, but later I saw the same thing in my son, an uninspired student until grade eleven, when he began parking himself nightly at the dining room table to study.

Discipline is quite a different thing from ambition. I've always put my personal relationships before my career, including my publishing relationships. In fact, the one time I decided to put career first (when, on the advice of a newly acquired agent, I broke with my first publisher, the Porcupine's Quill) I was traumatized . . . literally for *life*. Patrick Crean rescued me and I've followed him from one publishing house to another ever since without shopping my books to other publishers. Spending all those years at Key Porter and Thomas Allen out of loyalty probably sealed my fate as a B-list writer. The other unambitious choice I consistently made was to write things I was interested in without regard to whether or not readers would be.

The tussle with cancer definitely shocked me out of my former self. I went from being peer-oriented, highly social, and somewhat rebellious, to studious and serious. I started reading adult books while I was recovering from surgery, mainly the classics that were on our shelves, supplemented by biographies from the Sherwood Park library. I remember loving Dostoyevsky, Hemingway, Thoreau, J D Salinger. I once brought *Sons and Lovers* to school and left it on my desk to impress my English teacher, who tapped it and said I should be sure to read it again when I could understand it. She was right, of course; I was merely trying to be a serious, artistic person.

I also took ballet and piano (I was terrible at both), painting and pottery. Some of these classes were at the U of A; we had to go into Edmonton for anything cultural. My mother often took me to the Citadel Theatre because I loved drama; I won "Best High School Actor" in a provincial competition. I was crafty, too,

sewing my own clothes, knitting, spinning wool, even concoct-
ing my own natural dyes. I made Ukrainian Easter Eggs and muk-
luks. It seems that I experimented with every possible artistic
pursuit *except* writing. Possibly this was because almost everyone
I read was dead and male. Munro and Gallant came later.

Of course I wanted out of Sherwood Park after high school. I
was accepted into the department of fine arts at the University
of Alberta, but at the same time was chosen to participate in
Katimavik, a nine-month volunteer program that sent groups
of French and English youth to three different communities in
Canada, one of them Francophone. I opted for life experience
over art school. That decision led to my complete transformation
from a suburban artiste wanna-be to a feminist, peace activist
vegetarian. My mother was furious.

During Katimavik I lived in Kaslo, BC, working in construction; New Ross, NS, building log cabins on a Mi'kmaq reserve;
and Rouyn-Noranda, working at a co-op radio station where I had
to twist my Anglophone tongue around "Abitibi-Témiscamingue"
whenever I identified the station. In each of these places we had
a billeting period in the community as well, so in addition to
those miscellaneous jobs I wasn't particularly adept at, I also
spent time on a sheep farm, in a Quaker off-grid intentional
community, and with the family of a prominent peace activist
and feminist. After Katimavik, I went down to New York City
and took part in the million-strong march in Central Park supporting the UN Second Special Session on Disarmament. The
rest of that summer I spent in Philadelphia living in a "community" associated with the Quakers. I had hoped from there to
become a commune-hopping vagabond, but my father sent me
a letter threatening to disown me if I didn't come back and go
to university. (So I was not as rebellious and free-spirited as I
imagined.) I did refuse to go back to Alberta though, and instead

applied to UBC because some Katimavik friends were going to Vancouver and offered me a room in their house.

In some ways I wasted my university years. I had a full scholarship thanks to Dow Chemical. Yet I chose Education, which was laughably easy. I did take a couple of elective courses that were formative: Biblical and Mythological Roots in English Literature, where I read *Paradise Lost* and Ovid, and Introduction to Slavonic Studies. Both were taught by charismatic professors; the latter, Dr Peter Petro, is the model for the professor in my novel *The Sky Is Falling*. His course infected me with a lifelong passion for Russian literature. I also have to tip my hat to my required English 100 course, during which I discovered that Canadian writers actually existed. Not counting *Anne of Green Gables* and *The Secret World of Og*, the first Canadian books I read were *Obasan* and *The Wars*. Though I haven't read them since (intentionally) and can't say if they would satisfy my current aesthetic tastes, I vividly remember the experience of reading them, *Obasan* in particular. I was on a ferry coming home from a cycling trip on the Gulf Islands when I sobbingly turned the last page. Months later, I attend a reading by Joy Kogawa. I was sitting in an aisle seat and she passed close enough for me to touch her sleeve. I was awed. Yet it still didn't occur to me to try writing myself.

Now comes the embarrassing confession: why I actually did start writing. In my third year of university a new roommate, Roger, an American doing his PhD in something scientific, moved into our shared house. In hindsight, he was an interesting guy, or maybe it's just that he was the first person I met in possession of a *New Yorker* subscription. Regrettably, he disliked my cat, Minou Pushkin LeFou, who, I grant you, had some unappealing traits (a friend once told me he was the only cat she'd ever met who looked *greasy*). Roger mainly took umbrage at the fleas and would squash them and leave them on my pillow—ah, the joys of communal living!

One day I came home to Roger waving around a letter he'd received from *The New Yorker*. He'd pitched them (ha ha) a story about a woman's softball team. The letter basically said, "go ahead and write the story," giving no promises at all. They still do send genteel replies; I've received a few of them. Anyway, Roger strutted about like this was an acceptance letter and (probably intentionally) stepped on my cat while he was at it. And I thought, *Roger* is a writer?

I was a prolific letter-writer at the time and had always been complimented on their entertainment value. If Roger the Cat Hater could be a writer, so could I. The next day I phoned the creative writing department at UBC, found out what I needed to apply, dashed off some appalling poems and anecdotes, and was shortly accepted into, not the introductory class I'd applied for, but a 300-level class. Take that, Roger, wherever you are!

So a combination of egotism and revenge had brought me into the creative writing department, a dusty hallway of seminar rooms and offices, and a lounge full of vinyl furniture draped with affected student poets (unchanged when I taught there twenty years later). I found I liked it. The workshops and the lively, dusty atmosphere of the department were so invigorating compared to the insipid playground of my education classes. At the end of my first course, I switched my minor to creative writing, which brought me together with the first person who seriously encouraged me as a writer, Andreas Schroeder. I was still a hairy-legged peace activist at the time and Andreas was the perfect model, a motorcycle-riding Mennonite who had served time for drug smuggling, utterly passionate about Canadian writing, generous and eloquent. And he wore sleeve garters! I remember going to see him in his office and asking what I should read. He rattled off a list of names. At that time I had started keeping a reading log, a running list of every book I read (I've kept this up and have since transcribed it on my website, for anyone who may be interested).

My Canadian reading starts in 1985:

28. Marie-Claire Blaise, *Nights in the Underground*
29. Alice Munro, *Something I've Been Meaning to Tell You*
30. Alice Munro, *Who Do You Think You Are?*
31. Alice Munro, *Dance of the Happy Shades*.

Out of the Canadians, Atwood came up next, then Andreas Schroeder himself, followed by Audrey Thomas, Sandra Birdsell, Marian Engel, and Mavis Gallant. I was in good hands.

In addition to introducing me to Canadian writing, Andreas personally encouraged me in numerous ways. He had judged a fiction contest in which I was a winner (before I met him). At the end of the year, the last day of class in fact, he told me I should apply for a Canada Council grant. "What's the Canada Council?" I asked. He led me to the office, drew the yellowed file card out of the little plastic box the department secretary kept on her desk, on which the address of the Canada Council was manually typed, and copied it down for me. I applied. He wrote me a glowing letter of reference. While my later efforts at securing Canada Council funds were often futile (the more I improved as an artist, the less likely I was to get a grant, or so it seemed), I got this one. I was therefore spared the ordeal of teaching public school in New Orleans, where I went next. I probably would not have survived that.

The previous summer I had studied French in Quebec and started a relationship with a man from New Orleans. We carried on long distance until I graduated. Then I moved down south to be with him. As is often the case with these summer affairs, once we were under the same roof—it was a great roof, in a shotgun house on the ironically named Melpomene Avenue—our incompatibility became painfully clear. For one, we didn't share a sense of humour. There is no greater hell for a funny person to have her jokes continuously met with blankness or even sneers. In the long run, he wasn't important, but the experience of the city was.

I had my grant that allowed me to write all day long. I also tried to make literary connections. There was a literary magazine run by a fabulous woman (first name Lee, last forgotten, along with the name of the magazine) who lived in the French Quarter and had her office in a carriage house in the back. (It may have been the old slave quarters, I'm appalled to realize only now.) Anyway, she was large and dramatically draped and would read the submissions in an antique barber's chair (a detail I bequeathed to Ellen, in *Ellen in Pieces*). I would come round a couple of times a month and assist her. I also noted the local writers who submitted and contacted them about exchanging stories because I badly missed the community I had developed at UBC. I would walk or ride my bike around the city during the day. At night, you couldn't even leave the house because of the crime. It was hideously hot. The cockroaches were enormous and everywhere, even in posh banks and stores. I used to knock on the drawers and cupboards before I opened them, so I wouldn't be met with a six-legged surprise. Yet the architecture, the ambience, the food, and yes, the writing were indeed wonderful. I read Faulkner, Flannery O'Connor, Eudora Welty, Grace King, Ellen Gilchrist, Katherine Anne Porter, Shirley Ann Grau.

Our apartment was one of four in a pair of connected houses, meaning our balcony abutted our white neighbour's. She showed me the gun she kept on her bedside table. When a Black professional couple moved in across the street, she was apoplectic. My boyfriend's sister's fiancé would bring up the Civil War at every family gathering and jaw on about Yankee carpetbaggers (imagine being related to *that!*). Even if the relationship hadn't fizzled, the violence and racism would have caused me to leave the city eventually.

I returned to Sherwood Park and lived for a couple of months with my parents, which was utterly humiliating. I had nothing in common with my former high school friends; my father glowered whenever he saw me, his fallen daughter. Even worse, I imagined that I had actually finished the collection of stories I had been working on in New Orleans. I sent it off to many, many publishers, all of whom rejected it by return post. I had no job, nothing to do but to keep poking at those terrible stories. I still had absolutely no idea how to write. I remember reading over a passage and thinking, "That's too weird." I backspaced away everything original, leaving only the banal and the clichéd.

I was finally saved when, somehow, I found out about the Banff Centre and a writing program called the May Writing Studios. It was seven weeks long and I had just enough money left over from the grant to pay for it. I applied and was accepted. I remember meekly entering the room where the welcome reception was held. Don Coles, the poetry editor, came over and, on connecting me with my application, heaped me with praise then shepherded me around the room introducing me to everyone. I was literally stunned. The stories I'd submitted were, of course, awful, but maybe not *comparatively* awful.

The Banff Centre was where I met my next champion, Adele Wiseman, director of the Writing Studio at the time. She took an almost maternal interest in me. I went around in a vintage suede jacket, the collar of which I turned up in a desperate attempt to seem arty. Every time I encountered Adele, she would turn down the collar and give it loving pat. The following year, 1987, she selected me to take part in the short-lived Canada-Ireland Artist Exchange Program, another life-changer. All this generous attention, yet at the time she was dying from a brain tumour and had to be driven to the hospital in the middle of the night for intravenous painkillers.

I went back to the Writing Studio in 1991, after Adele had died and the wonderful Rachel Wyatt had taken over. Our cohort that year included Anne Carson, Michael Redhill, Steven Heighton, Karen Connolly, and many others who went on to become published and even well-known authors (famous in the case of Carson). Some became lifelong friends. This was when I really found my groove with the writing. It was quite magical. For example, I remember being on the volleyball court when, mid-game, it suddenly came to me how I could rewrite a story I'd been suffering over. I just walked off the court, ignoring the protestations of my teammates, and back to my room, where I started condensing what had been forty pages into ten. That was "The Chmarnyk."

In the end it took about eight years to write *Bad Imaginings* instead of the nine months I had proposed in that long-ago grant. Along the way most of the stories were published in literary magazines, as well as in *Saturday Night* and the Oberon Press anthology *Coming Attractions '92*. How they came together as a collection was through Steven Heighton, whom I'd met at the Writing Studio in 1991. He had published his wonderful book *Flight Paths of the Emperor* in 1992 with the Porcupine's Quill when John Metcalf was the editor there. I think Steve actually sent some of my stories to Metcalf; I don't recall submitting them formally myself. John Metcalf phoned me up and offered to publish the book. I said, "Sure!"

I remember being slightly disappointed by the editorial process because Steve had promised that John would write excoriating commentary all over the manuscript. Steve revelled in these baroque insults. But John was very kind to me and mostly said, "Anything more?" Only once did I receive the coveted abuse. I phoned John with a timid editorial question when he was obviously several sheets to the wind because he listened patiently, sighed voluminously, then said, "Caroline, you go ahead and do whatever the fuck you want," and hung up. I treasure that exchange to this day.

Published in 1993, *Bad Imaginings* did extremely well for the time. "The Chmarnyk" and "The Hanging Gardens of Babylon" had both won CBC Literary Awards. There were nominations for the Journey Prize and a National Magazine Award. The collection as a whole was a 1993 Governor General's Literary Award nominee, which was the only national literary award at the time, as well as a 1994 Commonwealth Writers' Prize nominee. *Bad Imaginings* won the 1994 Ethel Wilson Fiction Prize. Stories from it went on to be included in fifteen anthologies world-wide. Not only was I still doing readings from the book years after it was published, I accumulated a thick folder of reviews. Imagine! All that coverage for a first-time author's small press collection of short stories!

·

The last stories I wrote for *Bad Imaginings* were the longest ones, so I decided, timidly again, that I would expand myself lengthwise. I'd try the novella form. Around that time I read an article in *The New Yorker* about the ethical considerations of preserving and displaying the hair at the Auschwitz Museum. The first thing that struck me was: why hadn't I known about this room full of hair? I set out to explore this vague idea without any clear idea of where the search would lead. All I knew was that I didn't want to write about the Jewish experience of the Holocaust; it wasn't my place to and besides, it had been, and continues to be, explored as a subject by writers who *are* qualified. Instead, I began thinking about the hair and who cares about hair, which led me to my characters: two hairdressers who make a pilgrimage to the museum. About six months into the writing, I realized with horror that what I was working on was actually a novel.

Fifteen years after the publication of what became *A History of Forgetting*—the novel having fallen out of print when its publisher, Key Porter, closed shop—Biblioasis republished it in a revised version for their Reset series. At the time I was asked by *Canadian Notes and Queries* to reread and write about a book that had been important in my life. I thought my own first novel might be a fitting subject. What I wrote best summarizes the novel's troubled history.

A HISTORY OF A HISTORY OF FORGETTING

from Canadian Notes and Queries,
Number 93, 2015

This book has baggage. Or rather, I have baggage concerning this book, a steamer trunk full of bad, bad feelings about almost everything to do with it: the research, the writing, the publishing (especially the publishing), the critical response it received.

It was my first novel. I know what you're thinking: *First novel? Say no more!* But not every first-time novelist is as miserable as I was. Some tap out a work of brilliance on their first try: Mary Shelley, Françoise Sagan, Zadie Smith. Others have, of course, painfully abandoned early work, which just about happened to *A History of Forgetting*. For most of the fifteen years since its publication, I've sort of wished I *had* given up on it, except I'd probably have given up on writing as well. Instead, I've been dragging this steamer trunk around, opening it for anyone who asked. But what I haven't done until now was open that damn book. So let me unpack the trunk one last time, then I'll tell you what I think.

I heft the lid. A bitter, self-pitying odour rises up. Ugh! I reach in, grab the Challenge of the Form.

In 1994, when I began *A History of Forgetting*, I was a young short-story writer facing down the proverbial Loose Baggy Monster. I decided that my best course of action was to get the novel out onto the page however I could. And so I wrote, and wrote, every day, all day, except holidays and weekends. Words, words, words—a long limp string of them. What I didn't understand was that a novel is a dramatic form, that it's constructed in scenes. I was essentially writing a very long short story from which it took more than three frustrating, dispiriting years to untangle myself. Until then I kept on writing, word after joyless word.

I reach into the trunk again. This time I pull out Difficult Subject Matter. Difficult Subject Matter is what sensible authors save for their prime, when they have several books behind them and the necessary technical mastery. *A History of Forgetting* concerns two hairdressers who make a pilgrimage to the Auschwitz Museum. It explores how history ripples out and affects (or doesn't) people in another time and place, and the role compassion plays in memory. While not about the Holocaust per se, the Holocaust is the central motif and, in a way, the central event. In other words, for my very first attempt at a novel I picked a subject that has been thoroughly explored by exceedingly more qualified people, about which I couldn't hope to add much wisdom, one that required me to submerge myself for *years* in the darkest period of modern history.

And look. Along with Difficult Subject Matter comes the Bad Trip. They go together. My original idea was to research the novel from the Spartan comforts of my East Vancouver apartment, but I soon realized that the Auschwitz Museum was unimaginable. Today you can take a virtual tour, but this was the pre-internet world, a world that forced actual experiences on you, whether you wanted them or not. I won't elaborate on the Bad Trip here, or describe what a bitter and begrimed place Poland was in 1994. It's in the book, every word of it true. Some things you can't make up.

There's still more in my trunk, including what I find most painful to draw into the light: Fraught Publication.

For most of the writing of *A History of Forgetting* I had a tireless champion in John Metcalf, my editor at the Porcupine's Quill. As I grew more doubtful, John's enthusiasm only redoubled. Here are some of his comments from 1995:

> *You mustn't worry about your rate of progress … You say you've only got 26 pages. But I would reply: 'Ah, yes. But they're* ADDERSON *pages.'*

> *I send you support and encouragement by brain-beam every day.*

> *I've been absolutely unable to get out of my mind your hairdresser story. It is very rich and broodingly <u>dark</u>. So don't worry that you're <u>not</u> on the right track. It is hugely powerful.*

The Porcupine's Quill had ably published my first book, *Bad Imaginings*, in 1993. While I was perfectly satisfied, I had a writer friend, also a PQ author, with a legitimate complaint. They kept pushing his publication date back without the courtesy of informing him of the delay. The third time they did this, outraged on his behalf, I told him, "If they did that to *me*, I'd pull the book!" That's the thing about youth—you have extra energy for outrage. These days, I don't bother to enquire about publication dates. The box of books arrives. "Well, this is a surprise," I say. Not so then. I was easily fired up by injustice, probably more than usual because I was feeling so insecure.

In the summer of 1997, with *A History of Forgetting* supposedly finished and in production, I was about to get married.
Hoping to read through the proofs before the house filled up
with guests, I phoned the Porcupine's Quill to find out when
they would arrive.

"Oh, didn't anyone tell you? We've pushed back your pub date."

In my own defence I'll say that I was a stressed-out bride
who was quick to transfer her indignation for her friend to herself. *I'd pull the book*, I'd said. I didn't, not yet. Instead I contacted an agent who loved the book (she said). She *instructed* me to
pull it so she could place it with a publisher who would respect
me. There would be multiple offers, she breathlessly assured
me. That was when I pulled the book, when I had someone else
on whom I could blame my bad behaviour. I felt wretched and
John was heartbroken. Every night from the Napa Valley, where
we were on honeymoon, I phoned Vancouver to retrieve the
agent's messages about the multiple offers.

There were no messages.

When I returned home, honeymoon nearly spoiled by anxiety, I called for an update. All the big publishers had passed.
The agent suggested I borrow some stationery and send the
book out myself as she didn't have any more time for it.

So through my own egotism and hotheadedness, I'd lost not
only a publisher, but the only person who believed my novel
(and therefore *I*, the writer) had any merit. The only person
who would ever send me daily brain-beams of encouragement.
There I was, at the nadir of my writing life.

Except there turned out to be one other person who believed in me. Patrick Crean had heard that I had a novel
(obviously from all those publishers who'd rejected it) and he
contacted my too-busy agent and asked to see it. It wasn't ready,
in his opinion, but he said that he would be willing to work on

it with me. With gratitude to last a lifetime (Patrick and I have stuck together ever since), I signed with Somerville House. Shortly after, they filed for bankruptcy.

Would there be no end to my torment? Yes, but not for many more months. Eventually, Patrick Crean joined Key Porter who in 1999 finally published *A History of Forgetting*.

I'm digging down deeper in the trunk now. I'm pulling out the Reviews. *The Toronto Star* called *A History of Forgetting* "a disappointing failure." "Ho-hum, the Holocaust again," half of them seem to say. The headline in the *Globe and Mail* read "Another Bad Hair Day." I went to bed for a month. Well, I felt like it, but I'd had a baby by then. To this day I wonder, only half-jokingly, would I have survived my first novel if not for maternal instinct?

And now that I've picked out and shown you all these shameful scraps, I think you'll understand the reason I have baggage. Hiding underneath are good things, of course. For example, five months after its uneventful release, *A History of Forgetting* was nominated for the 2000 Rogers Writers' Trust Fiction Prize. I flew to Toronto for the award luncheon and while I was there, a fairy tale thing happened. A British publisher offered me a two-book deal. In pounds! Lots and lots of them! So Toronto was a Good Trip. Then came the Better Trip. In 2001, my British publisher flew me to London for the book's launch and a four-day publicity tour: an interview and excerpt in *The Independent*, a dozen radio and television spots, signings in bookshops. Everywhere I went, they told me, "Peter Carey was here last week." *I was following in the footsteps of Peter Carey!* Instead of feeling vindicated, I fretted that someone would phone Canada and find out I was a disappointing failure. All the British reviews were raves. Back home, a Canadian film-maker optioned the book, which gave me a little extra, much needed money for seven years. There were other nominations: the Ethel Wilson Fiction Prize, and the *prestigious* Guardian Bad Sex Award.

More than any other book of mine (there have been six now, as well as many for children), *A History of Forgetting* has resonated for readers. Some connect with the novel because they have, or had, a loved one suffering through Alzheimer's, or they appreciate my frank portrait of an aging gay couple. I fear, however, that I've let some of these readers down. I mean the ones who approach me at readings to say how much they loved the novel, to which I reply, "It's my *worst* book." Then I point to the steamer trunk, which I take everywhere with me.

I recognize the look on their faces then. I've had the same experience—been excited to meet an author, only to discover he's a dismissive jerk I wish I'd never met and will certainly never read again. The truth is that I could never fully enjoy or believe the good things that happened to *A History of Forgetting*, or appreciate the praise it finally did receive, with all that baggage I was dragging around. So it was with these kind readers in mind, the ones I had let down, that I suggested *A History of Forgetting* when Biblioasis approached me about rereleasing my out-of-print books.

Now, fifteen years after filling up that trunk, I've reread the novel. Twice. I found parts of it overwritten and overwrought. There was just too much damn theme. At every opportunity I pushed it, like an overeager mother with a homely daughter. "Here's my theme. Say something, honey." There were needless, distracting subplots. Also, while funny, it was *bleak*.

And how did I *feel* reading it after so long? Foolish. All those years ago, I was hurt by the unenthusiastic response the book received in Canada. I felt hard done by, unappreciated. But now I felt that I'd got exactly what I deserved. First this book tortured me, then it humbled me. I'll stuff that in the trunk, too, if there's any room left.

The good news was that much of the stuff I didn't like could be cut. I set to slashing. Midway, I took a four-day holiday, which was when a miracle occurred. During those four days, I thought obsessively about the novel. Not about the contents of the trunk, but the people in the book—Alison and Christian and Malcolm, especially Malcolm—and not the way a novelist does, but a *reader* might. I no longer saw them as my own creations, but as actual people in my life. People I cared about. This was what had happened for those readers who'd been moved by the book: they had felt compassion. I'd claimed that was my object yet failed to achieve it myself. Now, for the first time, I saw that the book just might transcend its many flaws, transcend them because of the very human, suffering people whose story it tells. And not only that. If it could transcend its flaws, and if I was now excising those flaws—or as many as I could find this time round—might the novel actually be half-decent?

You tell me.

.

Shortly after the fizzled release in Canada of A History of Forgetting, before the good things happened, I experienced a reckoning. I had a young baby and very little time. I was (and still am) married to an auteur filmmaker, meaning we couldn't survive on his income alone. Was it feasible to keep writing? Did I even want to anymore?

This was the period when Canadian literature had exploded internationally and it seemed that fame and fortune were hanging low off the tree just waiting for a Canadian novelist to wander past and pluck it—but not me. Though I only considered quitting long enough for mulishness to set in, this dark period allowed me to reconsider why I wrote. For success? How was that possible? As soon as you focus on the finished book and its certain glory (ha!) rather than the writing of it, you've doomed yourself. Ultimately, I decided to keep at it and make my continued development my objective. Back then, as now, I seem to learn more from failure than success.

Since A History of Forgetting dealt with such dark subject matter, I decided to write a novel that progressed toward joy, which naturally lead me to … spinal cord injury. And Buddhism. This mad choice of subject matter was influenced by the fact that I'd been working on a failed screenplay for a number of years that included these elements (as well as a pig that escaped from a slaughterhouse, which did not make it into the novel version.) As for what I "intended," this probably changed during the writing as it usually does. I never seem to have a clue what I'm really writing about until I've gone through several drafts. At the outset I just wanted to write a decent novel that wasn't plagued by a burdensome backstory. I also wanted to play with point of view and allow characters with a previously established point of view to have thoughts in each other's sections—sort of a merging of third person limited and omniscient. Later, I saw Sitting Practice as a companion piece to A History of Forgetting, which was essentially about empathy. Sitting Practice was about the inverse feeling: pity. Iliana becomes wheelchair-bound early in the novel. Other people's post-accident attitudes about her prove much more difficult to deal with than her actual disability.

Researching the novel was fascinating and rewarding. In a book about sci and female sexuality, I learned that women who are paralyzed still achieve orgasms. I then interviewed six women with sci by email over a nine-month period, asking questions about their lives pre- and post-accident, questions that gradually became more personal. At the time, I was occasionally prevented from accessing different streets and buildings myself because I had a baby in a stroller; this simple fact helped me identify much more with the main obstacle for people with mobility issues: accessibility. When I finished writing, I hired a local woman with sci to read the novel and make sure that I had succeeded in my portrait of Iliana. She found only two tiny technical errors concerning the functioning of the wheelchair, which was so gratifying. One of the great pleasures of writing, possibly the reason I still do it, is to enter the consciousness of people very different from me—the ultimate act of empathy.

The novel was published by Thomas Allen and Sons in Canada in 2003, where my editor Patrick Crean went after Key Porter folded, and by the UK publisher review as the second of my two-book deal there. Review did nothing to promote the book, but it did get quite a few wonderful reviews, including this one from *The Independent*: "It could just be that Adderson has come up with the definitive test for the putative creative writing student. 'Write an explicit, funny and touching passage in which a paralysed woman has a passionate affair with a spotty youth, while her husband wrestles with his Buddhist beliefs and falls off his bicycle.' Adderson does it so well that few could match it for skill and wisdom. When I interviewed her, she told me that we must all put ourselves in other people's shoes or we're doomed. Put yourself in her elegant, snappy, beautifully crafted shoes and you'll feel all the smarter for it."

Sitting Practice received a couple of nominations: the VanCity Book Prize and the City of Vancouver Book Award, both in 2004. It won the Ethel Wilson Fiction Prize for the best work of fiction published in BC. It also became my most successful novel internationally. As well as the UK, it was published in Serbia (world's ugliest book), Bulgaria and France, then the US five years after its Canadian publication. Its success internationally I put down to the unusual subject matter and the fact that it's quite funny. In Canada, funny books aren't considered "serious," which is something I've never quite understood.

I was especially grateful for the US publication, which was with Trumpeter, a short-lived literary imprint of Shambhala. They had asked for a number of small changes relating to the Buddhism in the novel, but I was also allowed to make any changes I wanted. I excised some recurring language tics, as well as some flabby bits. As a result, the now out-of-print American version is, in my opinion, far superior to the ostensibly in-print (at least there are still copies in a warehouse somewhere) Canadian version. And for it I received my only review from *The New York Times Book Review*: "All of Adderson's characters are rounded and all have utility, not simply as plot devices but as part of a striving, suffering whole."

It took the better part of a decade to write *A History of Forgetting* and *Sitting Practice*. With the former I was trying to teach myself how to write a novel. With the latter I was practising what I'd learned. By then I was really missing the short story form, which is probably my forte. I was also afraid that I would forget how to write stories if I didn't exercise those particular muscles. Although I knew that a collection of short stories would probably not sell internationally (I was right), I decided to treat myself nonetheless.

To my mind, novels are a dramatic form. Like plays or films, they require at least some degree of technical aptitude, particularly in their structure and pacing. Short stories, on the other hand, though they may have some of the same elements as a novel, are a more poetic, language-driven form. You can write them by feel, the way I wrote *Bad Imaginings*, with no idea of what you're doing. But after ten years in the novel camp, I now had a toolbox full of techniques and so, when I set out to write another collection of stories, I decided to employ those tools.

Most of the stories in *Pleased to Meet You* started out as technical experiments, though by the time each story reached the final draft, the nature of the experiment often fell away. For example, the title story "Hauska Tutustua" ("Pleased to meet you," in Finnish) started as an experiment in micro fiction. I wanted to see how little I could put in the story and still have a story. A lot more than I thought, as it turned out! I kept adding and adding until the story, while not "macro," wasn't remotely micro. In "Shhh: Three Stories About Silence" I was looking for a way to string standalone stories together in a meaningful way. I also played with form in my use of cartoon captions. In "Knives" I was experimenting with bookending, though in the end I cut out the second bookend. "Falling" was an experiment in using poetic techniques in a story about poetry.

The story I had the most difficulty with was "The Maternity Suite," which I had started writing years before, but had been unable to finish. This is actually the work that I've laboured over (another pun!) more than any other, including all my novels: nine *years*. Since it's about an hysterical pregnancy, I structured the story in three trimesters, with each section told in a different character's point of view: the grandmother of the non-existent foetus, the mother, and the father. I just couldn't figure it out. Eventually I recognized the problem was mistaken character motivation. For most of those nine years I had assumed, understandably, that Anna, the hysterically pregnant mother, wanted a baby. One day I pulled the story out of the file cabinet and, reading it yet again, realized I had been blinded by the trimester structure. There are actually four main characters in the story, as Anna's sister, Pauline, appeared in all three sections. Once I gave Pauline her own section and point of view, what had been there all along became obvious: what Anna actually wants is *what her sister has.* In this case it only happens to be a baby. It's a story about sibling rivalry, in other words, not the deep longing to reproduce. After that revelation, it took about three days to finish the story.

Pleased to Meet You was published in 2006 by Thomas Allen. Five of the stories in the book were previously published in magazines and a three were anthologized, including in *Best Canadian Stories* 2002. "Falling" won second prize in the CBC Literary Awards and "Hauska Tutustua" was made into a short film. The collection was a best book in the *Globe and Mail,* the *National Post,* and the *Toronto Star.* I also received my only Scotiabank Giller Prize nod (longlist) for the book. Two thousand six was also the year I received the Marion Engel Award for mid-career achievement (now the Engel-Findley Award).

I'd like to say a few words about my writing for children, which I began around the time I was writing the stories in *Pleased to Meet You.* This is the other half of my writing career. There's only one other writer in Canada with a completely dual career in literary fiction and children's literature—the wonderful Cary Fagan.

I started writing for kids when my son was five. That summer, whenever we came home after an outing, I'd think: what happened today? That was a story! At first I thought I'd write down these funny adventures so that he could read them when he was older. I'm not sure why it didn't immediately occur to me that I could write for children too; I'd certainly read enough books to him. Eventually I did show them to my agent and she shopped them around, unfortunately as picture books, which at the time I didn't understand were the pinnacle of the genre. But they were eventually bought as a collection of short stories for emerging readers, and published by Orca in 2007. I've now published more than twenty books for kids.

Over the years I've turned into a bit of a proselytizer for kidlit, trying to get other authors to come over to the sunny side. Here's why I love it:

Firstly, as a tragic-comic writer, I get to have fun with my purely comic side.

Secondly, there are so many forms to challenge yourself with: picture books, chapter books, middle-grade, young adult (YA), graphic novels, novels-in-verse. I've tried them all. The only form I disliked was YA, which didn't exist when I was a young adult and therefore seems redundant to me.

Thirdly, unlike with literary fiction, kidlit actually sells. Both public and school libraries buy it. People who wouldn't buy an adult novel if you came at them with a hot poker will buy a book for their child or grandchild. There is still a robust reviewing culture supporting all this. And, get this: your book keeps on going! It's not dead in three months! People keep reproducing and those kids need something to read. That first book of mine, *I, Bruno*, which sells for $6.99, is still going strong. Years after publishing it, I still get modest cheques twice a year.

Fourthly, children's editors are supremely talented, kind, and optimistic, unlike their depressed and overworked counterparts in literary fiction. I have a particularly wonderful relationship with Groundwood, the kidlit arm of Anansi. Rather than rejecting something that's not working yet, my editor Shelley Tanaka will say in the kindest tone, "We don't think it's *quite ready* to contract yet." I haven't burned a bridge by showing something too early. This gives me a sense of safety and, because I feel safe, I'm able to risk more in the stories I tell and experiment with new forms.

Fifthly, many children's books are illustrated, so you get to see an artist's version of your story. I can't express how much delight this brings me.

Sixthly, because of its simplicity—which is why it's so difficult to write for kids—writing for kids has helped my adult writing immeasurably. I doubt I would have come up with Ellen McGinty if kidlit hadn't taught me the absolute necessity of an active protagonist who makes and solves her problems on her own.

Finally, I love children. I think they are the world's most important people. If the books we read in childhood stay with us all our lives, then writing for children is an honour.

Back to the adult track! My next project was *The Sky Is Falling*, a novel about the fear of nuclear war and the love of Russian literature. The original idea came to me around the time I turned forty—the prime age for a look back. I found myself reflecting on two contrasting periods of my life. One was my early twenties, when I was at university and a passionate anti-nuclear activist utterly convinced that the world was about to end unless I, personally, pitched in to prevent it from happening. The other was when I was fifteen and diagnosed with thyroid cancer. Once I reached middle age and could fairly objectively observe my own past, it struck me as interesting that I'd never felt imperilled as a teenager despite having a potentially life-threatening disease, yet I was so anguished as a young adult about our theoretical death.

How our sense of mortality changes at different ages is one of the ironies in the novel, which is about a group of anti-nuclear activists in the 1980s who shelter a teenager runaway who turns out to be fleeing from cancer treatment. The teenager, Pascal, engages so completely with life that his own situation doesn't even register. Jane, the protagonist of the novel, and her friend Sonia are so focused on nuclear war that they are, practically speaking, scared to death.

The Sky Is Falling is my only novel that is remotely autobiographical (beyond being emotional autobiography, which all writing arguably is) and the first of my novels where I reference reading, in particular, the great nineteenth-century Russian authors Chekhov, Tolstoy, and Turgenev. It has always struck me as odd, or sad, that characters in Canadian novels rarely read. As well as the fact that it fit with the Cold War theme, I incorporated the Russian literature element in the book because I, like Jane, took that life-changing course in Russian history and literature in first-year university. I had no idea at the time that this Russian literature thing would carry on through two more books! It's more than just motif or allusion. It's a technique, which Douglas Glover informed me has a name: "intertextuality." A fictional character engages with a pre-existing literary text and considers her own situation through it. The two texts then layer each other.

The Sky Is Falling was published in 2010 and was on best books of the year lists for the *Globe and Mail*, *Quill and Quire*, and Amazon.ca. It was also nominated for the 2011 Commonwealth Writers' Prize and the 2012 International IMPAC Dublin Literary Award (longlist).

After I finished *The Sky Is Falling* and was fishing around for what to write next, I noticed a marketing trend in fiction: books that were clearly collections of linked stories had the word "novel" slapped on the cover. These were great books, books I loved— *Olive Kitteridge* and *A Visit from the Goon Squad* in particular— but they weren't novels in my opinion. I found it annoying that publishers thought readers couldn't tell the difference between a novel and stories, and that they thought so little of the story form that they wouldn't even admit to publishing it. But soon I got to thinking. Would it be possible to write a novel, one with an inciting incident, rising conflict, a climax, and a denouement—the whole Fichtean curve shebang—where each chapter actually *is* a standalone story? I wrote *Ellen in Pieces* to find out.

Where Ellen came from is a mystery, but I suspect she's a bit of an alter ego: tall, big-boned, large-breasted, sexually forward, impulsive, in-your-face. I'm decidedly not *any* of those things. As I mentioned, her genesis I credit to kidlit. The most important rule for writing for children is that the protagonist solves her problem on her own without the help of an adult. In other words, the protagonist always has agency. After I started writing for kids I realized that the protagonists in my books for adults tended to be, if not passive, certainly reflective and sometimes the least interesting person in the book. The moment of that realization— *boom!* Ellen kicked in some door in my head, a protagonist who fucks up her life, then fixes her own messes.

I wrote *Ellen in Pieces* as ten discrete short stories. Every story-chapter was built around a moment when Ellen positively affects another character's life. Usually I write chronologically so I can watch the story unfold and follow its causal implications, but with *Ellen* I jumped around much the way the individual stories themselves shift in time. For example, I first wrote "Poppycock" based on my own father's breakdown after the death of my mother, but it's the second story-chapter in the book. To keep track of all the points of view and time shifts, I created a long chart that I taped to the wall above my desk.

My intertextual Chekhov obsession came up again in "Your Dog Makes Me Smile," where Ellen reluctantly adopts a dog and, in trying to name him, rereads "Lady with a Lapdog." I also did something in the book I considered quite daring; I dropped Ellen's point of view for the second half of the novel. I did this to recreate for the reader the experience of losing a dear friend. Ellen, with her boundary issues, reveals so much of herself in Act One that I hoped readers would develop the same love-hate relationship with her I had, cringing one moment, wanting to embrace her the next. Then, just as in real life, when Ellen gets her cancer diagnosis, she withdraws. We are no longer inside her as readers, but among the friends and family whose points of view take over the rest of the novel as they try to come to terms with Ellen's imminent death. Some reviewers, citizen and professional alike, criticized this and considered it a *mistake*. They didn't seem to understand it was a technical choice designed to achieve a certain effect. Many also thought Ellen was a bad mother and therefore disagreeable to read about.

I certainly was "at ease" writing this book. I enjoyed every minute of it. It seems now that I just sat back and let Ellen do her thing and tried not to censor or control her or the sentences. I remember this especially happening in "Divination" with the image of Ellen carving a pattern on a pot, working around it and wondering if the pattern will match up with where she started and how she doesn't particularly care if it doesn't. That's exactly what I felt writing that story, that I just wanted to be absorbed in the experience and I didn't care where it ended. Then it just ended itself. It felt like a little miracle.

Of course when I finished and strung all the stories together, they didn't work as a novel at all. There was far too much repetition because each story had the same narration that filled in the backstory of Ellen's life and loves. Thankfully it wasn't too difficult to go in and excise the repetitive bits. In the end, probably none of the story-chapters in the published novel work as standalone stories, but I rather like that they exist. There are actually two different works: the novel version of Ellen and the short story version.

I published four of the Ellen stories individually and they did pretty well. "Erection Man" was longlisted for the 2013 *Sunday Times* EFG Private Bank Short Story Award (the world's richest short story prize at the time), along with the likes of Junot Díaz. (Weirdly, it was rejected by all the magazines I sent it to.) The same year "I Feel Lousy" was nominated for a National Magazine Award for Fiction along with "Ellen-Celine, Celine-Ellen," which won the Gold Medal. "I Feel Lousy" won the Alberta Magazine Association Gold Medal for Fiction and was nominated for a Western Magazine Award for Fiction. Ellen stories appeared in *Best Canadian Stories 12, 13, and 14. Ellen in Pieces* was a CBC Best Book of 2014 and a 2015 Ethel Wilson Fiction Prize nominee.

Although I continued writing and publishing books for kids after *Ellen in Pieces*, and was trying to work on another novel, I became sidetracked for a number of years by a non-fiction project that grew out of a Facebook page I created in 2013 to protest the rampant demolition of character homes and gardens in Vancouver. "Vancouver Vanishes" eventually became a book of non-fiction essays and photographs, *Vancouver Vanishes: Narratives of Demolition and Revival.* I wrote three of the essays, commissioned the others, and contributed most of the photographs. I also spent close to five years advocating on the issue: creating a petition, giving talks (unpaid), writing op-eds (unpaid), organizing a demonstration, speaking at city council, etc. My interest in the subject had less to do with architecture, of which I know little, and more with my repulsion over the hypocrisy of a civic party elected on a green mandate allowing the annual destruction of more than a thousand livable homes for luxury redevelopment during a housing affordability crisis.

Later, however, I came to realize that a lot of my passion was about narrative. Old houses are repositories of narrative. They become so first because of the natural materials they are made from. (Anything that comes from nature has a story, particularly wood, because it was once alive.) Embedded in the old house, therefore, is the story of the trees and the story of the people who hand-logged them, and the story of the people who built the houses by hand, without power tools. And then there are the absorbed stories of all the people who lived in the house through the decades (story layering again!). A new house won't accrue stories in the same way because it is mass-produced from mainly synthetic materials and, besides, the standard of build is only around fifty years. Even twenty- and thirty-year-old houses are torn down in Vancouver.

And now we are nearing the end.

The novel I started thinking about after I finished *Ellen in Pieces* was something completely different for me. I had brought Chekhov into two novels. Why not write about him? At the very least, I thought, it might help me get over my literary crush.

My original idea was to explore Chekhov's late-life marriage. A prodigious breaker-of-hearts, he finally gave up his "bachelor habits" three years before he died when he married the Moscow Arts Theatre actress Olga Knipper. Despite this, he continued to live with his sister and mother, with Olga only making infrequent conjugal visits. I delved into the research and pretty quickly realized that such a novel would be woefully short on dramatic action. Plot summary: a dying man in a boring seaside town quarrels with his female relations.

By then I had discovered the story of Lika Mizanova, Chekhov's model for Nina in his breakthrough play *The Seagull*. In the play, Nina is an innocent young woman who yearns to be an actress. She falls in love with a famous writer, runs off with him, and is abandoned when she becomes pregnant. Her reputation is ruined; her baby dies. Pretty much the same thing happened to Lika, except Chekhov himself didn't ruin her. After he tormented her for years with indecision, they had brief affair. When he dropped her, she tried to make him jealous by taking up with the playwright Ignati Potapenko, a close associate of Chekhov. Potapenko got her pregnant. The terrible irony was that Lika's baby died three weeks *after* the premiere of *The Seagull*; the play presaged this tragedy. I could hardly believe that the novel hadn't already been written.

More research followed, including a trip to Russia and multiple revisitations of his stories, plays, and letters. For almost a year I struggled with point of view: first or third? Whose? I tried to write from Chekhov's point of view, the way Colm Tóibín wrote from Henry James' in *The Master*. It was leaden. Just awful.

Naturally, I was curious about that steady presence in Chekhov's life—Masha—not only his sister, but his amanuensis, housekeeper, secretary, bookkeeper, and confidante. Though Masha never married, she did receive four proposals in her lifetime, offers she refused when Chekhov made clear his disapproval. It's easy to jump to the conclusion that he wanted to keep Masha close so that he could have a "wife" without the emotional complications of one, but given their difficult childhood, I think there was something more complex going on. Ultimately, my interest in those complications won out and Masha took over the novel that became *A Russian Sister*.

Even after I had settled on Masha, however, I still had trouble bringing the novel to life. I had decided that I wanted to stick as close to the historical facts as possible, which resulted in my writing many drafts of what was essentially biography. I was terrified of barging into the consciousness of actual people, of misrepresenting them and making errors. Also terrified of the opinion of academics who I thought would say, "How dare you!" My breakthrough came when I realized that my Masha, Antosha, and Lika were *fictional characters* as much as any character I've created from scratch.

The novel was published by HarperCollins, Patrick Crean Editions, in the late summer of 2020 (Year One of the Plague), two months ago as I write this. I'm hardly the only writer affected by the pandemic. A further issue has been the near-collapse of reviewing in the mainstream media. Thus far I've had a scattering of reviews, some enthusiastic, others less so. A couple have ended by claiming that Chekhov himself would approve of the novel, which is good enough for me!

As for what I plan to do next, I have to admit that our uncertain future bears down on me hard, as it does for us all. I have no grand ambitions, only sparks of ideas. I'll probably indulge myself by tinkering away on short stories for a while, if only for the pure pleasure of stringing words together and seeing (and hearing) their effect.

I really do mean tinkering. Only part of my writing process involves getting the *story* down on the page. Probably three-quarters of the time I work on getting the actual words right. In the early drafts, these two aspects of the craft happen simultaneously. On a given day I might write a page, sometimes more if there is dialogue. The next day I start from the beginning again, rewriting what's already there, only adding new material to move the story forward once I've perfected what already exists (perfected for *that* day at least). The changes I make to the language affect what will come next. For example, I might change a word for one more striking or original. That new word is loaded with different associations that may influence what *happens* in the story next. Or the change in the rhythm causes me to change more words, and then the dominos fall from language to plot again. I keep working this way, always starting from the beginning, until I get to the end (in the case of a short story) or I get unbudgeably stuck. (Novels I tend to work in sections or I'd never be able to move forward.) Once I finish a draft, I put it away and work on other things until enough time passes that I either don't care what I wrote or I can't remember it. That allows me to see it objectively. When I go back to it months later, every wrong word jumps out at me.

Why is it wrong? Again, it often has to do with how it sounds, both in my head and when read aloud. It's partly rhythm, partly poetic association. I also want the words and images to be interesting and honest.

I think it's best explained in an example. Here are a few sentences from "Poppycock." Ellen goes to visit her father in the psychiatric ward after his suicide attempt, bringing a fruit basket. She trips on the way and the fruit spills out. When he won't speak to her, she goes to wash the fruit in the sink and thinks:

The average human heart is the size of an apple. Where had she learned that? A McIntosh apple all mushy with bruises.

I worked on that story chapter for two years, which is typical for me. Every time I read this passage a sour note rang in my head. Then one day I got it.

The average human heart is the size of an apple. Where had she learned that? A McIntosh apple all bruised to mush.

The imagery is the same, but the sound is different. Now the last line ends with four one-syllable words, which seem to me to mimic the very blows that might inflict a bruise. There's a melding of meaning, not just in the imagery of the apple-fragile heart, but the sound of the words.

That's what I'm after.

THE PROCEDURE

CAROLINE ADDERSON

Ketman was driving back from the clinic, wiper blades whupping across the glass, the lashings of water reminding him of a car wash and how he used to take his son Kenny to wash the truck. The boy would scream and giggle as the brushes whirred to life, his small hands clinging to Ketman so he wouldn't be swept away in the deluge. So there *were* good memories of Kenny!

Out of nowhere, a cyclist materialized dressed all in black, begging to be hit so that he or his grieving relatives could sue Ketman. Normally Ketman would have laid into the horn, but the doctor came to mind then, smiling like he was trying not to. In the clinic, his lips had compressed in his boyish face and his eyes, unlocking from Ketman's, had flicked to the side. This doc—the luck of the draw at a walk-in—was half Ketman's age and weight. Half the man that Ketman was, in other words, and that much farther from death, sitting there on his swivel stool trying half-assedly to conceal his smug amusement. *That* was the moment when Ketman should have brought up what had happened to his mother, which really was suable, though Ketman had taken the high road.

"Two years ago. She went in for a knee job. Came out dead," he told the tyke doctor who was not, in fact, in the cab of the truck with him. "So I have a good reason to feel it's not worth the risk."

Ketman nodded several times, the last to his own reflection in the rear-view mirror.

.

Shelby wasn't home, but the cats greeted his arrival like faithful dogs whose crap you didn't have to pick up. They wove themselves around his legs—loam-coloured Linus, Muffy the calico—while Ketman checked the fridge for inspiration. He rustled around in the produce drawers, sniffed inside containers.

A few years back, to help burn off the slack season's unexpended energy, Ketman had stepped in as cook. (It was the counsellor's suggestion, so not a complete waste of money.) With Shelby's Hilroy of stained recipes as his guide, Ketman faithfully reproduced her uninteresting meals then, encouraged by his success, bought an actual cookbook, one with a golf-shirted guy on the cover. "Guy" as in the type who held his knife and fork in fists on either side of his grub-filled plate, guarding it. Blue-eyed, muscular, stiff brush of blond hair—much like Ketman in his youth, right down to the nose destined to overwhelm his face. Ketman boiled and basted his way from Beer Dip to Bananas Foster, then struck off on his own.

At last he settled on half a butternut squash perspiring face-down on a plate. Where was Shelby? The gym, probably. It would irritate her if he phoned.

The doctor had called him *Mister* Ketman. Nobody did that, not even his landscaping crew. Nobody called him Ken either. He was just Ketman, checking the cupboard now for Arborio rice. At fifty-five he must have seemed prehistoric to that smirking medical minor. The risks of the procedure might have been "minimal," but *puncture* was one of them.

There was nothing to do now but wait for Shelby, so Ketman went downstairs in search of televised distractions. He was still there watching the Food Network with the cats when the back door slammed an hour later.

"Shel?" he called.

"Just a sec! I'm texting Kenny!"

Ketman waited through the next commercial then transferred Muffy from lap to couch. Linus had a diagnosis, Petting Aggression, and couldn't be handled. Ketman stood, forcing the cat to leap.

Upstairs, he found Shelby in the kitchen, bags at her feet, her rain-sprinkled glasses seemingly suctioned to her forehead as she twiddled. Ketman's bratwurst thumbs were barely opposable. He'd never got the hang of texting.

"What's the matter now?"

"Exams. He's nervous." She had yet to take off her wet coat or make eye contact. Did she even remember he'd gone for a physical?

The onion waited on the cutting board. Ketman got started peeling it, wondering, not for the first time, what was the point of going away to university if you ended up texting your mother ten times a day. Yet Shelby looked so much happier when she was communicating with Kenny. In a week he'd be back for Christmas, a reunion Ketman dreaded. The kid would barely look at him. He spoke to Ketman in grunts. Ketman got more conversation out of guys on his crew, some of whom barely knew English.

The phone blooped. She lowered her glasses and gathered up her bags. "I'm just going to change," she said, walking out.

Shelby was gone as long as it took to make the risotto and when she finally appeared, she was texting again. "Tell him we're eating," Ketman said.

"I just did."

She took her seat across from him and smiled. Though her face was thinner from all the hours she clocked now at the gym, her hair was comfortingly the same, adding inches to her height, dyed auburn to cover the grey. Ketman's moustache, chest and stubble were still only lightly sprinkled with age. He'd gone beige instead of grey, his work-weathered skin too. He pictured his own reflection in the rear-view mirror driving home—aghast and mushroom-hued—and cut to the chase.

"I finally got that insurance thing done."

Shelby was eying her risotto. "This looks great, Ketman. But why's it orange?"

"That's the squash from last night."

Nodding, she took a bite. A root ball of hurt formed in his chest, but where in the past Ketman wouldn't even have recognized its presence, now he grabbed his mental shovel and attacked it.

"The physical. Remember?"

She glanced at her phone. "Oh, right. Everything okay?"

The doctor had provided a pamphlet. It would have been easier just to hand it to her now, but he'd left it in the truck. Linus sashayed over. Ketman heard his motorized purring, felt soothed when Linus rubbed against his leg. He found his words. The procedure, its risks. He spared her the unspeakable *puncture*.

"What do you think?" he asked.

Shelby was forking at the risotto like she was aerating a compost heap. "What do you mean?"

"Should I have it?"

"Everybody's supposed to, right?"

"So you think I should?"

"Of course."

Ketman recalled the doctor's face. Now this matter-of-fact response from Shelby, who seemed to have forgotten what had happened to his mother. That had been a minor procedure too. The morning he was supposed to pick her up, she'd phoned Ketman to say she was being discharged and would be in the waiting area. Barely an hour later Ketman had walked unawares into a scrum of white coats and flowered scrubs.

"I'd have to have a general," he told Shelby.

Her dark high school eyes, magnified by the stronger prescription of her glasses, met his. Finally, some sympathy! The dregs left over from Kenny, no doubt.

"It'd take longer to recover from the anaesthesia than the procedure. Are you worried it's going to hurt?"

"I just don't want to be awake for it," he said. "I mean, would you?"

"For heaven's sake, Ketman. Do you know how many medical indignities women are subject to?"

Ping! Beside her plate, the phone lit up. Shelby pounced.

.

The next day, Ketman called the clinic. "Knock me out. That's all I ask."

The receptionist laughed and gave him a date four months away.

Christmas came and brought Kenny with it. After a couple of days of watching his adult son stretched out on the couch, laptop on his chest, body a sleeping platform for cats, Ketman asked Shelby, "The kid still can't find two socks that match?"

"So?" Shelby replied, which brought back those 150 buck-a-pop sessions where she'd perfected this devastating syllable.

Ketman got on the computer himself and booked an all-exclusive in Puerto Vallarta before he blew his top.

In Mexico, while Shelby and Kenny scuba-dived or caught the shuttle bus to town, Ketman conversed brokenly with the grounds men. He checked Kenny's browser history just for the hell of it and discovered yet another aspect to their generational divide: hairy pussy on one side, shaved on the other.

Halfway through the trip he observed to Shelby that she wasn't only swimming in the hotel pool, but in her bathing suit.

"I'm okay, Ketman," she said.

"Come. I want to treat you."

In the shop in the lobby, he stationed himself outside the change room. A pink one-piece. He couldn't convince her of the bikini.

"Hot mama!" Ketman told her when she emerged. Before she could escape, glaring, back into the cubicle, he stepped in front of the mirror with her.

"Look at us, Shelby. Thirty-two years and going strong." An arm around her shoulder, he pulled her to him with the whole raw force of his love.

In the mirror Shelby's head snapped to the side, setting her glasses askew on her face.

The days grew longer, the rain less torrential. *Galanthus, Muscari, Crocus.* Whether Shelby had finally accepted Kennylessness, Ketman couldn't say. He was back on the job and outside, not "breathing down her neck all day." And Shelby was too busy managing the work schedule to go the gym. She joined a women's book club instead.

This time of year, yard maintenance overtook the design side of Ketman's business. He hired extra crew, stepped in for the no-shows. Then, after a long day power raking and pruning, he would putz in their own yard, meaning they ate dinner later. Over one of those twilight meals, Shelby brought up the procedure.

Ketman was jolted in his chair. "Did they call?"

"It says on the schedule that you're supposed to confirm it," Shelby said.

Now he remembered. He'd written it down himself then apparently frittered away the months of his reprieve. He could hear that outside, among the bud-swollen *Camellia japonica*, the birds were laughing at him.

"Could you confirm it, Shel?"

She was in charge of the phone. He'd put her on the payroll around the same time she'd stopped cooking, which had made no sense to Ketman—his money was already hers—but the counsellor said to.

"No, Ketman," she said now. "It's not a work thing."

He felt his whole being sag. Elbows on the table, head propped up on his fingertips, he scrubbed worriedly at his eyebrows.

"I understand," he said, though he didn't.

The next morning, Ketman went to the room they called her office. It was decorated with Kenny memorabilia, the shelves lined with dusty consolation trophies and Mother's Day crafts: tissue-paper roses in a papier-mâché vase; a pottery turd. The schedule, kept in a large rectangular hardbound book, lay open on her cluttered desk. Ketman cleared it off, replaced the cordless phone in its stand to charge, set aside the nail file and clippers. The miniature scimitars of his wife's trimmed nails he swept lovingly into his palm and deposited in the wastebasket.

Now the week spread before him, his own back-slanted hand surrounded by Shelby's sweetly looped letters. Each day was overcast with pencilled addresses and phone numbers, except for the clean coming weekend. There was nothing on the Friday, even.

Good Friday, Ketman read. *Easter Monday*.

Easter? They'd just had Christmas!

Ketman clutched the edge of the desk. His mind's eye saw the bubble gum Crocs again and his mother's legs immodestly splayed on the floor. Ketman had bought her those Crocs himself, but failed to recognize them at first.

He lifted the phone back out of its stand and dialed. To the receptionist who answered, he gave his full, consonanted name, heard her clicking it on the keyboard. He remembered how the funeral home had blown his mother's floral arrangements. Ketman had specified no lilies. There he'd sat, wreathed in cloying scent, stewing in the pew. Beside him, his brother Mark sobbed freely. Ketman had asked Mark to pick up their mother from the hospital because he, Ketman, was supposed to be out in Langely xeriscaping an industrial park that day. Mark, whose office was twenty minutes away, had said no. Yet if Mark *had* picked her up? She might have died in the arms of a son, her own flesh and blood, instead of surrounded by strangers.

According to the receptionist, the complicated pre-procedure instructions had already been emailed to him months ago. She re-sent them now, along with the list of dietary restrictions.

"Easter dinner," she said, as if the statement were a question.

"Pardon?" he asked.

"Watch the rolls. No seeds."

"Got it." Ketman said, and hung up.

·

Ketman left for work, but for the rest of the day he fretted. About the procedure. About his mother and the way she'd died. Fretting led to haranguing. One guy on his crew got surly and muttered a Punjabi expletive that Ketman knew. *Chittertort.* Ketman blew his top.

Ketman's brother, too, was on his mind. Mark who only had him, Ketman, his big bro. Yet Ketman and Mark hadn't spoken in more than a year.

When he went to bed that night, he found Shelby reading her outdated feminist tome. She left the radio on all day, tuned to the CBC. Ketman was pretty sure he'd heard there that were three sexes now, possibly more.

He asked her about inviting Mark and Sunita to Easter dinner. Shelby's eyes widened. "Seriously?"

"Remember what you said to me after mom's funeral?" Ketman asked.

Shelby didn't.

"'Mark is your flesh and blood.'" His only remaining blood relative, apart from Kenny. "Without Mom and Kenny here, what would be the point of cooking a ham? But I won't ask them if you don't want me to. We just won't do Easter."

Weariness settled in her voice and on her face. "They don't bother *me*, Ketman. And you're the one cooking."

"It will be three days before the procedure," Ketman reminded her as he got up to pee.

When he flicked on the bathroom light, the cats appeared as if by magic. Linus batted at the toilet paper hanging off the roll while Ketman stared down into the bowl. Urine streamed as from a hose. At least he had no prostate worries.

He preferred it when Shelby participated in the decision-making. Apparently, though, he over-consulted, or so she'd complained in counselling. Shelby didn't want to consult on everything. The problem was that even when Ketman heard the alarm bells—*ding-ding-ding*—that signalled an error of judgement, he ignored them.

Because, despite the *ding-ding-ding* clearly audible now over the flushing toilet, despite the fiasco of their last holiday meal with Mark and Sunita, he couldn't ignore this fact: with his procedure only six days away, it might be Ketman's Last Supper.

Ham, scalloped potatoes, minted pea soup, lemon pie. Ketman went a little crazy with the meringue. Mount Fuji in his oven. The reasonable foreboding in the concrete six-pack of his gut he'd channelled into a pussy willow centrepiece with matching sprigs for the napkin holders.

Shelby was mad at him. After hours of the silent treatment, with their guests about to arrive, she suddenly had at him again while she tucked in the pussy willow sprigs, her sole contribution as his helpmate.

"What you are, Ketman, is a bully."

His latest no-show was to blame, the worker who'd got surly a few days before. He'd called the office line that morning demanding a cheque and giving Shelby his version of what had happened, which apparently counted for more than Ketman's.

"The guy swore at me," Ketman said—again. "What do you expect me to do?"

"What did you call *him*?"

"He was dragging his ass around. How come I never get credit for *not* blowing my top? I only get demerits when I do."

The doorbell interrupted them. "Don't mention the procedure," he told Shelby. "I don't want Mark to worry."

Shelby made a sound through her nose and went to answer the door.

There were cries of surprise from down the hall, followed by exclamations. "You've lost so much weight," Sunita said. "Isn't that he-man feeding you anymore?"

When Ketman joined them at the door, Sunita thrust the chilly bottle she was carrying into his hands. A lawyer like Mark, she was dressed in a teal blue shalwar kameez embroidered in gilt instead of her usual drab pant suit.

Sunita scooped up Muffy and the sisters-in-law headed for

the kitchen, as though Shelby had something to do with what was happening there.

Mark had removed his shoes and now stood blandly in his socks. His grip when Ketman shook his hand was slippery and soft, as though he'd applied lotion in the car. Behind the chunky glasses, a curious look. He was probably wondering about this sudden invitation.

"Beer?" Ketman said, waving him through to the living room as he carried off Sunita's prosecco.

The women fell silent the moment he entered the kitchen. Shelby frowned. Then Sunita exclaimed, "Ketman, this pie!" She pointed to where it towered in his mother's Pyrex pan.

He took down a pair of flutes from the cupboard. Shelby and Sunita watched while he opened the bottle and poured them each a glass, Sunita smiling as though she couldn't believe Ketman possessed the fine motor skills required for the task.

With two beers in hand, he left them to it.

In the living room, Mark had installed himself on the couch, dress shirt straining across his paunch. He looked heavier, or maybe it was the beard. With a smile that seemed worked with strings, he accepted the bottle from Ketman.

"Did you want a glass?" Ketman asked.

"It's fine."

Ketman sat in an armchair, took a sip and rested the cold bottle on his knee. Mark stared at the rug. In one room, the women were gabbing ruthlessly, in the other the men were at a complete loss. Why the hell had Ketman invited them?

Linus leapt onto his lap. Distracted by the tension, Ketman petted him. Predictably, Linus bit, prompting Ketman to react exactly the way the vet had told him not to in the case of Petting Aggression. He swore and shoved Linus off his lap. Mark puckered with disapproval.

"I'm having a procedure on Wednesday," Ketman blurted out.

Mark's brows lifted above his designer frames. "What kind of procedure?"

Shelby and Sunita entered then, prosecco off-gassing in their flutes. "Is this men's talk?" Sunita asked. "Should we leave?"

Shelby dropped into the other armchair. Ketman tried to signal to her his distress, but she countered his look with one approaching dislike. He'd seen it so often since Kenny went away that it was becoming her default expression. *This* was why he'd invited Mark and Sunita. He didn't want to have Easter dinner alone with his wife.

Sunita settled next to Mark, tucking her legs under her broad rump and resting her beautiful bangled arm on his shoulder. "Oh, *the* procedure. I thought you would've had it by now, Ketman."

"Nope," he said.

"I haven't either," Shelby told Sunita. "Have you?"

"I'm only forty-eight. Mark, you should have it."

"Ketman's freaking out," Shelby said.

"I am not!" Ketman said.

But Mark nodded. "Because of Mom." He grew pensive, the sandy brows sinking below the fancy frames. Ketman could hardly believe that his brother understood him. Just as he became convinced of it, Mark put on a faux-British squawk.

"No one expects the Pulmonary Embolism!"

Everyone laughed except Ketman. He went to the kitchen to check the potatoes.

Done. Gruyere convulsed under the foil. The others were still laughing in the living room over his mother's corpse. The sooner they ate, the sooner they'd leave.

Just then Shelby slipped into the kitchen and pulled her phone from her cardigan pocket. "I'm wondering if he opened my Easter package yet." *Bloop* went her departing message. At least she offered to carry in the soup.

He ladled at the stove while Shelby delivered the bowls to the table, one at a time. Either their guests, or the prosecco, had taken the edge of her mood. "It's going okay so far," she whispered on the last trip.

Ketman took his place at the head of the table, Jesus's place, and fixed his eyes on the pussy willow centrepiece.

"But seriously, Ketman," Mark said. "The procedure? Is this a fear of death thing?"

Partly, yes, he wanted to say. But over the last few days Ketman had begun to sense a murkier terror. He shrugged, sending Shelby a yearning glance at the same time. "I've lived a good life."

Sunita said, "Well if it's not a fear of death, then it could only be one thing."

Mark nodded. "Squeamishness."

Sunita said, "It challenges his heteronormativity."

"His what?" Shelby said.

Sunita took Ketman for a redneck, which technically he was. The Redneck Gourmet. (The time she'd called him that, Ketman imagined his own cookbook with that title or, better yet, a Food Network show.) While Sunita and Mark took turns explaining Ketman's toxically masculine world view to his wife, Ketman bowed over his bowl and began delivering soup to his mouth in a steady, crank-turning motion. Impossible not to recall the fiasco of their last get-together the Christmas after their mother died. It had started jokily too, with Mark telling Kenny he was lucky to be an only child, but had ended up as a free-for-all of accusations going back to boyhood. Sunita even brought up how Mark used to walk himself to school. "Can you imagine?" she'd told Shelby. "Six years old. A busy road to cross. Ketman was supposed to walk with him."

"There was an underpass," Ketman said.

Yes, the underpass! The underpass with scary graffiti! No

molester had been lurking there to snatch Mark. He wasn't struck by a car.

"He was lucky," Sunita said.

What next, Ketman had wondered. Mark's longstanding grievance regarding the unequal division of Hallowe'en candy? What were these whingings compared to letting your mother die alone on a cold floor? he'd asked Mark, who'd taken umbrage and stormed out with Sunita.

Shelby was listening to them now as she sipped her soup, wearing the same expression she wore while reading—a Rip van Winkle fascination at everything she'd seemingly slept through. Main course, salad, then pie. And if they tried to linger, Ketman had the excuse of needing to rest up for the procedure.

He went to get the ham, wobbly as a buttock, smeared with mustard, doused in maple syrup. When he returned, Shelby finally spoke.

"Actually, you're both overthinking Ketman. He's a big baby, that's all."

Ketman released the platter two inches above the table. It thunked.

The rest of them held out their plates for him to load.

.

The next day, Easter Monday, Ketman drove out to Delta to pick up some compost for the backyard. Shelby, in a hurry to finish her book, made it clear she didn't want him hanging around the house.

On the drive, he pondered Shelby's comment to Sunita and Mark. Had she been defending him? Possibly. But then the argument over the no-show squelched his hope.

Bully.

Ketman wasn't as heteronormative as they thought, though.

Not with his preference for cats over dogs. (Practically *effeminate*.) Or his cooking. He'd doted on his mother. And what about the centerpiece he'd spent two hours creating, that no one had commented on?

Ketman was nearing the Massey Tunnel by then and when he realized it, he pictured himself pitted against Sunita in court, citing this further, irrefutable proof of his tender nature: every time he drove through the tunnel, he thought of Princess Di.

Irrelevant, said Sunita, who was not, in fact, in the truck with him.

No bottleneck on a holiday. Ketman breezed right through, remarking—also as usual—its untagged state, where every other stretch of bare concrete in the Lower Mainland bore the spray can's jagged testaments.

He spent an hour shovelling in the compost. Its sour aroma infiltrated the cab of the truck all the way back home.

.

That night, Shelby claimed she wasn't hungry. So Ketman's actual Last Supper before the dreaded liquid fast was a plate of leftovers he chomped through at the counter. He swallowed the pills from the kit he'd picked up at the pharmacy, then went downstairs to pace the den.

Nothing happened.

Shelby still had a hundred or so pages to go in *The Second Sex*, eyes glued to it as he climbed into bed.

"Fasting tomorrow. You'll have to go it alone."

"I'll survive," she told him.

What happened to us, Ketman wanted to ask her then, but didn't dare.

The next morning, he concocted the slippery solution from the foil packets and drank it down. Something happened then—a purging the likes of which Ketman had never experienced. The litres sluiced through him, a car wash in the penultimate stage before the hot air starts up. But instead of being inside *it*, *it* was inside *him*. By the end of the day, he felt like a discarded rubber glove.

An image came to him, ignominiously, while he was still sitting on the throne. He pictured the Massey tunnel again, but not clean like it actually was. The murky thing he dreaded waited there. And in the middle of those gangland ciphers, actual legible words. His full legal name and, beside it—*asshole*.

The possible jagged truth of himself, sprayed huge.

·

The next morning, Shelby dropped him off at the hospital entrance and drove off without a backward glance. Ketman rooted himself on the spot, confusing the automatic door behind him. It opened and closed, opened and closed, while he stared at the Honda's blinking indicator. He couldn't see Shelby. She was shorter than the headrest. The car merged into the flow of traffic, then vanished.

Signs pointed the way to *Gastro-enter-ology*, where they handed him a gown. In the change room, his thick fingers struggled with the ties, then the weird socks their no-slip fish scales. Clothes, wallet and phone loaded into the plastic drawstring bag.

A large, regal, grey-permed nurse handed him a clip-boarded form to fill out in the intake area across from the nursing station. A few minutes later she came over and saw his shaking hands.

"You must be cold."

She returned with a blanket, which she tenderly spread across his lap. With the majesty of a cruise ship berthing, she slid her bulk into the chair beside him, took back the clipboard, cooed the questions and ticked the boxes on his behalf. Checked his pulse and wrote it down. Ketman thought of his mother's loving ministrations, the honey-sweetened aspirins crushed in a spoon, the thermometer slipped under his tongue.

"Please," he said. "I have to talk to my wife."

The phone was at the very the bottom of the drawstring bag. The nurse found it for him.

"What?" Shelby answered.

Ketman heard café sounds in the background. She'd said something about meeting someone for lunch. "Come back, Shel."

"I'll be there at three like I'm supposed to be."

"Now. *Please.*"

"Ketman? It's a colonoscopy. Grow up."

She hung up before he could speak of his love, before he could vow to submit again to the counsellor and her pitiless judgements, submit to anything Shelby wanted. He loved Kenny too, he wanted to say. Of course he did! It was just that Kenny irritated Ketman, much the way he, Ketman, irritated Shelby.

"Better now?" the nurse asked.

She escorted him to the holding area beyond the nursing station. A half-dozen beds separated by curtains. He lay down. Another nurse took charge of him there, cheery and round-faced, who lifted his hand and began gently slapping the back of it, as though to scold him. She was coaxing out his veins. The iv port slid right in.

"You're putting me under, right?" Ketman said.

"You'll get a sedative. You might fall asleep."

"I asked to be knocked out," he told her.

Another gurney wheeled in, bumping Ketman into the hall. As they traded places, Ketman saw the back of the incoming patient curled on his side. Deflated shoulders, the freckled top of his bald head with a wispy brown fringe beneath it. He seemed shrunken. Destroyed.

They left Ketman, whose breathing came now in fishlike gasps.

Crepe-soled orderlies brisked back and forth. A poster hung on the wall above him. He read it to calm himself. Code Grey: Disruptive Individual. Code Green: Internal Evacuation.

Ding-ding-ding-ding-ding.

Then a new face loomed above him, young and rosy, his actual nurse. Staring up at her nose-ringed innocence, Ketman understood that his mortification would be boundless. "I want a general," he whimpered.

A gapped smile. "You'll be fine," she said.

The nurse wheeled him across the hall into a huge, night-black room where the blinking eyes of the machines in one corner were the only source of light.

"Turn onto your left side please, Mr. Ketman."

The doctor must have come in then, or she'd been lurking in the shadows the whole time. She introduced herself, placing a warm hand on his shoulder.

"How do you feel, Mr. Ketman?"

"I asked for a general. They said it would be okay."

"Why? Don't you want to watch?"

She began rattling off the terms of the consent. Hearing that word again—*puncture*—Ketman gave up. Meanwhile, the nurse was fiddling with the IV. He felt the vein in his hand stretching to accommodate an incoming flow, distracting him from the same intrusion elsewhere, the actual *chitterchort*.

A scene bloomed on the monitor just above his head. He knew the place. He'd been there, either in a nightmare or in one of those computer games he used to play with Kenny. A long pulsing passage glistening with moisture.

"All right, Mr. Ketman. Here we go."

There are mysteries. Drowsy already, less agitated, Ketman accepted their existence though his inclination had always been not to dig too deep, to stay in the topsoil, far from life's profundities. He wasn't interested, preferred instead the beige surface of things because, in the end—was that what this was, the end?—his life, however unexamined, satisfied him. Shelby, the cats. Business was good. Kenny might come round. Ketman didn't have huge expectations. His one complaint? He missed his mother.

"Here's the first corner."

He saw it up ahead, a bend, and now a sour taste flooded his mouth and he wanted to call out to the doctor to slow down, but his tongue only lolled, he, too, helplessly under the control of she-who-moved-the-cursor. She was pushing him deeper inside his own slimed coils, into the more distant loops where his fear had organized itself into that monstrous shape, where it squatted in the extended cave of who he actually was. Except, when he did round the corner, the same pink walls came into view.

"You're doing great."

Maybe it was relief, but he sensed a different presence now, not malignant, the opposite, an almost universal benignity, a protecting and fostering spirit maternally gathering him up, his own mother in fact, here with him, always, even in his colon, infusing him to the cellular level with such a ludicrous sense of hope that when the next corner appeared he abandoned all resistance and moved glad-heartedly toward it, so certain was he that she would be there when he rounded that curve—smiling, her heavy arms open, glasses fogged from the humidity. She understood and loved him. She loved him best.

She wasn't there. His disappointment gave way to shock, then to the shocking truth of her absence. Its permanence. He dug in his feet to stop himself, but got no purchase from the socks. What had he been thinking? His mother would never come *here*, not with her lifelong distrust of germy places, especially public toilets—which was secondary to the fact that she was dead.

Dead, dead, dead, dead, dead, dead, dead.

"We're near the end, Mr. Ketman. It'll be over in a moment."

He wanted to close his eyes, but couldn't. Around, then around again to the penultimate bend until he saw it hunkering ahead—the thing he dreaded. Ketman was alone with it. Ketman alone.

KRISTYN DUNNION

KRISTYN DUNNION *is the author of six books, most recently* Stoop City *(Biblioasis, 2020), and* Tarry This Night *(Arsenal Pulp Press, 2017). Her short fiction appears in* Best Canadian Stories 2020, Toronto 2033, Orca, *and the* Tahoma Literary Review. *Dunnion was raised in Essex County, the southernmost tip of Canada, and currently lives in Toronto.*

FIGMENTS AND FICTION

I grew up in Kingsville, Essex County, on the shores of Lake Erie. My entire youth it was a one-stoplight town. Mostly farming, some fishing. A lot of dads worked in Windsor at the car plants, but not ours. I was born in 1969, the year of FLQ bombings, Manson murders, Woodstock. The year astronauts landed on the moon. Nixon was US President, Pierre Trudeau was prime minister, and Britain invaded Northern Ireland, officially.

My parents came from divergent worlds and met while teaching at Western Tech Collegiate in Toronto—fireworks, by all accounts. They were high school basketball coaches, and their early courtship involved dates at Vesuvio Pizzeria and Spaghetti House in the Junction with their entire teams chaperoning. My mother is the eldest daughter of a conservative, Protestant family. Her coming of age during the 1950s brought inevitable conflict with the patriarch, her unyielding grandfather, who, together with his father had built parts of the old town of Kingsville. Her cousins regale us with stories of their grandfather lording over painfully formal Sunday dinners following church. All rules were shattered in the 1960s, however, when an uncle invited his liberated Dutch girlfriend, who shocked the family by wearing pants and by sparking up a cigar in the men-only study after dinner. Perhaps a similar rebellious streak led our mother to choose our dad, whose working-class Irish Catholic parents arrived from counties Donegal and Derry in 1929.

My paternal grandparents met in Toronto, married, and raised four children in what once was a rental area for new immigrants, now known as the affluent Annex. Our dad never said much about his upbringing, but according to his sister Kay (deceased 2019), meals were carefully stretched and their hard-working mother often went without. My grandmother cleaned for a family in Rosedale, worked at a dry cleaners, and later at Eaton's, where she'd buy deeply discounted gifts each January, tucking them away for the following Christmas. Her frugality, which saved the family, made a big impression on my father. I remember a tireless baker of gingerbread and chocolate chip cookies, a tiny, devout lady who attended daily mass, but who also loved to watch wrestling. She taught me to leave offerings on the sill and in the garden for the Fair Folk: top of the cream, first sliver of cake, or a dram of whiskey when my uncle was into it. My aunt said their upbringing was shadowed by my granddad, a labourer who liked "the drink" and had, in those long-ago years, a demonstrable cruel streak. Having made a recent pilgrimage to Ireland, I know Donegal's wild beauty—rocky cliffs plunging to brilliant sea, miles of desolate peatlands and thorny gorse, the unexpectedly alien sand dunes—must have haunted him from afar. In places, the Northern Ireland border still shows signs of combat, struggle, and poverty to this day, some reasons he and countless others left. Granddad was rough but also loved animals—my aunt said when he was a boy he'd seen his dog shot in the street by a British soldier, cementing his aversion to the invaders. I've read it was a strategy, to round up and kill dogs from a particular village—so they couldn't bark warnings when the army materialized, but mostly to crush villagers' spirits.

So my parents married in 1966 despite many hurdles—religion, class, familial expectations—and returned to my mother's hometown to multiply: my brother, then me, a sister one year later, and a "miracle baby" girl several years after that. My dad went to law school in Windsor to upgrade his occupation, while my mom raised toddlers in the county. One day, unannounced, she agreed to buy her grandfather's historic home—Georgian Revival style, completed in 1923 and now a dedicated heritage site—the venue for all those anxiety-provoking dinners. After her grandparents died, it'd been left to her aunt, an opera singer who'd made her home in Detroit, instead. The house, boarded up and abandoned for ten-plus years, had been claimed recreationally by the town's teenagers. It was haunted, filled with ancestral and Victorian relics, many of them broken or defaced.

In those years (Dad in law school, Mom at home) there wasn't much cash. My mom gardened, cooked, preserved food, sewed many of our clothes. A family friend gifted an enormous dog to guard us—part German Shepherd, allegedly part wolf—one that had been liberated from its miserable, abused existence, elsewhere. "Prince" permitted us to rub our faces in his thick ruff, to ride him in the yard like a pony, and when the original owner came looking for him, tried to tear that man to pieces. Some of my mom's family lived across the street, others farther away; their lawsuits, political forays, and infighting wove a dramatic childhood tapestry. Our great-aunt, the opera singer, was our first real-life diva. I worshipped her! Her perfume (Opium by Yves St Laurent) would infiltrate the yard several minutes before she made her bejewelled entrance, calling in her contralto stage voice, "Come, Aunt Nora's precious darlings!" She wore a black "fringe"—a French bob, a wig, as we learned years later, and dressed entirely in white or in pink, or sometimes a white-pink combination. Even her garbage can over in Michigan was pink.

Our maternal grandmother (sister-in-law to the opera singer) was raised by a Methodist preacher in the prairies, and met my grandfather at the University of Toronto's Victoria College. Detail-oriented, introspective, a librarian before she married, she edited the academic works of her sons, lived in Zambia during the 1970s with my grandfather, an engineer who volunteer-built irrigation systems with the Canadian International Development Agency. In the 1980s, widowed and living alone, she'd been targeted by local thieves so much that she moved in with us for the next decade. Despite increasing struggles with Alzheimer's symptoms, she was a source of comfort during my rocky teen years.

After graduating law school, our dad worked at a firm in Windsor and later opened his own practice in town. In the early 1980s, his office was destroyed by fire and he had to start over. My mom became a supply teacher (she subbed for my health instructor the day we studied male anatomy—excruciating!), then a full-time French teacher. Finances became more manageable, but continue to be a point of difference between them. To this day our dad obsesses about saving money, "shopping deals," something we three eldest siblings replicate, helplessly. Whenever they could, my parents prioritized fixing the antique furnishings in the house. They still live there. It is beautiful and sombre, with mahogany doors and oak floors. I'm bound to it, though never able to write under that roof—heaviness, restlessness invades me. It's a place of confused magic, both the house and surrounding land: a sorrowful, hare- and deer-occupied ravine, a winding, seasonally flooding creek, a steep hill bordering the town cemetery.

I was the chubby one, ravenous compared to my three picky-eater siblings, whose plates I coveted. I read constantly from age four, anything I could get, and spent a lot of time at the library.

By six I had prescription glasses and heavy orthotic shoes for some foot problem. Being nerdy, dressed strangely, plus living in this huge house confused other kids. If we were so rich, why didn't we have new winter coats, designer jeans? Why did our dad drive such a crap car? Curious about the house, schoolmates were universally wary of our father—that's how we learned he was stricter than other dads. Now in his eighties, our dad says we were raised in a free environment, that we "ran with the wolves, with the foxes," however we chose. And relative to his own upbringing, this is probably true!

We spent a lot of time in the valley, fording Wigle Creek, and up the far crest to the graveyard. Dressed in the abandoned clothes of our forebears, we'd traipse through the wilderness, playacting. Summers, in those formative years, were spent at Cedar Beach on the shores of Lake Erie, a kid's paradise. We combed the beach for treasure, and spied on the Jesuit priests at their nearby silent retreat. We watched a lot of bad TV in the 1970s, read endlessly from the strange collection of books shelved throughout the house. Despite a radical attempt to downsize, there remains a thrilling and bewildering mix of publications from any given era: vintage comics, paperback novels, nineteenth-century etiquette manuals, and early science texts predicting the possibility of a planet called Mars.

Generally happy but prone to outbursts, I was spanked the most, often for my emotional reactions. I was not like the others! Overly sensitive. Dramatic. Screaming about a spider, despairing about injustice, real or perceived—such exaggerated acts of terror and protest were not tolerated. I'd weep when Charlie Brown was picked on by other Peanuts characters in the TV holiday specials, for example, so much so I was occasionally exiled from the family room. Our dad was incensed by rootless bickering, particularly when trapped with us in the car.

The only trips we took were to visit his family in Toronto, four or five hours cooped up together. Without fail I'd laugh, meeting his eyes in the rear-view mirror, augmenting his fury. After years of this—the car pulling onto the road shoulder, me being hauled out and spanked as a public warning, a cautionary tale for brats in oncoming vehicles, silencing all occupants in the back and the back-back of our red station wagon—my mother became convinced my behaviour was evidence of some form of hysteria and diagnosed me with a *nervous condition*. I still laugh inappropriately—helplessly, obnoxiously—when confronted by male authority (see police!).

I remain emotionally connected to the underdog. Books that describe cruelty and injustice rip me open, leave me inconsolable. There are scenes from *Sounder*, by William H Armstrong, imprinted since those early years. As a teen, *In Search of April Raintree*, by Beatrice Culleton Mosionier, left its mark. For me, books remain the most potent way to connect to a life lived differently, and to develop empathy, a vital building block for compassion.

At six or seven, my mom signed me up for Brownies (the organization has since been renamed Embers), ostensibly to make friends, and I was to walk to a nearby church after school. Shyness or some other forcefield overtook me; I could not enter that church. I hid in the bushes and waited for little girls to come out at dusk, like bats. Then I walked home for supper. After weeks my secret was somehow revealed; my mom asked if I went (I lied), and what we did together (I fabricated something), and, finally, said she'd accompany me. Terrible! My mother, then and now, defies the clock. She moves at her own infuriating pace. We walked to the damn church, very late. All the girls were shut inside. Dozens of small shoes lay piled in the foyer. The mystical wisps of faery song escaped solid oak doors. I was nearly hysterical in my desire to abort the mission, but my stubborn mother wrenched open the church doors and gave me a push. Silence. Stares. The girls were collected in small groups around a magical centrepiece: a large, round mirror like a pond, a toadstool upon which sat an elf, a metallic box, flowers strewn around a piece of green Astroturf carpet. Witchcraft, I thought, and still do. The grownups—I would learn the multi-chinned, grey-haired smoker was Brown Owl, the one with the mushroom cut, Tawny Owl—clucked that I was sash-less, out of uniform, the only bare-headed child amongst so many brown berets, a no-no. I turned but my mother had slipped away, leaving me sock-footed, without my "dues," the fifty cents collected from each girl by the troupe leaders, jotted down in a special notebook using strict accounting with the pencil that clipped to her brown belt, then ritually deposited in the elf-guarded box at the centre. "You can pay double next week," said Brown Owl. Once in, I got the hang of things. I was a Sprite my entire Brownie career. But this hesitation to cross a threshold, this ghosting of gateways, existing in two places at once, and inhabiting neither of them fully, continues to define me in many ways, and inspires a great deal of creative work.

My mother wanted more children but miscarried twice and was seriously ill afterwards. In the late 1970s, hundreds of thousands of Vietnamese, many of whom were orphaned children, sought refuge as a result of the Vietnam War, and my mother decided to adopt. We drove all the way to Toronto to collect a boy—I was thrilled, I yearned for a little brother—but we returned empty-handed. The child in question would struggle growing up in such a white, homogenous town, said the social worker, and my bereft mother finally conceded. The almost-adoption brought racial self-awareness, possibly for the first time. We knew several kids who weren't white, but I'm not sure I'd previously imagined how they might feel, being so outnumbered at school. My parents made concerted efforts for us to learn languages, to meet people from different backgrounds. They instilled in us a curiosity and respect for difference. My dad, who had come from a diverse immigrant neighbourhood in Toronto, didn't want us to get too comfortable in this small town. He wanted us to leave, expand our horizons. Instead of adopting, my parents fostered two boys over the years. One, the same age as my youngest sister, was ultimately taken by his father, a biker in a local gang, to Vancouver and never seen again. The next, a boy my age but held back in school, died some years later in Windsor police custody.

At age eleven I announced to my mother's friend that I would neither marry nor have children. She made me promise to not tell my mom; it would upset her. Somehow, I sensed that the path peddled by almost everyone I knew would suffocate and betray me. I didn't know why, and wouldn't. Not for many more years of painful, late-blooming discovery.

Salvation came in occasional opportunities to attend an all-girls' summer camp, paid for by my maternal grandmother and featuring bilingual programming, a mix of woodsy survival activities, athletic endeavours, and the arts. Here I met girls from all over the country and beyond, many from posh backgrounds. The camp itself was rustic: unassuming tents and cabins perched on rocky wilderness acres facing the inevitable lake, the swimming dock a breeding ground for massive dock spiders and furtive water snakes. Camp lore and singularly bizarre customs—chants, non-denominational morning prayers, songbooks, uniforms—it was Girl Guides times a thousand. Alienating and overwhelming to a newbie, these rites and routines consoled the indoctrinated! Camp was a strange mix of communal living, rigid daily and evening programming, and fairly large chunks of unsupervised "free" time, which invited unparalleled acts of hilarity with daring tent-mates, and also dark moments of terror, homesickness, and profound ennui. Although we bemoaned the lack of boys, it was a relief. We could simply exist. Above all, there was space to investigate the Self. Who were we, anyway? Purveyors of contraband junk food after covert "tuck shop" raids. Surreptitious smokers. Ghost story raconteurs. Architects of elaborate, irreverent pranks: switching the sugar out for salt, toads in the sleeping bag, undies up the flagpole.

Summer camp was very much like my boarding school fantasies (based almost entirely on the film *The Trouble with Angels*, minus Rosalind Russell). This was where I first met astonishingly cool budding artists and kindred spirits, where countercultural ideas began to spawn. A vegetarian Buddhist counsellor loaned me *Jonathan Livingston Seagull* by Richard Bach. Was I, too, a "one-in-a-million bird"? When I aged out as a camper, I returned to the camp as a counsellor and once as a dishwasher. Fevered letter-writing campaigns to my new faraway friends, the beginning of a lifelong passion, helped assuage loneliness when I returned to our woeful hometown each fall. Sometimes I visited camp friends in other cities, including Montreal, which captivated my imagination. I was determined to get myself there, someday.

My mother blamed any number of my antisocial behaviours on "that bloody camp." Although I continually struck out, summer camp seemed to be a hotbed of lesbian activity, and almost no one was the wiser. I gravitated towards mopey, flamboyant, or utterly deranged types, but instead of hooking up, I settled for experimenting with personal aesthetics. It was harder to keep up my new persona back home. Not that there weren't interesting people there—but my terrible awkwardness and self-consciousness, my stuck-ness, made it hard to connect. In a hometown sea of headbangers, there were a few goths, new wave-ers and, my ultimate crush, a punk rocker named Jenny who was several years older and completely unattainable, with whom I conversed only once. Her genius manifested itself in outrageous attire. Once, she wore a pair of Adidas trackpants that she had slashed open on either side, and reattached using a few hundred safety pins, revealing two strips of bare flesh from waistband to ankles. I fairly swooned, as did Mr Ogle, the school librarian, who threw her out in disgust.

Though never as daring as Punk Jenny, I'd also been guided by an inner fashion compass that confused and eluded others. Clothes battles—often my pairing of outlandish or verboten items—began with my mother when I was about three. As teens, my sister and I and a handful of our friends shopped the Goodwill and other second-hand stores, then piloted our looks at school, where we were derided and mocked mercilessly. Compared to workaday adults, we had a lot of free time and poured much of it into outrageous fashion and lunatic self-discovery. I'd wear men's pyjamas, long shredded shirts, vintage jewellery, micro kilts with cleated golf shoes, and hand-painted denim jackets. Some outfits were forbidden; those were tucked into the abandoned doghouse in our yard and retrieved, straw-covered, on the sly. My mother sometimes intervened. I was forever picking my oeuvres out of her rag cupboard or the garbage, muttering lines from Sylvia Plath's poem "Lady Lazarus." Our father lined up my year-younger sister and I in the front hall for inspection before we were allowed out to such festivities as the local arena dance; we often had to change or subdue our make-up, and once he hollered that I looked like "a harlot from the Left Bank." Years later, when I actually read about the Parisian Rive Gauche, I was utterly delighted. My People, certainly, although lost in time—artists, lesbians, feminists, and prostitutes—free-thinking women!

From grades nine to eleven, I was one of a dozen or so kids enrolled in an experimental school program that can only be described as misguided. With admittance based almost entirely on the results of a poorly administered IQ test, participants were quarantined from regular "advanced" and "general" classes, a mix of all five grades housed in one room, pioneer-style, where we more or less taught ourselves math, English, and Independent Studies—a radical departure from the 1980s rural Ontario curriculum. Labelled "gifted," we were socially disadvantaged, to put it mildly. This room terrified the teachers, and held a strange mix of mathletes, science geeks, and art nerds. For me, it meant three years of reading randomly across the library shelf, pursuing personal obsessions (including a research paper on "Homosexuality," an obvious and pathetic cry for help), and disregarding mathematics almost entirely. When I returned to the regular-advanced stream in grade 12, the program finally condemned by the local school board, I was mathematically illiterate, even less responsive to authority, and branded a complete nerd. The upside: I'd met and been influenced by some interesting kids and, finally, had a small social circle.

Living in that most southerly provincial tip (south of Windsor, south of Detroit, trust me), we had access to a range of American television and radio stations. Our dad forbade cable television—that cost extra—so no Much Music. Classic rock, in competition with rap and R&B, dominated the Detroit airwaves. Back then, bafflingly, one couldn't like both. Mixtapes, the calling card of burgeoning friendships and potential romances, were the order of the day. My cousin William Power sent tapes and records from Toronto, and I credit him with turning me on to so many crucial bands—punk, hardcore, industrial goth, post-punk, anarcho-crust, you name it. A lifeline! So too, the all-night alternative CBC radio (Brave New Waves and Nightlines), which I played relentlessly in a shared room with my seven-years-younger sister, brainwashing her. I'd scribble the names of riotous bands in a bedside notepad in the dark. Totally illegible, when I tried to read it in the morning.

The closest record shop was in Windsor, an hour's drive away. But even if my parents made the trip (to the Devonshire mall, the most sought-after retail destination), they couldn't be convinced to park downtown near the derelict shop or, if they did, to allow us to enter such seedy premises. Not Fast Eddie's drug den arcade, either! These separate trips became clandestine operations that required elaborate cover stories: a car, a driver (hopefully licensed), cash, suitable get-ups. For live music we had to cross the border to Detroit—infinitely more dramatic—and procure fake ID, since the legal drinking age in the US was twenty-one. Cobo Hall, Joe Louis Arena, the Pontiac Silverdome, St Andrews Hall, and the Grande. So many shows are gone from my mind, but I vividly recall a deranged Billy Idol getting handcuffed and dragged off-stage during his opening number after he dropped his fitted leather pants and bared his ass to the audience. My half of the bedroom was covered in evil-fonted posters: leering Sid and Nancy, Siouxsie and the Banshees, the Ramones, Crass' poster of a severed hand on a barbed-wire fence. The ceiling above my bed was reserved for Billy Idol's pouting snarl. My sister's side boasted Strawberry Shortcake, Sweet Valley High books, an oversized print of the Pope and endless rosaries from her French Catholic school, which I routinely stole to wrap around my wrists, neck, and forehead.

With few exceptions, I had little respect for our teachers at school. But they had nothing on my piano instructors—the Ursuline nuns in Windsor. These broads were tough; you didn't fuck around. Strict, almost ruthless, whacking my knuckles with a metal-lined ruler while I played scales and arpeggios, up and down the keyboard. The same week I began with the nuns I had my first sexual experience; coincidentally, a friend took me to see the film *Agnes of God*, in which a young nun gives birth, kills the infant, then is interrogated by a psychologist to determine if she can stand trial—a palpable, personalized warning against fornication! Convinced I'd share this fictional nun's fate, an unprecedented fear-motivated discipline had me playing three to four hours per day, as if playing the piano could serve as some retroactive birth control. You couldn't lie to nuns, they KNEW things; I was sure they could smell the sin all over me. Their terror campaign became more twisted the few times our dad drove to the lessons. He made liturgical "jokes," had them blushing, ankles crossed in front of their long skirts; the old gals loved him! He'd been raised by such wolves. He knew what made them tick. I completed grade ten in the Royal Conservatory, sat exams, performed a recital or two, and never touched a keyboard again. Years later, I put that musical theory to use with my phat bass sounds in queer rock/metal bands (*Heavy Filth*, 2008–2011; *Bone Donor*, 2013–2017). Sister Theresa, who softened over time and gave me her favourite Chopin record (which she specifically hid from the invincible and eternally disapproving Sister Elizabeth), no doubt shuddered in her grave.

Meanwhile: me, comatose at school, working as a weekend lifeguard, of all things, and cleaning the CPR manikins for extra cash. I hated putting my face underwater due to wearing contact lenses and, thanks to the film *Jaws*, had an irrational fear that while swimming lengths, the dark grate at the bottom of the deep-end would open remotely and a blood-thirsty shark would be released—probably the only reason I was able to swim fast enough to earn my "levels." Vintage Hollywood films with my grandma Sunday afternoons, both of us spellbound by the stylish, iconic stars: Joan Crawford, Bette Davis, Katharine Hepburn (her favourite). I consider Lucille Ball, with whom I share a birthday, a spiritual guide. *Ziegfeld Follies* made its fateful impression, although it chased my Methodist-raised grandmother from the room. I dated a series of more-or-less interchangeable boys, placeholders, who all thought I was a headcase. I was trying to draw critical attention *away* from myself (so I thought), but only complicated things in our gossipy town, with our strict parents. They were terrified my sisters and I would get knocked up and be trapped, branded forever. I was frantic, buying time until university. Understand—I couldn't have cared less about academic pursuits. But university was the only sanctioned escape route, a distinct privilege, without which I hate to think what might have happened.

Because of their conflicting religions, my parents had decided we should choose when we were older, and did not have us baptized. However, our mother performed her own ritual at the deep kitchen sink, presumably in case we died, in hopes that our baby Souls would not go to purgatory or Hell, or wherever she feared they might end up. She now denies that particular blasphemy, but I think it's radical and downright cool. We were dragged to pretty much every church and bible school over the years. Once, during a sermon at the United Church, the visiting minister condemned abortion and I walked out, furious. I would've been twelve or so, maybe a bit older, and it spurred some talk in town. When we came of age, however, our mother did an about-face and insisted we each pick a church, any church, or else we would not receive her blessing to leave home. Most of us chose the closest one (Anglican). The priest at that time was a lovely man, a sculptor, sensitive to my plight when I confessed having trouble accepting some of the doctrinal premises. It was the night before I was to be baptized and confirmed, and I'd been attending confirmation lessons, as required. He suggested I just not speak those particulars out loud. For example, if I didn't believe in ghosts I could "skip" the part about the Holy Spirit. "No, no," I said, "I definitely believe in ghosts, our house is full of them." He asked what troubled me precisely, and I replied, "I'm just not convinced Jesus is the *actual* son of God." He blanched. "That's rather central to the whole belief system," he said. I was eighteen and *urgently* wanted to go to McGill in Montreal. I explained the catch-22. Our parents insisted we attend post-secondary school; it'd been drilled into our heads since childhood. They and we had saved finances especially for this purpose, but suddenly my mother wouldn't let us go unless we'd been "properly" baptized. The priest was kind, and the ceremony went off more or less as it was meant to, other than I remained mute for most of it.

I wanted out! I wanted to meet artists. To create. Montreal was a do-over. I needed a focal point for my great restlessness, that specific boredom and rage that fuels most teenaged girls, and, if harnessed properly, could bring down the government. Luckily for the government, all I could manage to do was register for classes: film studies, dramatic literature, French and German instead of math or science. Back in 1988, computers weren't in common use and nobody had a phone. For information, you had to ask other humans or look it up in a book. Despite my conviction about moving, I wept after my dad dropped me at the girls' dorm (Royal Victoria College). I'd been assigned a creepy basement room with pipes running through it and one small ground-level window looking onto a misshapen bush near Sherbrooke Street. A perfect match for my dreary state.

I made confused attempts to locate and express myself, while at the same time search out kindred spirits. Riveting courses on the gothic novel, feminist performance art, and the history of children's literature are all that I retain from my undergraduate efforts—that, plus vocal instruction, and a theatre class led by an Eastern European eccentric who had us bouncing "like bas-ketballs" around the classroom, then "sprouting, sprouting like an onion!" My stage credits from campus productions include beyond-Broadway cameos: as a pinhead in *The Elephant Man* (the director insisted I didn't need a costume since my shaved head with pink ringlets was weird enough); a wig-wearing cho-rus member in *Lysistrata* (old men used to offer up bus seats when I wore the waist-length black hair); and my showstopper, a notorious Crawford-inspired "Mommie Dearest" role in *Psycho Beach Party* wherein I beat my daughter (the inimitable Shannon Quinn) with a jock strap and pontificated about the inferior-ity of men. The *Montreal Gazette* review declared it had "less depth than a toilet." Through theatre, hanging out in the local arts scene, and skulking around downtown bars, I met wildly creative, brainy, and hilarious people, many of whom remain vital to my very existence.

Pinnacle Montreal moments: infiltrating gay bars in peculiar, off-the-mark outfits (tree branches for antlers, tutus with striped stockings), rendering me completely unfuckable; blasting Nina Hagen and Kate Bush out the windows of a series of decrepit apartments; a police raid at Les Foufounes Électriques, where I was deliriously trapped beside the most beautiful Cosma (Mon-treal's "Punk Jenny"), while her jealous girlfriend glared from across the bar; dancing at the Thunderdome the night it burned down, oblivious and under the false impression that an extra dose of dry ice was billowing through the club.

At the other end of the spectrum, second year was marked by tragedy. The Montreal massacre—December 6, 1989—four-teen female students shot and killed at their college by a man who hated women, hated feminists. Devastating then, it haunts me still. It spurred me to join a feminist collective at CKUT-FM, where I co-hosted radio shows that embraced a platform for issues affecting girls and women. Then, the Oka Crisis, summer of 1990; Mohawk burial grounds were to be dug up to accommodate the expansion of a luxury golf course in Oka, Quebec. I was working in the Laurentians, north-west of Montreal, and this conflict was omnipresent in the news—the intervention by the Mohawk people; the violent response by the Sûreté du Québec, the RCMP, and the Canadian army; the hate crimes in neighbouring white communities. It was the first time an Indigenous conflict with the Canadian government had been so thoroughly captured by media.

As a child in public school, every morning we'd recite the Lord's Prayer, sing *God Save the Queen* and *Oh, Canada!* What did I know? Only what had been taught in our colonial classrooms: the taming of a vast wilderness, the extraction and exportation of invaluable natural resources, the battles with competing invaders, the erasure of whatever and *whomever* had been flourishing, long before the arrival of Europeans. The Oka Crisis shook my understanding of nationhood and land politics. So began a life-long re-education process. I owe my growing understanding of historic and ongoing human rights abuses perpetrated against Indigenous communities to the surging body of irrefutable cultural evidence written, created, and produced by brilliant Indigenous artists—Alanis Obomsawin, Louise Erdrich, Lee Maracle, Rebecca Belmore, Tanya Talaga, Kent Monkman, to name only a few.

Back in 1990, the artist and musician Joellen Housego and I spent countless hours illustrating elaborate comic books, cutting and pasting and photocopying them nearly to death. I was working out issues related to the female body, violence against my own person, among other things. These masterpieces granted us entry to the punk zine underworld, where we swapped with the Mad Hatter creators of other confessional or pop cultural works. Zines connected us to radical bookstores around North America and abroad. I later wrote a master's research paper about this underground movement, and still cart around boxes of archaic comic zine first editions every time I move house.

After graduation I was loath to leave Montreal, but work was hard to find. A friend helped me apply to graduate school—Guelph, a place I couldn't pronounce and knew only one thing about: Dr Mary Rubio, who compiled L. M. Montgomery's life's work, taught there. My vague plan was to write and illustrate a children's book in the new MFA program; I'd been making some beautiful little hand-painted books, which had been included in a gallery exhibition for children's books illustrations at Concordia University. But when it came time to leave Montreal, I panicked and deferred for a year. I tried my hand at "regular" living. A souvenir and sports regalia shop on Rue Sainte-Catherine was hiring—Joellen worked there—so I trotted down in a respectable outfit (worn at Halloween to dress up as "the girl my mother wanted me to be") and was told they'd forgotten to take down the sign, the position was filled. Joellen insisted this was certainly not the case, so I returned in the same outfit, wearing a chestnut-coloured wig on my mostly shaved head. I was hired on the spot! The owner, a total dick named Wayne, used to singsong, "Oh, Miss University, can you take out the g-a-r-b-a-g-e?" Making $5.78/ hour, it wasn't a glamorous life. But it allowed me to stay another year, during which time I co-wrote and performed a play (with Bridget McFarthing), *Blatantly Sexual*—wherein my character confronted her queer identity, and Bridget's character expounded lustily on the joys of sexual adventure—that was remounted twice at Buddies in Bad Times Theatre in Toronto.

Meanwhile, in the Plateau where I lived, an unknown assailant was climbing the city's landmark fire escapes, slipping through windows left open for a summer breeze, and setting women's hair on fire while they slept. It terrified me. This, and so many other acts of male violence. During a *Take Back the Night* march we were heckled by dozens of men, had to dodge hurled beer cans all the way to the edge of Parc LaFontaine, the site of a recent, brutal rape. During a rousing speech, I saw an old man lurking in the bushes, swilling from a bottle, laughing at us, his zipper undone, offering his small, drooping contribution to the domain of regenerative organs. More than demoralizing! I felt isolated, and friends were moving on with their lives, doing god-knows-what. Being stalked by a mime in full face paint was the last straw.

Off I went to Guelph, clutching my zines. I hoped they'd serve as introduction and connect me to like-minded people—a business card for freaks. They did, after a fashion. Grad school was a procrastination tactic, a means to avoid an actual or—god forbid—adult life. The MFA program I'd originally applied to hadn't taken root, so I joined the MA stream in literature. Theory mainly: literary criticism, post-modernism, post-colonial feminist thought, egads. I was to read Kristeva and Foucault, when all I knew was Valerie Solanas' S.C.U.M. *Manifesto.* I struggled, but made the best of it. I'd hoped to take a creative writing course but the gatekeeping professor said my sample excerpt (from the aforementioned play) was too vulgar, and I was not permitted to register. That play might've been crude, but it got great laughs from packed audiences, night after night! Perhaps my writing would've been elevated in that select venue amongst her worthy protégées? We'll never know.

Hoping to meet chicks, I left my comics on a coffee table in The Womyn's Resource Centre. By my next visit, I learned something awful had transpired, something lewd and terribly hurtful. A special meeting was announced to discuss this very serious matter. A larger room had to be secured to accommodate the growing turn-out of distressed womyn. The agenda item: hand-drawn obscenities discovered on the coffee table, now safely locked in The Pornography Drawer.

My comics. Banned in Guelph! Totally misconstrued, accused of criminal intent, *Mudflaps by Nytsirk Noinnud* succeeded in offending nearly everyone. After hours of circuitous discussion, someone suggested "the artist"—dare I say felon—speak up. I thanked them as sincerely as possible, explained I was new and had hoped to make friends, adding, "At least I know who *not* to hang out with."

Guelph in the nineties was the Canadian equivalent of *Portlandia*. Nevertheless, it's where I met committed activists: animal liberators, prison abolitionists, anti-racists, anti-fascists. Here, too, I encountered solidarity movements for Indigenous rights, for Central American revolution. It was less psilocybin-costume-party than Montreal, more dumpster-diving-potluck. Fugazi, not Motörhead. In Guelph I was forced to confront politics and theory head-on. Identity politics—which many grapple with after leaving their families of origin—are potent, even volatile, and "recruitment through seduction," a thing in many activist circles, definitely complicated the matter. Add in never-ending meetings: hours of minute-taking, consensus decision-making, rotating chairpersons. *Hives are breaking out as I write this.* People embracing new-to-them ideologies are sometimes uncompromising, resulting in social quagmires born from confused rivalries and peer-policing, all in the name of justice. (Regrettably, this dynamic seems to have only intensified with the advent of social media.)

The anti-racist, anarcho-punk, animal-rights folk were the most fun and also the most politically effective—shout-out to dear Mark McAlpine! I stopped eating meat entirely, have been vegan pretty much since. It took several potluck dinner meetings with the International Socialists—who spread their celebrated "working class" crabs via an infested office couch, love lair for many a young Marxist—before it became evident: they only invited anarchists for the food. Not one of the I.S. males cooked!

While slogging through the MA program, I washed dishes at a local restaurant and was a collective staff member at CFRU-FM, the campus radio station, where I (once again) ran into trouble. Listeners lodged complaints with the Canadian Radio-Television and Telecommunications Commission accusing me of obscenity, a hot-button issue in the mid-90s. Books and magazines celebrating queer sexuality were being seized at the US border. The bookshops that stocked those titles were charged under pornography and obscenity legislation; same with publishers that produced the material. Sex radicals and LGBT activists were being silenced, again, and I hosted live readings from the banned authors on my show: hence, hot water. (All my obscenity charges were eventually dismissed.)

Despite the drama and growing pains, I cherish my enduring Guelph friendships. After graduation, I worked at the radio station until Toronto, however impersonal, beckoned. I yearned to explode into some kind of queer femme monster, and so I took to the stage as Miss Kitty Galore: burlesque cabarets, drag shows, fetish parties, and punk fundraisers in dirty basements. Performance art—text performed with costumes, makeup, music, lights—unleashed the female, feminine and/or feminized body, the site of so much violence and control, the battleground of the patriarchal corporate project. In a few minutes you can do a lot of damage to mainstream expectations; you can vanquish assumptions. I'd get double-booked for Halloween gigs due to my spooky aesthetic, often at Buddies' main stage or Tallulah's Cabaret—my Virgin Mary strip show, Zombie Love series, Lesbian Serial Killer, the Angry Poet—demented characters stretched slightly beyond my own experience. I didn't petition for gay marriage, but I hosted an uproarious party to celebrate the legalization of gay divorce.

Upon arrival in Toronto I joined the *Who's Emma?* collective (named for anarchist Emma Goldman) in Kensington Market, and volunteered at the punk music and radical bookshop, a venue for anarchist free-school, all-ages punk shows, and general DIY culture. A hub that attracted misfits and rebels, it's where I met and collaborated with many people who continue to figure in my life. I refused to attend collective meetings—as I'd been to more than enough in Guelph—which undermined the project substantially. For a few years I helped organize Toronto's annual Anarchist Bookfair, and promoted fiction alongside inevitably dry theory and personal zines. A losing battle! Fiction, in this social context, has the unfortunate reputation of being considered decadent or somehow politically unnecessary—which is completely laughable. Why must we, who yearn to abolish current power structures and who dream of nonconformity, conform to literary genres? Margaret Killjoy, in an effort to counter this, edited a book of interviews with anarchist fiction writers, including the beloved Ursula K LeGuin (*Mythmakers & Lawbreakers*, AK Press, 2009), in which Lewis Shiner describes anarchism as a "defiant gesture in the face of overwhelming authority, in defense of the compassionate human spirit." This resounds in my core. To make real change in the political landscape you need to also change culture, and art can sometimes do that. Books have definitely done that for me—it's why I write. The art I love most, regardless of medium, subverts a capitalist and patriarchal mindset, celebrates positive images of defiance to greed and misused power. This is at the heart of everything I do, and where I hope to contribute.

I got a job supporting psychiatric survivors in a café setting, and urged my sweet friend Mark Karbusicky, whom I'd met at

Who's Emma?, to join me. He would become known as a video editor/producer, primarily in collaboration with his long-term partner, transgender artist, sex worker and animal rights activist Mirha-Soleil Ross. Later, I found work in community mental health services as a tenant advocate, and Mark eventually followed suit. Decades later, its work I continue to do; it pays the bills and keeps me rooted in the concerns of some of the most vulnerable community members: poor, homeless, or marginally housed people with severe mental illness. This work profoundly informs my world views, and the ways in which I understand power, privilege, conformity, and autonomy.

In the late nineties, *Who's Emma?* closed due to financial pressures and I revisited the idea of writing, with the goal of reaching the children of the dominant culture. Working alone appealed after so much consensus decision-making. Peter Carver, the Jedi master of Canadian children's literature, ran a writing class out of Mabel's Fables bookshop. He found me, a punk in ripped jeans, nervously pacing the ground-floor retail area, and worried I was there to rob the joint! After proving I'd registered, I was permitted upstairs, where I met published authors—Anne Laurel Carter, Carolyn Beck, and so many others—all developing new work and supporting others to do the same. A homework assignment to recall one's childhood neighbourhood grew into *Missing Matthew* (Red Deer Press, 2003), my first book. Peter Carver was a great source of encouragement; he edited this and my first young adult book for Red Deer Press. I tried to connect the various threads of my life in *Mosh Pit* (Red Deer Press, 2004), a queer girl's response to S E Hinton's *The Outsiders*, a coming-of-age story for the kids I'd see panhandling at the all-ages gigs, inventing themselves in fierce and vulnerable ways. During a visit to a local arts high school, the librarian revealed it was their most stolen book. I was delighted! I'd get handwritten notes or random emails from kids who'd hopped freight trains, were squatting, living rough, and had somehow come across a copy. My next young adult novel, *Big Big Sky* (Red Deer Press, 2008), edited by Nalo Hopkinson, examined notions of global militarism, anti-authoritarianism, and queer revolution in a speculative genre. I revisit themes, but each story has its own way of needing to be told, so genre experimentation is a must. My soft spot: fabulist, magical, speculative elements, and far-out thinkers.

On a personal level, getting published is fairly legitimizing and undid decades of parental disappointment. They continue to be really proud. If a wildly enthusiastic octogenarian tries to sell you one of my books, it's probably my dad. Being a published author compensates for my confusing pansexuality, for refusing to marry or have kids or drive a car or eat meat, and even for earning so little money. From an industry standpoint, I like working with independent publishers and booksellers. Everyone has the conviction that what they're doing is vital, and so do I. My books are intended to be defiant omens, aimed at various institutions—organized religion, government, the conjugal family, the military, police.

In 2007, Mark Karbusicky, the friend with whom I'd worked for years, committed suicide. I was gutted. In 2010, Will Munro, artist, DJ, scenester and Vazaleen party organizer, also from *Who's Emma?*, died of brain cancer. At his memorial I danced with beloved Luscious (Elizabeth Baxter), who died one month later due to complications following gastric bypass surgery, leaving me and countless others completely forsaken. Our communities were traumatized. I grieved a very long time. Luscious was my model date for all the best parties and to this day I find it impossible to attend certain events without her. I continued to lose friends, more than a dozen since, many to suicide and overdoses: roommates, collaborators, co-workers, neighbours. To list them would be too painful.

Basically, I sobered up.

Not *literally*. Heavens, no. But my concerns changed drastically. I had no framework, spiritual or otherwise, for accepting these deaths. Ghosts—fiction for other people, a literary device, perhaps—have always been real to me. After years of social distraction, they were back in full force. I could see, hear, and sometimes *feel* them: those loved ones didn't stay buried. They visited, night after night, and their very existence forced a change in my thinking. Did I have a legacy? What was my purpose? By then the scene was less queer, more mainstream gay; to me, it mocked itself. And looking around the clubs, all I could see were those now absent. My brilliant, generous, and creative friends should've been sidling up to the bar beside me. I stopped going out quite so much, and began to amuse myself at home.

Ergo, I had more time to write.

The Dirt Chronicles (Arsenal Pulp, 2011), my first book for adult readers, explores queer punk street life. There's autonomy and celebration, but also the violent reality of racial profiling and police brutality. My goal was to make the issues real, the characters likeable. So that collection had heart, and aimed to call out youth predators. When I read excerpts to street-involved youth, they'd often ask if I was writing about a particular cop by name. In fact, the nefarious acts depicted in the book were compiled from crimes that members of the Toronto police force had been accused of or charged with, in the year or two prior to writing it. I was trying to go back to a dropped thread in an earlier book (*Mosh Pit*), a particular kind of violence I couldn't bring myself to write. And in *The Dirt Chronicles* I forced myself to follow that unseemly trail of abuse and neglect.

Of course, I didn't know how to write literary fiction. It wasn't until later that I began to understand what a short story is meant to do, or what great prose is capable of—lighting a stick of dynamite inside your head. My first arts residency in 2012 was at the Banff Centre for a short fiction intensive facilitated by Sarah Selecky. I was in that fallow post-publishing period, and needed to kick-start something new. Ours was a talented group, and more than half of us kept in touch—exchanging work, giving thoughtful critiques—in the years to follow. I met the then-unpublished-yet-already-formidable Paige Cooper. Jani Krulc and Frances Key Phillips, with their sharp intellects and generous feedback. I reconnected with the witty and succinct Sheila Toller, a crucial friend from early camp days, and Phoebe Tsang, a magical poet and librettist I'd first met in Winnipeg touring *The Dirt Chronicles*. Was it the altitude or the fresh mountain air? Being in the same room with these writers, reading and discussing our work for days—a first for me—provoked a seismic shift.

I understood that I had no idea what I was doing when it came to short fiction.

Informed by years of studying theatre (including an audited course with Uta Hagen at Wayne State University), in my early books I was comfortable exploring character through dialogue and scene work. That's still more or less how I go about writing: plot germinated through character development. In committing to short fiction—which I initially, erroneously, believed would be faster than writing novels!—I began to focus on craft. To read short fiction consciously and critically, the only way to learn technique (unless you are part of an oral storytelling community or culture). All theatrical elements—rhythm, movement, conflict, drama, etcetera—rely on the performance of language itself, not on an actor embodying speech on stage, in film. Obvious, I suppose, but I was finally getting it.

This changed the way I read, which, in turn, changed the types of books that excited me. Authorial intention is still of primary importance, but these days I'm particularly fond of thumping a book in delight after reading a really good sentence. A knock-out sentence that astonishes with its precision, with its complete audacity. Huh! Language, our trade's tool, at the height of its power. Example: "*I did not give a rat's ass about America. There was no such place*" from *Heartland* (Restless Books, 2018), the debut novel written at age seventy by Cuban-born Ana Simo, co-founder of Dyke-TV and the direct-action Lesbian Avengers, made me sit up and shout.

Excellent fiction isn't easy. You can't escape, or breeze through. You don't drift off to sleep reading Angela Carter's imperative *The Bloody Chamber* (Victor Gollancz Ltd, 1979), for example. It's hard to read more than one of her stories at a time. Her syntax is hypnotic! Reading Annie Proulx and Joy Williams and Shirley Jackson is as endlessly instructive as it is joyful. Cormac McCarthy, the old grump, injects stark prose with lethal imagery. A fantasy: we drink rounds of bourbon in a malodourous and poorly lit bar, then slash tires in the parking lot. Beyond benevolent and even more out-there is Richard Van Camp, whose infinitely humane stories balance urgency and horror with generosity and humour. It's his narrative voice that carries us through, no matter the landscape.

The poetry and prose of Dionne Brand.

Rebecca Solnit, period.

China Miéville enthralls, from expansive-mind-fucks like *Embassytown* (Del Rey Books, 2011) to the more brutal, poetic novella *This Census Taker* (Pan MacMillan, 2016). Reading Miéville's list, or Anne Carson's, you get a sense of the scope of their brilliance; their experiments with style, structure, and genre support immensely complex ideas that, frankly, leave most of us scrambling to catch up. Carmen Maria Machado's collection *Her Body and Other Parties* (Graywolf Press, 2017) and her memoir detailing same-sex partner abuse *In the Dream House* (Graywolf Press,

2019), broke open a mental barrier that had me compartmental-izing so much lived experience, keeping it safe from the clutches of my fictional pursuits. Encountering the vivid works of a writer whose under-represented experiences or identity reflects and overlaps with mine is truly cathartic.

Since that first Banff trip in 2012, I've dedicated pretty much every weekend to reading and writing at home, every vacation for residencies. The occasional arts grant has allowed me to take un-paid leaves from my front-line work. I invest increasingly more time and energy in writing and less in unrelated efforts, which makes me happy though fiscally irresponsible.

It bears mentioning that, previously, I feared abandoning my so-called life—job, girlfriend or lovers, social scene. Things un-ravelled when I left, even for a weekend. Stuff would go missing. I worried about my cats. Evidence of a real barnburner: overflow-ing ashtrays, a forgotten bag of empties, panties strewn around the apartment, that sort of thing. By 2012, I'd chosen a different kind of personal relationship—someone not an emotional wreck, not debilitated by trauma, not intent on harming or undermining me. My cats, family to me, are well cared for during these artistic forays. Home (whatever apartment at the time), becomes a bea-con, a place I yearn for and can believe in. Home exists even if I'm not there, holding it together. I met John MacDonald—where else, but at *Who's Emma?*—and for decades he was a friend, com-rade, and arms-length buddy at almost every punk and metal show in town. Hilarious, loveable, and a reliable partner, he's one reason I can focus on writing.

I began to amass rejections from an infinite list of literary journals. Rejection is tough, of course, but allows the opportuni-ty to improve a story without the embarrassment of being caught, pants-down, in print, forever. I can experience a great deal of excitement about a project early on, when it requires the most work. In the past, I've confused that private enthusiasm with a public desire to share material: never again. When I'm asked to read excerpts from early works, the page is utterly littered with corrections and omissions and deliriously critical self-talk, such as, *Imbecile, what were you thinking?!*

One story, concerned with scarcity, religious dogma, and misogyny, grew into *Tarry This Night* (Arsenal Pulp Press, 2017), edited by Susan Safyan. This book is very Old Testament. Much of it was written in the bleak stairwell of my apartment building. I listened to epic doom metal, researched the prepper movement and impacts of climate change, posed as a minister to request bunker blueprints for "my congregation." I read the poetry of Marita Dachsel, recommended by Marina Endicott, who was my mentor at Banff in 2014, in the now-defunct Wired Writing program. Marina read through the horrible first draft of that manuscript and took me by the hand, as it were, basically showing me how to edit. She asked tough, necessary questions, which allowed me to sink deeper into the terrifying world I had called upon. This kind of dedication, this focus—what's actually required in the revision process—had previously eluded me.

At the Vermont Studio Centre (2016) I rediscovered my love of painting—the three-dimensional aspect of manifesting art, using one's hands, making a sloppy mess, stimulating the brain's image centre and shutting down those restrictive, judging parts. I appreciate the curiosity and openness with which visual artists approach the act of *seeing*. Writers can learn a lot from other artists. For me, writing is such an interior, highly intuitive process that it's difficult to express what I'm trying to do. The unpopular truth: integrating knowledge takes time. Practice, creative exploration, and living *mi vida loca* improves my writing. Mostly, I thank the judicious critiques I receive from smart writers, so much so that I can't conceive of completing the process in isolation. Public readings also reveal what's working, what needs revisiting. I pull tarot cards for my characters—don't laugh. I sketch, map, and collage my way through. I consult Lucille Ball, whose portrait by artist Cheyenne Randall sits at my left hand. (For the record, she doesn't typically answer.) I read Greek myths. I bible-dip. Not the most efficient process, alas.

Connecting with international artists has been incredibly gratifying, and mitigates loneliness. In an unfamiliar environment I become hyper-alert. I breathe, see, *think* differently. I (sometimes) get a lot done. The Banff Centre and Artscape Gibraltar Point on Toronto Island are energetically charged havens. Hambidge Arts Centre in north Georgia, where the spiders grow as large as my face and I helped rescue a malnourished puppy; Annaghmakerrig in Ireland, where I chased apparitions of my forebears and my familiars; La Porte Peinte, with its extraordinary, clairvoyant director, located in a French medieval village, is where I wrote "Oort Cloud Gets a Makeover," completing the *Stoop City* collection. Arts residencies offer respite, not unlike those scintillating summer camps back when I was a confused witchling. Each place resonates with its own his/stories—rocks and waterways, plants and animals—and those energies influence my state of mind, worming their way into handwritten rough drafts.

When I'm broke (often), I settle in at my desk and get to it.

Stories included in *Stoop City* (Biblioasis, 2020) were polished over the course of several years before I even submitted the manuscript. Edited by the supremely articulate John Metcalf, this collection (and I, myself) benefitted a great deal from his enthusiasm for the lively performance of language. He was the first person to really pay close attention to and celebrate the technical aspects of what I, what any of us writers, are trying to do, and the first to point out, in no uncertain terms, what improves the work. "Last Call at the Dogwater Inn," which closes the collection, was rejected by a dozen journals before winning the 2015 Machigonne Fiction Contest and being published in *The New Guard*. And "Daughter of Cups," which marinated in a drawer for years, was published in the first issue of *Orca: A Literary Journal* in 2019—an editor fished it out of the first reader's rejection pile by chance. "Daughter of Cups" was re-printed in *Best Canadian Stories 2020* (Biblioasis), edited by Paige Cooper, and won the Metcalf-Rooke Award, generously sponsored by Steven Temple Books. Although fiction, it's set in my hometown in the 1980s. Even this tiny truth feels scandalous. Like my young adult novels, it explores the maiden quest, a specifically gendered hero's journey. Depicting a girl's ill-advised sexual initiation without embracing a totally disempowering narrative was my goal; so, too, was blending small-town realism with the influence of deep magic, a monstrous matriarch rivalling the adult male protagonist and the sway of his motorcycle club.

Long, long ago at a CANSCAIP workshop, Brian Doyle, beloved Canadian children's author, voiced his opposition to MFAS and writing circles and the like; instead, he advocated for literary apprenticeships with the deceased. He urged us to read the classics…and copy them, shamelessly. How else could one learn craft and the skillful pacing of dramatic tension? Apprenticing with a dead author also meant avoiding potential copyright lawsuits, he explained. His advice provoked an uproar! Nevertheless, he led participants through an activity of total plagiarism, rewriting an infamous Charles Dickens passage about *fog*, replacing it with *snow*, what Canadians know best. I cheered his clandestine can of Molson Canadian at the catered lunch by way of thanks.

Good writing often embodies a numinous quality, sifting through the echoes of other lives lived, connecting clues in an attempt to find meaning: ghost hunting. In reading and writing,

I want to be reconnected to myth, to the animal body and primal impulse. To shuck off the repression and restriction imposed all around us, either using characters who cannot help but undermine those social constraints, or by the careful, meticulous peeling back of surfaces, to peer at the damage beneath. The more I learn, the more there is to learn; I hope I never tire of not knowing. Curiosity suckles the tendrils of obsession. Writing, painting, performing—it's all ritual to me. This is the beginning, middle, and end of it, the circular framework I invoke at my desk when I sit down to work: the pen, poised; the candle, lit; the tea, brewing.

LAST CALL AT
THE DOGWATER INN

KRISTYN DUNNION

First, there is Jimmy's six-pack of o.v., warm and bereft. I keep it company, washing down a handful of prescription pills from his bedside table. Jimmy's door is open and the afternoon sun is a lake of fire drawing and curling and surging to smite me as I perch on the edge of his bed. All the motel rooms are laid out similarly, but Jimmy's smells like shoe polish and mothballs and faint traces of diarrhea. Like denture powder and Old Spice cologne. Like a man who lived and died alone.

Inside the tiny bedside drawer is a well-thumbed pocket bible, St James edition. A pair of dollar store reading glasses. Round white candies that may have once tasted like mint. Swaddled in a handkerchief is a feather, probably pigeon, like a time-sanded relic from the Holy crèche. Scraps of paper penned in his furtive scrawl say, *St Barbara among the heathens!* And, *Cripple Civilian Society—Villains!*

I wouldn't exactly call it living, but I've been next door three years, ever since Delia chased me out of Detroit, back to my side of the border. I rarely set foot in Jimmy's room. It is void of many niceties. Obviously, no television; the man railed against them. No computers or electronics of any kind. "Ray," he'd say, pointing at my bedside radio, "That's how they track you." And he'd lower his hat to deflect the lobotomizing frequencies. He often shout-sang to ward off evil as he paced up and down the block, fists at his side or threatening the sky: *Bop wop a doo-dah, bop wop yeah!*

Jimmy deranged me at first, all that humming and tapping, those scat vocals puncturing the thin wall between us. I was not at my best. I'd paid a week's rent, cash. Locked myself in that room on the tail of a lethal bender, heartsick and determined to end it all, but, miracle, I survived the unconscionable mix of dope and pills and bourbon and poison I'd brought with me. *Addict loser no-good asshole.* Delia's accusations drummed down on my wretched remains like a flash flood, a summer rainstorm with brimstone and thunder and bolts of lightning that zapped my last tender spots, killing them, but not the rest of me.

Plan B—forcible detox, since I couldn't walk, had no tele-phone, knew no dealers in this part of town. If I died, at least I'd have succeeded with the original plan. I lay cramped, sweat-ing. When my bunged-up bowels finally moved, I shat myself profusely and couldn't crawl to the shower. Worms writhed my skin. I was beset by demons, which I later attributed to Jimmy's incessant, singsong voice, his abrupt barking and jazz hacks. Hours, maybe a day later, dragged along the crumbling balcony, I pounded his door, yelling, "Hie thee, Satan!" Jimmy opened a chained inch and said, "The government send you?" Which struck me as hilarious—that the government might send a shit-stained, detoxing maniac as a reliable representative. Jimmy unlocked and slipped me a lifesaving can of warm beer—o.v, always o.v.—which I shotgunned, and, instead of bashing his head in as I'd imagined, we became friends.

I rock back on Jimmy's cot, plastic creaking under the polyester coverlet. Roaches scurry to the corner. "They deserve a life, too," he'd say. A piece of foolscap taped high on his wall announces: *Do not impeach Biggie Smalls!* Jimmy alone campaigned on Biggie's behalf during a recent mayoral race that involved evangelical street-shouting and handwritten placards. (She got seventeen votes.) The candidate never once appeared in public.

Whenever I made crass jokes Jimmy would say, "Biggie Smalls and I cannot abide ignorance, Ray." One afternoon he said, "Biggie and I are heading to the beach, care to join us?" As Jimmy and I sauntered toward the lake, I wondered aloud, "Will we meet Biggie there?" "Ray," he said, "Biggie is with me wherever I go, unless she is breeding or feeding or otherwise feeling poorly." Jimmy spoke intimately to the crook of his arm and, later, into the depths of his coat pocket. He turned his head to listen for Biggie's response. Biggie, I assumed, was an imaginary slice of Jimmy's scrambled pie.

Stirring in a dim alcove above the note crouches the largest wolf spider I've ever seen; magnificent, furry, and somewhat familiar. A flash—me, drunk at the bar, and Jimmy lifting a palm-sized thing to his face adoringly. At the time I thought it was a hairpiece. Another hazed memory—me, collapsed on the rug in my room while Jimmy dances endlessly to a song I can't hear, his right hand extended for balance, his feet lifting and clopping, one-two, one-two, a furred lump creeping along his shoulders. *Biggie Smalls, straight outta the Georgia Woods*, Jimmy screeched.

Could it be? This, *this* is Jimmy's friend? Biggie Smalls in all her webbed glory, who will crusade for her now? A toast to Jimmy and Biggie is in order. I don't speak, just hoist the tin of beer.

Shadows fall upon me. Neilson, that rural numskull, appears in the sunsoaked doorway with a sickly little hustler. I'm not one to judge, but.

"Heard about Jimmy," says Neilson, and removes his hat.

I nod.

The hustler freezes like a hare and peers through dirty bangs at the ground.

"Come to pay respects," says Neilson, bathed in embers blown to flame.

"Door's open," I say, and that scares him. He'd rather a punch to the gut, that anti-social wolf.

Shadows liven their golden faces. Voices. I recognize Darlene's. She says, "I can't believe it. Just can't believe it!"

Darlene's mom rams her bedazzled walker past Neilson, makes straight for the only chair, and sits, heavily. Dust puffs out from around her rear end. Her entourage follows, crowding Neilson and his street trade away. The door pulls mostly closed and a dullness rides the room. It's cooler but gloomy. I blink to rid myself of red coals that shoot behind my eyelids. Now it's me and Darlene and her mom and the manager's niece, a glue-huffer whose name I don't know. Darlene is wearing something shiny around her neck, a wide collar, possibly made from aluminum foil. Her earrings are dangling styrofoam balls.

I feel woozy. The room closes in.

"Isn't it terrible, Ray? Just terrible," says Darlene's mom.

"We seen the cops leave, so we come up," says Darlene.

I succumb to Jimmy's flat, discoloured pillow. My jaw relaxes; saliva pools in my mouth. It takes all my strength to lift each leg and stretch it the length of the mattress. How many pills did I take?

"Darlene, see what he's got in the kitchen," says her mom. "I'm peckish."

My vision obscures to a blurred wash-out. I hear but cannot see Darlene wander off the carpet onto the linoleum, humming. The cupboard hinges quibble when she forces them. I feel each pressed-board slam in my marrow.

"Lipton Cup-o-Soup," Darlene shouts. "Saltines from the diner!"

"I'll take crackers," says her mom, and then the violence of her press-on nails tackling the plastic wrap. Crackling and crumpling and, finally, the seismic rupture. She crunches. Slurps. Stops to pick masticated lumps from her molars.

I cover my ears, whimpering.

The huffer darts and her hand closes over the pill bottle beside me, shaking it.

"Leave it," I mumble.

She unscrews the lid and peers inside. "Oxy, oxy, no oxy," she says, and sets it back down. Her face looms; eyebrows kneel in the centre of her lined forehead, her beak poised to stab.

"Gone," I whisper, and her eyebrows broaden and sink with despair.

Daryl's postnasal drip alerts me to the fact he has joined us and still has a baggie on him—the incessant tapping of fingers on that same pants pocket. Like my mother worrying her rosary, God in her skirt. Daryl has brought his dog. I can smell her dogginess, not unpleasant, not compared to the rest of the room and its occupants. She sniffs my bare toes, whiskery lick, presses her moist nose and snorts. *Shangri-La!*

More resident miscreants arrive to say farewell and snoop Jimmy's stuff. It's getting crowded and that anxiety-prone beast nurtures a quiet whine in the back of her throat. The jingle of her expired tags tracks the spin of her muzzle from Daryl's jerking movements to the rest of the unpredictable bipeds, back to her tweaked-out master. She turns a quick circle then scrabbles under the bed.

"Ray, Ray, you know Jimmy?" says Murray, the halfwit who lives with his mother in two-oh-seven. He passes a bottle. I slug off it. Sour mash.

"Cops shot him," Murray says, "then they tasered him."

"Domestic terrorism," says Mary Louise, his lesbian sidekick, the rockabilly butch.

"As if," sniffs Daryl.

Jimmy's voice haunts—*Let it be a lesson to any opposing the Western corporate regime: fast food, auto-oil, the Godwars!*

"To Jimmy," says Mary Louise.

"To Jimmy," we mumble. A clinking of bottles, the popping of beer-tin tabs, the rush and fizz of foam. Slurps. A few tears are shed. Darlene and her mom and the girl were there when it happened, been laying low ever since. They talk the most in order to quash their guilt about the loot they scored at Ernie's TV and Appliance, three blocks east on Bloor, where Jimmy took his last stand. Where Jimmy incited an actual riot in his perpetual war against electronics.

Tear gas! A shootout! Bender or no bender, how had I missed this?

An impromptu service of the funereal kind begins, and I would gladly desert, but those pills have kicked in and I have no control whatsoever over my limbs. I hope they're still attached to my torso, which rises higher, higher, floating near the stained ceiling squares. Hovering, I see it all: my body splayed on the cot, mourners encircling me, hungry for one last piece of the dead man.

Voices lift from the knot of bodies a galaxy away. Darlene's mom says, "Remember the time he hijacked the main office because the tax man was onto him?"

"Ha, that was funny."

"Was not, they held our cheques for three weeks," says Darlene.

Murray says, "We were on the news. On the TV!"

"Nearly gave him a stroke."

True. Acting out his beliefs, Jimmy was captured in photos and write-ups in the local paper, which only confirmed his suspicions. He'd say, "They're spying on me, Ray, I knew it!"

Everyone feels pretty bad for Jimmy, though I also feel bad for myself. The last drug-addled jazzman on the planet to give a shit about me, gone.

I descend back to my body, re-inhabit it. Jimmy's scent is in my nose, my hair. Lying where he slept each night, decked out in an open coffin, that's me, a spectacle. Friendless. I may as well *be* him, although I am white, debatably less crazy, and at least two decades his junior. Now I seep into the lumpy mattress, drip through rusted springs, and puddle onto the dog shivering on the filthy carpet below. I burrow deep beneath the floorboards, the concrete sub-basement, into the ravenous, wormy earth.

Take, eat, this is my body.

Above me, Jimmy's other things are shared out amongst the neediest, the loneliest. Everyone claims a memento. Housecoat, slippers, good suit, a fine hat wrapped in tissue paper and stored in an old-timey box. A cardigan with mismatched buttons. His checkerboard. The sum of a man—is this it?

I'm not too proud to accept his ancient record player, which someone lowers sombrely onto my stomach. The weight of it propels me back from earth's bowels and up into my flesh. I sold off my vinyl eons ago but can keep an eye out. Used to find records at the end of each street on garbage day—people couldn't wait to junk them when they bought CD players. Now everyone tosses CDs. What next?

Daryl says, "He's in a better place now."

Darlene says, "The morgue? Won't someone have to get him?"

"He has a daughter," says Mary Louise.

"Huh."

I cannot begin to describe how the police dragged Ernestine, the muttering manager with the large ring of mislabelled keys, from her untidy office. How I crept from bed and peered out the eyehole. Who wants to see a broad expanse of uniform and badge first thing? Not me, but I hid my gear and stumbled into pants, a shirt I buttoned haphazardly, a jacket to cover the bruising along my inner arms. Barefoot, I opened up to bid them good morning.

"Afternoon," said the pink-complected ginger cop.

Ernestine eventually cracked Jimmy's door, and while the police searched the premises, she told me they'd shot him. Sixteen times. She said, "The daughter was sick of getting calls, so he put you down for emergencies. I been knocking since yesterday."

"What day was that," I asked, and she sucked her teeth.

"Raymond Jacobs?" The blond cop rustled papers and pointed to sign, "Here and here. Oh and here."

"We're holding his things pending investigation," he said. "SIU."

The itemized list includes: one wallet (worn soft as a seal; I know it like my own); one leather belt (frayed at the end and notched tight to tie off with); one pair white sneakers (splattered red in my mind); one shirt; one pair pants; two dress socks; boxers; one brown fedora. Clothes no doubt folded stiff with blood.

"What about the bullets?" I said, and had to repeat myself since twat cops never listen.

"The sixteen bullets. They belong to him now? You gonna put them in the bag too?"

Gingersnap ignored me, but the blond had the decency to blush when he said, "I don't think so."

"He never hurt a fly," I said, and my voice trembled. I pressed a fist to my lips to stop the rush of what had swum up my throat from my churning wet belly.

Ernestine said, "Watch it, Ray, or they'll shoot you, too."

When the cops could find no proof that Jimmy had been the spokesperson for simmering student revolt nor for the anti-poverty group that immediately endorsed his actions, they prepared to leave. Normally they lock a place back up, but since there didn't seem to be anything of value, they left me sitting on the edge of Jimmy's bed, barefoot and stupefied, the door swung open.

Now the huffer hauls Jimmy's codeine cough syrup out from

behind the rusted can of Drain-o under the sink and it makes the rounds. A few good hits take me below seawater, to a new level of pre-consciousness. There's a deadening of the body, enhancement of certain senses, most notably hearing.

Darlene yaps again about the corpse, "Think he'll cree-mate? It costs, you know, you can't just dig a hole, someone's got to pay."

"Welfare," says Daryl.

"The daughter," says Mary Louise, "if there's no wife."

Me, I wonder.

And Darlene's mother nods vigorously. I can hear the flubbery shake of her goiterous neckskin. The creak of vinyl purse straps grasped tightly in her fingers. Polyester pant legs shimmering, pressed by hamhock thighs. The stretch of the nylon stitching that fights to keep those pants sewn together. A flesh orchestra—throat clearings, saliva swallowings, scalp scratchings, spine crackings. A soft gust of air being expelled from somebody's anus. Knees pop when someone's sorry weight heaves from one foot to the next.

I cannot move or speak.

Is this death?

After some bickering about his room—is it larger than the others, who has seniority and gets to switch—they leave, almost all at once. Even the dog skitters out after Daryl, who beats it back to three-oh-six, probably to snort a bump, and Jimmy's door swings open to sunset. Daylily and ripe tomato and burst peony.

"Don't go," I say, but no sound comes.

I remain prone.

I am gratified to survive the ritual. If this is survival.

I am one with Jimmy's berth.

Now I turn my mind to the beat of my heart: steady. The jumping skin at my wrist, my neck.

Once Jimmy and I were drinking at Penny's Open Mic and he

stood in line to take his turn with the slam poets and folksingers, the indie-rock douchebags. Jimmy had wolfgrowled and yodelled and shouted about tuberculosis, his childhood quarantine.

"Locked up with the freakshow! Ten years of suffering, suffering. Sanatorium released me to wander the streets, how kind! My family, *poof*, gone. Threw me in jail, said I disturbed the peace. I said, what peace? Ain't nothing peaceful left in this life!"

Poseurs clapped and bought him pints of draught. By way of thanks Jimmy said, "Got this plate in my head from the pig battering I took on the way downtown."

Poor old Jimmy.

A drink would be nice, whisky or bourbon. I'm not one for Scotch, Jimmy neither. Drinking and doping take me from misery, at first. Sooner or later they U-turn straight back to Delia or the times before—evictions, incarcerations, disinheritance—all my bantling failures, and often end in staggering tirades up and down Lansdowne Avenue while I try to purge myself of venom.

I'd shout, "Fuck you, Delia, fuck your greedy suck mouth!"

Jimmy'd smoke a cigarette and wait for it to pass.

"Jimmy," I slurred on more than one occasion, my arm around his neck, "every time I touched that woman, she'd push away. Then complain I wasn't interested. She'd lie there, fuming. That woman gave me the limp dick. Used to like mowing the lawn; I couldn't get that right for her, either."

"Ray," Jimmy would say, "Biggie and I cannot abide coarse talk," and he'd shield his jacket pocket with a hand.

I'd say, "That woman was sent to test me, she was born to bring me down. Even my mother couldn't stand me. Even my father. I never finished anything, never had the chance to get it right!"

He'd said, "Bullshit, Ray. You made yourself into who you are. Now it's time to move on."

What kind of man says that? That's for fathers. For men of the cloth. Or a certain rare combination of the two.

When I picked fights, which was often, he'd step between me and the sonofabitch I'd provoked. He'd brace his hands on my shoulders and look me in the eye. He'd say, "You don't have to do this, son, you are better than this." Once my screaming subsided and my fists dropped, he'd say, "I got an itch to dance, Ray, let's smoke a bowl and listen to your government music box." My guess is that that man had single-handedly kept me out of jail the better part of three years. To think how I scored that H and tucked it away, wanting it all for myself—enough to feign illness to Jimmy's comprehending face and hole up for days, shooting it, dreaming it, filling my blackened soul with its magic—while out there, somewhere, Jimmy took his stand without me.

Twilight in Jimmy's bed: the blue hour, bruised plum bled to dusk. The grind of cars and trucks rounding the curve out on Lansdowne Avenue, honking, revving, squealing to brake at the light. Beeping: a city bus kneels to let widows and strollered mothers climb aboard. Planes pass overhead and their sonic rumble effects a loosening in my guts; it's a frequency I've heard all my life but never paid mind to. This vibration could be some sort of answer. When the Go Train counters with its relentless engines, its momentous reclamation of suited suburbanites, I feel the bedframe tremble and believe I might aneurism or per-haps orgasm with the drama. *Bee bop, diddily whop, bap bap, yeah!* These are sounds that bury a man, sounds a man can never climb back up and around, never in his miserable shit of a life. I spread my arms wide on Jimmy's cot.

Above me, Biggie Smalls spindles in the corner, lays her thou-sand cotton-swabbed eggs, sits the night in wait for prey. Later, later, the teeny tiny speckles shake themselves to life. They spin and descend the besmirched wall toward my cooling flesh. Creep their way to the dawn of a forgotten universe.

CYNTHIA FLOOD

PHOTO: DEAN SINNETT

CYNTHIA FLOOD's *stories have won numerous awards, including* The Journey Prize *and a* National Magazine Award, *and have been widely anthologized. Her novel* Making a Stone of the Heart *was nominated for the City of Vancouver Book Prize in 2002. She is the author of several acclaimed short story collections including* The Animals in Their Elements *(1987),* My Father Took a Cake to France *(1992),* Red Girl Rat Boy *(2013) which was shortlisted for the BC Book Prizes' fiction award and long-listed for the Frank O'Connor award, and* What Can You Do *(2017). She lives in Vancouver's West End.*

HOW I BECAME A WRITER

FAMILY

I was born in Toronto on 17 September 1940, much-wanted by my mother certainly. My only sibling, Philip Creighton, was eleven years older. He made me toys and a dollhouse, taught me canoeing, took me skating with his high-school friends. He also gave emotional protection, because our father frightened me. When stifled anger replaced fear, Phil showed sympathy. As adults we lived very different lives, but love persisted. Laughter too—Phil died in August 2018, having phoned a fortnight earlier to tell me a joke.

What a little girl experiences, what an old woman understands: hard to resolve. Donald Creighton's anger, in predictable and unpredictable forms, dominated my experience of family life. I tried to avoid him, often dreaded his presence. Yet Dad invented amazing serial stories for me (Mr Jumpy, Oswald Leftover), read aloud with enthusiasm, engaged in flights of verbal teasing, and joined in social events with delight. All that, though, could vanish in a second.

My mother, Luella Bruce Creighton, cut a much more reliable figure. She told stories, embroidering what the butcher said, a tale overheard on a streetcar, the neighbours' *peculiar* actions. She laughed, often acted on impulse. She wrote novels and stories, also books for children; she enjoyed gardens, cooking, summers at Muskoka. Mum formed long, close friendships. Her rare angers occurred for a reason: I'd been rude, careless.

ELEMENTARY SCHOOL

In the 1930s my parents couldn't afford private school for Phil, but in the 1940s I got it. Other girls at St Mildred's talked of special white dresses for communion, so I asked to be baptized. This startled Mum and Dad, who'd long ago rejected Methodism, but they found godparents for me. Except for arithmetic I liked school, and I remember some teachers warmly, both lay women and nuns.

Some key memories:

Boredom while listening to others struggle through Dick Jane Spot Puff. I paged ahead, in our "reader."

Tears at the blackboard in grade two because I couldn't do some arithmetical task.

Struggles with inkwells, fountain pens. In time though I took pleasure in writing the upright hand the nuns taught us.

Reading Housman's *Wake: the silver dusk returning / Up the beach of darkness brims.* What did that mean? I read it again, again.

Writing poems, stories. A tale about a horse led to a reprimand from my teacher. "Where did you copy this from?" "I didn't!" " Oh yes you did." Humiliated, I told no one, for years saw no compliment.

Learning *fallow* and *sallow* the same day.

Puzzling over why other girls read so slowly.

When I was eleven we moved to England, and for two years I

boarded at Uplands School in Bournemouth. (Mum finished writing her second novel, meantime.) I felt no homesickness except for Muskoka. My accent got mocked of course, but I made friends, and in Miss Ludwig found a fine teacher. We read *Midsummer Night's Dream*, Kipling's *Captains Courageous*, Paul Gallico's *Jennie*. I regret not trying to find Miss Ludwig, on later visits to England.

At Uplands, arithmetic problems metastasized. *If Joe has 6 pencils at 10 cents each and Jane has 13 at 4 cents each*—that sort of query, bad enough in cents and dollars, grew to terror in pounds, shillings, pence.

Latin's presence in English surprised me.

I wrote stories, poems.

In my last term, my class toured the school's science lab. They'd enter it, after the holidays. I understood nothing of what went on there or why.

SECONDARY SCHOOL

In Toronto, just turned thirteen, I entered grade ten at Bishop Strachan School (nunless). My classmates, all older, had periods, boyfriends, illicit make-up. Such a shock. I never again "played," i.e., ran freely about with friends, except at Muskoka. Grade ten's only bright, no, brilliant spot: our English teacher, Mrs Wybrew. We read Addison & Steele, incredibly but for me enjoyably, and *Julius Caesar*, deemed suitable for youth because no sex occurs in it.

Geometry, a new hell.

I didn't know about the difficulties my father then faced as chair of U of T's history department. He brought his bad temper home. Phil had married. Our mother missed him, and focused on her own writing. Likely I puzzled her because I didn't want what she expected, clothes, records. I had no social life; she tried, embarrassingly, to arrange one. Mum at my age had been combative, determined, but I kept my disagreements underground. Also I was religious.

Over four years at BSS my shyness lessened. I learned to write a good essay, to keep my ideas to myself, to feel superior. I wrote poems and stories, won school prizes that meant little (no real competition). At the end of grade eleven I was alleged to have passed algebra, and thereafter studied only English, history, languages. So happy! So ignorant. I missed worlds of metaphor and imagery.

In grades eleven and twelve with Miss Seaman we read Cather's *The Professor's House*, Eliot's "Animula," Shelley's "Ozymandias," Lawrence's "Piano," Saint-Exupéry's *Night Flight*, Goldsmith's *She Stoops to Conquer*.

During Religious Knowledge class in grade twelve I asked a question about the Forty-Nine Articles of the Anglican Church, then the focus of our study. Shocked, our gentle RK teacher responded, "Cynthia, that is heresy!" In my head a sensation of collapse began, like a sandcastle when water's poured on it. Within days my religious faith had gone. Some loneliness persisted for a few months.

In grade thirteen the teachers appointed me head girl, a leadership role I didn't want and performed poorly, in my own and my classmates' opinions. (This presaged similar roles later in life.) I longed for school to end, though I enjoyed studying *Hamlet* with Miss Grace Macnaughton. She spoke as if acquainted with all the characters, and her Scottish accent enhanced her readings of the text.

Beatrix Potter, *King of the Golden River*, *Just So Stories*, *The Jungle Book*, *Alice*, *The Old Curiosity Shop*, *David Copperfield*, *Five Children and It* etc., *Anne of GG* (all, repeatedly, even awful *Kilmeny of the Orchard*), *Bobbsey Twins*, *Tanglewood Tales*, Enid Blyton, *The Wizard of Oz*, the *Green Red Yellow Pink Blue* etc. *Fairy Books*, *Little House on the Prairie* etc., *The Middle Moffat*, *Donegal Wonder Book*, *Green Dolphin Street*, *National Velvet*, *Little Women* etc., *My Friend Flicka* etc., *The Sword in the Stone*, *Mary Poppins*, *The Rose & The Ring*, *Five Little Peppers* etc., *Swallows & Amazons* etc.

I remember no Canadian writers except L. M. Montgomery.

To be absorbed in a new story: marvellous. Rereading felt nearly as good, sometimes brought surprises—things I'd not noticed the first time through. (Always a fast reader, sometimes careless.) I reread some scenes often: Meg recognizes her family's poverty, Laura smells fire. Why did I read so much? I loved it. Also I loved dolls, hide-and-seek, tag, snowmen, swimming, canoeing, jacks, skipping, checkers, roller- and ice-skating, card games.

Early on, I met in fiction one of life's great pleasures. It's never faded. I enjoyed studying poetry at school, but the experience rarely offered the intensity of reading narrative prose. It still doesn't. Also, as in youth I've remained an eclectic reader.

At the University of Toronto I specialized in English literature. In my last year, after a two-term course in US literature, we got six weeks of CanLit—Lampman, Carman, MacLennan, Callaghan—tacked on.

What I read by choice in high school and university: Wodehouse, C. S. Forester, Maugham, Bennett, Spark, M. R. James, Wilkie Collins, Faulkner, Mrs Gaskell, Brontës, Gabrielle Roy, Austen, Trollope, Swift, Greene, Dos Passos, E. M. Delafield,

Dreiser, Dickens, Mann, Tolstoy, Damon Runyon, Dodie Smith, Orwell, Kathryn Hulme, Forster, Winifred Holtby. Also Tey, Christie, Ross Macdonald, Simenon, Ambler.

Why I read so much: the usual. Lonely, out of place in high school, I'd found company in fiction and hid my love of reading except at home. At university things changed, though I did meet methodical English majors, aiming to teach high school, who read *only* the assigned Austen. *Done*, tick. But good friends I made at U of T loved books as I did. Talking with peers about Hemingway, Sagan—marvellous. Those friendships have lasted.

Did I read and reread because I sensed it was good training? Not consciously. I wrote poetry, got excited if any appeared in university publications, and wrote stories too—but I didn't see writing as a career. I expected and was expected to marry soon-ish. Probably I imagined my mother's pattern, writing on the side. As graduation got closer, anxiety increased.

TWENTIES

I won a fellowship to Berkeley, and on arrival learned that I couldn't write a thesis but must take an oral exam. Terrifying. (Not what the calendar said, either, but to push back never occurred to me.) I wrote little that year, took a weird miscellany of courses. Key memory: standing alone on campus and saying aloud, "This isn't where I should be." Dropping out never entered my head. WASPs don't. I nearly failed my MA oral.

Two years of secretarial work and lively social life followed, in San Francisco. I fell in love, started stories, threw drafts away, formed no literary connections. Maybe get a PhD in comparative lit? (This idea came after a binge of Zola.) I filled out forms, tore them up, then moved to New York. Again, zero literary links. I temped as a Dictaphone typist, walked the city, produced wads of handwritten sheets, stories abandoned, unfinished. One tale, set in San Francisco, did stay with me.

In 1964 I met Maurice Flood, by chance, at the Museum of Modern Art, where he worked as a guard, and in 1965 we married. We lived briefly in the Village, then moved to Toronto. An anti-war activist with the *Catholic Worker*, Maurice had fought a hard fight against the draft and wanted out of the US.

I worked at U of T Press and wrote about lives I imagined for our elderly landlords. In 1967, visiting Expo, we fell for Montreal and decided to move there. I got work at McGill University Press, and at last finished the San Francisco story, "On California Street." *Wascana Review* published it in 1968. Total thrill.

Wanting to see more of Canada, we quit our jobs in the impulsive way people did then, and moved west in August 1969. In Vancouver I easily found secretarial work. Then, early in 1970, we dove into the city's radical political scene (both of us), the women's movement (me), and the new gay liberation movement (Maurice). A core memory of that time: standing by the Vancouver Court House on Georgia to watch the Abortion Caravan depart for Ottawa.

My second education began.

POLITICS AND WRITING

For years I wrote and edited articles, briefs, letters, speeches, leaflets, broadsides, editorials, pamphlets, and a few stories. I joined a series of feminist and socialist organizations, participating fully. My two daughters arrived, Isabel in 1973 and Margaret in 1976. I remained sole breadwinner as Maurice became a public figure in the struggle for gay civil rights. By a fluke, in

1972 I landed work teaching Business English at Langara College. I taught part-time, keeping space for politics and writing.

Somewhere in those years I got hungry for narrative. I can't find another way to say it.

By 1974–75 I started writing fiction again. One summer I had six weeks to do so, in a tiny "study" in the rented house we shared with other politicals. So happy! I had three stories on the go, went back and forth. I still work that way. Later on I hand-wrote a novel, and in 1976, pregnant with daughter #2, typed the final version.

During these years I learned that literary and political people often saw each other as time-wasters, though feminists weren't quite so rigid. I didn't connect with any of the established literary groupings in Vancouver. Men dominated these elites, as far as I could see, and my Trotskyism doubtless didn't attract. Way too serious!

My stories began to appear in feminist literary magazines, *Makara* and *Room of One's Own*, and in more standard magazines like the *Journal of Canadian Fiction*. By this time I thought of myself as *someone who writes*. I longed for more time, but *artist* wasn't on my radar.

My mother expressed distress at the subject matter of some stories, finding their characters and situations ugly. However, she praised my skill, applauded me for working at writing. She regretted not doing more, herself. Once Mum said, of a recent publication, "It deserves to be in a better magazine than this." A complicated compliment!

I don't recall responses from Dad. Have I repressed them? By the mid-seventies he was already ill, despairing because he saw his life's work as useless. He didn't approve of how I lived, so likely had small appetite for my fiction. Once, when I came to Ontario to visit my parents, Dad told me, "The important thing for a writer is to build up an *oeuvre*." Instant silent rage. My childhood home, my parents' home at that moment: completely organized to meet his needs for solitude, for long quiet hours at his desk.

Not long before Dad's death in 1979, my parents came west. When my father and I were briefly alone together, he asked about my writing. What I felt about it. How I saw it in my life. I didn't shout *Where've you been?* I turned the talk. Perhaps we spoke of Wodehouse.

WRITING WHEN POSSIBLE

By that time I'd grasped that I *needed* to write. Not writing led to a sense of dysfunction, alienation. Writing has taken me through many troubles because, at the level where writing happens, I'm still okay. In 1980-81, though, writing couldn't do that. My marriage entered a disaster zone. Break-up came in December 1981.

Big changes.

My daughters Isabel and Margaret, singly or together, began to live alternately with me in Vancouver and with Maurice in San Francisco. Irony: their long, painful absences gave me writing time.

At Langara, I participated in founding the Women's Studies program, and later taught in Canadian Studies. I developed a course in Native Indian Literature (a first in the BC college system), and wrote a parallel course for the Open Learning Institute. (Distance learning, via Canada Post, on paper, with telephone tutorials. Incredible now!)

Then, in 1984, Langara College offered me permanent full-time work in the English Department. I hesitated, but—more money, summer months free for writing, a pension. *Yes.*

In 1985, through involvement in a left-wing newspaper project (*Out of Line*) I met Dean Sinnett, then a radio tech at the CBC. At those long, serious meetings we made each other laugh, and a connection began. We've been together now for thirty-five years.

By the mid-1980s I'd published enough to think of A Book. Penny Goldsmith—a good friend and small press publisher—knew Vancouver's publishing scene. She led me to Talonbooks, which published *The Animals in Their Elements* in 1987. Mary Schendlinger edited the MS, and Penny found Josie Cook's fine painting for the cover.

A favourite in *Animals* is "Beatrice," for its evocation of left-wing political life and the role of women comrades. "Evelyn and Rosie" I value for the two voices and long timespan. While writing, I saw it as a feminist documentary. Through "A Young Girl-Typist Ran to Smolny" discovered how footnotes could work. (I'd never read Jorge Luis Borges.) Several stories run too long—"Twoscore and Five," "On the Point," "Roses Are Red."

With the sacred mark of book publication on my forehead, I applied for membership in The Writers' Union of Canada. So happy! Off I went to my first meeting and got well-snubbed by the good old boys. Soon I connected with more welcoming members, and became much involved in TWUC activities. Very satisfying, that membership, then and now.

In 1987 my story "My Father Took a Cake to France" appeared in *Malahat Review* and won the Journey Prize. I worried about my mother's response. Visiting Ontario, I brought her a copy of the magazine, and while she read I left the room.

I came back to find Mum tearful.

"You have got him. To the life."

Gratitude, beyond words.

In 1992 Talonbooks brought out my second book, *My Father Took a Cake to France*. Again, Mary Schendlinger oversaw its production.

Karl Siegler, the publisher, and I talked about possible designs for the book. I wanted a type cover. What colours? Karl pulled out his pack of Parliaments, wrapped in pale gold and burgundy. Perfect!

Dadcake, to use its family title, even achieved a second printing, in 1993. In this collection my favourite is "Gold, Silver, Ivory, Slate, and Wood," for its landscapes and for Ray's slow learning how to see. Feminist perceptions from two decades of activism guided "Schooling of Women" and "Winter Into Spring."

During the 1990s, although much time went into a novel, *Making a Stone of the Heart* (see below, in *Novels*), I also published six stories set in a girls' boarding school in England. I talked about both projects in a women writers' group I belonged to, Sex Death & Madness.

SDM didn't workshop, but focused on writing and its companions—blocks, fatigue, inspiration, failure. Also, we pooled information about editors, publishers, agents. Members included at various times Bonnie Klein, Carmen Rodriguez, Christine Hayvice, Claire Kujundzic, Jena Hamilton, Kate Braid, Kath Curran, Joy Kogawa, Margaret Hollingsworth, Sandy Shreve, Sheila Norgate, Tana Runyan, Thuong Vuong-Riddick. Our meetings went on for a decade.

In the mid-2000s, I focussed again on my fictions about England in the 1950s. At a writers' conference around 2005 I met John Metcalf, who told me about his and Dan Wells' new publishing company, Biblioasis. He encouraged me to submit. I did, got accepted, and received good advice from John on linking *The English Stories.* The book appeared in 2009. I didn't then know the term "a novel in stories," but TES does exemplify that concept. Its cover design delighted me.

The research for "A Civil Plantation" absorbed me for months. Mr Greene's voice, so neurotic, came to me clearly. "Miss Pringle's Hour," because of its diary form, pleases me still, while

"Magnificat" exposes the era's hypocrisy about sex—even worse then in the UK than in Canada. "Early in the Morning" came from a friend at my English school contracting polio. (She lived on till her mid-twenties.) I kept the writing plain, to let events carry the sorrow and to make prominent the inconsistency and deceit of adults.

Since then I've published two more story collections with Biblioasis, *Red Girl Rat Boy* in 2013 and *What Can You Do* in 2017. Like the earlier three, they show family interactions, feminism, children in an adult world, left-wing politics, old age, schooling of various kinds.

In RGRB I most enjoyed writing "Eggs & Bones," "Dirty Work," "Red Girl" itself, and "Blue Clouds." With "Eggs," I imagined a split screen with the two versions of the marriage showing at once. (In a way that story resembles "Evelyn & Rosie," though antagonistic instead of loving.) "Dirty Work" pleases me still, so full of incident and covering such a long timespan that it clearly could be a novel—but *isn't*. As for "Clouds," when the idea came of ending it with the painting I laughed with happiness. I did that again when Biblioasis sent me the proposed cover design.

Red Girl's also special for me as my only book to be nominated for BC's Ethel Wilson Fiction Prize.

What Can You Do (2017) received good reviews too. In the title story a middle-aged couple realize their answer is *Not much*. "Apology" shows the spite that often erupts in old age, while in "History Lesson" I enjoyed trying a male voice to present old Harold's lefty life. "Dog and Sheep," a favourite, uses an account of a walking tour in France to explore the cruelty of privilege and class structures.

My stories have always varied in length. *What Can You Do* (2017) contains the most *really* short ones (five are under ten pages), but *Animals* (1987) comes close, with nine stories under

12 pages. *English Stories*, because I often wrote formally to match the characters, has five longer than 20 pages. *Dadcake*'s stories range from eight to sixteen, while those in *Red Girl* tend to run longer, many from fourteen to twenty.

Length *in itself* doesn't have much effect on the difficulty of writing fiction. Some of my long stories reached solid form in days, while the shortest in *What Can You Do* went through thirteen drafts over the course of a year.

NOVELS

In the mid-1970s I wrote *The Woman in the Window*, about a feminist involved in the feminist movement of that era. I remember little of the story, though it ended with a demo of some kind. Press Gang Publishers turned it down. Second Story might have also? Probably TWTW fell into the category of earnest realism.

During the late 1980s/early 1990s I wrote *A Private Manifesto*, set in Seattle in the 1970s. This novel concerns a girl with parents heavily involved in the radical movements of the time. They disappear, she goes into "care," and later as a young adult tries to search out the truth of their lives. Lots of good stuff in the ms, last time I looked. The opening chapters might have made a novella. (I tried, couldn't make it work.) The rest had way too many characters and settings.

In the later 1990s I wrote *Making a Stone of the Heart*. This novel arose because of a newspaper article about a woman with a pregnancy in which the fetus died, then calcified. Lots of symbolic value…Also I'd read a short English novel (Martin Amis' *Time's Arrow*) structured in reverse chronological order. Fascinating! The notion of starting with old age and going back to youth appealed to me.

To cover the four principal characters' lives I did intensive research into Vancouver's history. In personal terms I'm glad I did so, because the process rooted me in this city even more. But but but—to write about four lives in reverse time order creates insoluble organizational problems. Several readers warned me about this while I worked on *Stone*. I persisted in completing my unusual book, even found an agent and a publisher. The novel came out in 2002 from Key Porter, which promptly collapsed into receivership.

KP's fall took down many books, including mine. Perhaps two reviews of *Making a Stone* appeared? Both sounded puzzled, as if the writers had wanted to enjoy themselves but couldn't. So—stubbornness, though sometimes essential, can do harm, and a writer is not always the best judge of her own work.

I wonder now. Did I write novels because I felt inadequate for "only" writing short fiction?

WHAT I'VE LEARNED

In 2017, a story I wrote in the 1980s, "Twoscore and Five," reappeared in an anthology (*Making Room: Forty Years of Room Magazine*, Caitlin Press, 2017). I hadn't read it in years, felt the work held up. So *long*, though! A frame story, yes, which explains some of the bulk, but really—*six thousand* words? Even with an academic narrator?

In the 1980s I greatly admired Doris Lessing's stories, and from the 1990s onward I even more admired William Trevor's and Nadine Gordimer's and Alice Munro's. None of these writers feared going on at length. Lydia Davis' experimental fictions, which I found in the 2010s, startled and pleased me. She freely invents story "forms," very spare indeed, or thick with incident and detail, or like short plays. I also came upon Carys Davies, another writer of unusual short stories. Plus Colm Tóibín, Jhumpa Lahiri, Camilla Grudova…

While reading novels, I often think *This would be so much better at half the length!* (Same for movies.) In youth I'd continue reading, out of respect for the writer's toil, but I quit that decades ago. Even fine writers can sink into the Too Long swamp. I deeply admire William Trevor, but some of his novels, such as *Felicia's Journey* and *Lucy Gault*, should have been short stories. They're fatty and sluggish, though Trevor couldn't write a bad sentence if he tried.

Now, when writing a story, I define the territory between 2,000 and 3,000 words as *long enough*. Past that I get nervous, fear rambling.

On finishing a day's work I make notes on problems, sometimes create a To Do list. I may spend a week working on Story A, then move to B, next to C. That way I don't get bored or careless inside one fictional world. Also, when I return from B to A or C, the staff in my head's back room may have solutions ready. I've learned to trust them.

To invent plot is way easier than to convey emotion without labelling it, also easier than to show an individual's particular way of being in the world. For those, imagery's crucial. Alice Munro excellently chose *magnet* to express its power. While looking at an early draft, I may note some energy-laden words I didn't choose by conscious design. How to use them? Not heavily. Don't lay down *clues* for detectives. A reader might notice, or not—yet enjoy going where those images lead.

After drafting a story, I often used to realize that the action needed to move up from page four or nine to page two or even page one. Fear of landing in glue, or fire, had led me to defer events. I've learned that writing full sentences early on can drag a story into this kind of trouble. Now I start with phrases, fragments, single words. By hand. *No* connective tissue. I fight the urge to organize, to type a page. Often I leave that potential story alone for a while, to work on one that's nearer completion. Days later, the scrappy notes may resolve.

Sentences, paragraphs: having taught college-level English, I easily write thesis-followed-by-evidence, so I check to ensure the story doesn't carry that classroom taint. Fictional design, though, makes its own demands, so I also check the rhythms. Find repetition (the boring kind). Discover omission, overlap.

Editing, I ask each paragraph and then each sentence, *Why are you here?* Sometimes, favourites can't answer that and must go.

Clean-up comes near the end. I like lists but try to limit them. Adjectives: attention-seekers. Adverbs: often evil. Copula verbs: same. Because the higher gears of English grammar can mangle a reader's interest, out go most pluperfects, expletives, passive voice, series of co-ordinating clauses.

I set the story aside for a month at least. Some small items or typing errors may greet me then. At the last, I follow a fellow-writer's surprising advice: read the story aloud, sentence by sentence, backwards *from the last page.*

Those liminal minutes just before going to sleep or on waking up—I've learned to trust them. I attempt awareness then, because good material may emerge to meet the process that generates fiction.

Whatever that is, I'm grateful, always, to my parents for passing on the relevant genes. Writing: one of the best parts of my life.

WRITING "CALM"

A big stable in Vancouver's Stanley Park is home for horses that pull wagonloads of tourists around the Park or serve in the local police force. Sometimes, two or four mounted police ride about the West End, where I live, stopping to let people pat the animals, ask questions. The horses learn not to freak out, and to hope for apples.

One October night in 2015 I woke to hear four horses clop-clopping down a nearby street. Why, at night? As the rhythmic sound faded, I began drifting ... and saw a boy, maybe ten, awake. Unhappy, lonely. He heard *clop-clop*. Looked out his window. Saw them? No. Too soon. But he could try to find them ... I went back to sleep.

Writing "Calm" gave me pleasure.

Early on, I watched videos about training army horses, circus horses, fox-hunting horses, horses that do dressage. All these and their trainers form close bonds. Mounted police horses specialize in working amidst noisy, hostile crowds. The animals move humans around by stepping sideways and at the same time sort of leaning, pushing against us. They're trained, through hearing many unexpected loud noises, *not* to startle at gunshots or explosions.

From my notebook:

26 October 2015:
Started new story re the police/horses that arrived last night. Hopeful re this. Sure feels better than battering at [a story later abandoned] *that's such a mass of problems.*
[*Practice for the big demo coming up next week*]—[*no, this is logical not image*]
A child hears? sees? follows?
A vagrant? ditto?

27 October 2015:

Feel as if I began way too fast, committed to too much, left gaps. Try handwriting.

He wasn't allowed to have a key.

THEY TOOK IT.

Yes, slower process better

28 October 2015:

He would shoulder them aside

strongly not roughly   his calm purpose

moving them to one side, aside   then behind him   then gone

We saw the horses yest while walking, in those stables nr Beaver Lake. So big. They expected treats of course. Take oats next time!

One of the training videos says horse senses heartbeat of rider. Knows if scared or anxious or calm, resolute, etc.

Move desc of riders UP.

?? Well, it is on p 2. See what overall shape is, later.

He'll have to see a sign s'where for the demo. Alley? Or just the map? Pasted on lamp-post?

Has he ever seen the stables.   NO.

16 November 2015:

Good potential.

Add map, mapping—key. How? Boy has to see map showing stables.

Next day?

After the punishment?

Put more of the video stuff earlier.

terrain

lay of land

directions

mapping

re-use that scrap at p 5 re the name of that bird   silence his cold feet
The original first parag, at the very end—superfluous?
Print, next time—don't write more till you've checked the whole route

17 November 2015:
Don't get the map stuff too heavy
lay of land
ready to print & leave? 1392

[To check the boy's timing and identify where he'd scramble to reach a good viewing position, Dean and I took a midnight walk from the boy's home (near us in the West End) to Second Beach.]

18 November 2015:
more info re little maps, numbers down the side? images? check
incorp that detail
I like the ending a <u>*lot*</u>

19 November 2015:
Do the rider-cops have holsters? Yes
legend
add re guns
understory is ok

20 November 2015
take out street names—all, if poss. Yes.
underbrush   yellow reflective vests OK—*1356 words. Leave till Monday, full weekend.*
horses betw buses parked cars yellow reflective strips around "ankles"
has to be a ref to some upcoming EVENT *where we know but he doesn't*
that the horses will be used

23 November 2015
All done except for how to indicate pol event or upcoming crowds?
Resist? Yes, I think this works. Funny, used resistance *in emailing V*
yesterday. Must have been percolating.
take out ONE *resist? Yes.*
Printed. 1463

24 November 2015
Done, 1444. Printed.

CALM

CYNTHIA FLOOD

Strong feet stepped into the boy's dream, came nearer down the hall, and he sat up, but the sounds went past, outside.

Quick, to the window.

Down the dark, quiet street came four horses, two by two, with police on top. Streetlights shone on the animals' rumps, the riders' yellow vests. Clop clop. Harnesses glinted, tails waved, manes lifted and subsided. The horses too wore reflective yellow, in bands round their ankles. No heavy traffic here, though, not like the last time he'd seen them, at rush hour, walking calmly, single file, between a moving bus and a line of parked cars.

Hesitation. *Bad.* His bruises still hurt.

I have to know where you are, she'd said, you can't just wander alone. You don't know this big city. And stay out of the Park! Who knows what's hiding there?

Also, they'd taken his keys.

Clothes—he found them.

As he felt in the "secret" pocket of her rain jacket, from the other bedroom came sounds he disliked. Good, they'd sleep soon.

He left the building via the rusty fire escape off the third-floor hall. At the bottom he must swallow, then jump down to damp earth—better than taking the dim stairs to the basement door.

He hurried then. Clop clop, and the horses headed west past shabby low-rises like his, past the corner store with posters stuck on its outer wall. One said *Resist!* What? Then past the school, the one he went to, with a map of all Canada on the classroom wall. Vancouver, a dot. The town where he'd lived before, not even that. On the bewildering drive to the city, she'd kept saying *Look at the map, see where you're going!* He didn't. Hadn't ever asked to make this move. Back there, the cops only had motorcycles.

The boy kept half a block between himself and clop-clop, scuttling from hedge to street-tree to shrub. Where did they live? He'd seen the horses often, on busy West End streets or near the big beach. Sometimes the police halted them. Then people could ask questions or even pat those enormous heads. He saw the cops' holsters close up, and the animals' big nostrils, and their strange eyes, bluish-brown. Such big teeth. Soon the horses moved on. Their steady gait—lots of videos showed that, how the animals just kept on coming, calm amidst furious crowds. Did riots happen here?

As the quartet neared the big street he stayed further back, waiting while the traffic light changed and changed again. On the restaurant at the corner, someone had half-scraped off a *Resist!* poster. Near this intersection, he did know his way. Homeless men slept in store entrances, their hidden faces probably familiar to him from the network of local alleys, of bins behind cafes and groceries. Once he'd taken home a cold burger, untouched in its box. They'd found it. *Bad.*

When green shone a third time he sauntered across, then hastened after the lifting hooves. Along these blocks, richer landscaping fronted tall condos. To hide and move and hide: easy. Ahead waited greater darkness, though moonlight came and went as the clouds moved.

By day he'd wandered this terrain south of Lost Lagoon, grasping at its geography. Some lampposts in the Park and at its edges displayed a map, for tourists, so he'd learned some main routes. In the middle of the map's big green stood a tiny, surprising coyote. He hadn't known they could live in cities. Mum said *You never see what's right under your nose.* Not true. On his own he'd spotted a real raccoon snoozing in a tree, and a dead bird with a beak like a sword, and sleeping bags inside bushes, along with piled bottles and cans.

Once he'd even circled the Lagoon, peering up at the forest north of it, but had never before entered the Park after sunset. In the small town, he with other kids spent hours nightly in the local park, only vacating when the teenagers took over, but no map was needed. You could see right across.

Now he followed the horses into the darkness. Near-silence, but for the stepping animals. One lifted its tail. Plop plop, and that warm smell mixed with the night's leafy earthiness.

Would they turn at the tennis courts, head for the Bay? No. A right turn. Where to? At first following the horses, the boy then dared to move sideways into the damp understory of salal, laurel, giant rhodo—and then ahead, to crouch and peek as the nodding heads approached. Even when a rare midnight car drove past, the animals didn't change pace. The videos showed that, too, horses proceeding while police trainers waved flags and noisemakers in their faces, fired blanks, came unseen from behind to beat garbage-can lids. Calm.

Next they went west. On one side of that road, he knew, lay open lawn, on the other just patchy shrubs, low. All the way, streetlights. Now what? Could he scrabble downhill, unseen, unheard, to the underpass, and so move roughly west too? His insides heaved. No, not that tunnel in the dark—nor by day. It curved, so the exit wasn't visible from the entrance. *I'm not a little boy anymore. I'm not!* They'd laughed till they cried, though later Mum said *Sorry,* and then they smoked. Also, the meadow beyond the underpass gave no cover.

He slowed, guessing, and turned from the horses, south and then west in a long, watchful arc through both open and wooded areas. Breathed leaves, a trace of skunk, of cigarette. Uphill then, on to the high bank overlooking the ocean. Here he squatted under a shore-pine distorted by wind and weather, smelled algae, watched the incoming tide's long frills of white collapse on the sand. Soaked runners; cold sockless feet—he didn't care, looked north. *I was right.* Only a hundred metres away the quartet walked towards a ramp that sloped to the beach. Touching the concrete, the lead animals snorted, and the riders spoke gently, stroking.

When hooves met sand the four horses trotted south almost as far as the point, almost gone from view—then back again, under the boy's high perch, to and fro, to and fro. The animals' muscles created light patterns on their coats while the waves gleamed under the moon, fell into silver-marbled froth and made their *hsssh* sound.

When the riders headed straight at the water, the boy gasped. He couldn't swim. Nodding, the horses waded in. They stepped freely, splashed, came back to shore, reversed and went forward again into the waves, whinnying. *They're happy!* The riders turned them tightly, splashing through the shallows as if in an enclosure rather than the Pacific. Turn, turn—and out of the water they came, dripping, tossing their manes, to shoulder sideways, back and forth, steady pairs dancing while the sand bounced up by their hooves.

They stopped. One cop said something, and within a minute the horses walked two by two up the ramp and trotted eastward into treed darkness. Where?

Clop clop, clop clop, fading. At last the boy felt cold.

Once he slipped on wet leaves, falling.

Without the horses ahead, he got muddled in the darkness.

Emerging from the Park, he found the street wasn't his but took it anyway, for traffic lights winked ahead. *Resist!* was stapled to four street trees.

At the corner he checked a tourist map. *I'm just two blocks over.* By day he'd go again, figure out the lay of the land. As the signal changed, he noted at the map's edge a legend matching images to numbers dotted on the Park's green expanse. Seven: tiny horse. *Police Stables.*

Somehow the key's noise woke them at home. *Bad.* His wet, dirty clothes enraged his mother. The man never needed a reason, but used that one too.

In bed at last, he thought a bit about how one day he'd shove them off, shove as if they were an enormous ball, six feet in diameter, rolling about a training ring to impede his progress. As horses do when skilled in crowd control, he'd shoulder them. Lean against them, step sideways, step and step and another patient step till, like him now, they'd have no choice. Steady he'd be, calm.

Mostly he imagined stables. He'd stand close, look up. Touch? Feed? Once he'd seen a girl hold out an apple. Big teeth showed as the hairy lips lifted back, and the horse crunched the fruit.

The boy raised his hand, held his palm flat.

SHAENA LAMBERT

SHAENA LAMBERT's *most recent novel,* Petra, *published 2020 with Random House Canada, was inspired by activist and Green Party founder Petra Kelly, who changed history and transformed environmental politics, only to find herself caught up in a triangle of love, jealousy, and murder. It won the Ethel Wilson Prize for Fiction. Lambert is also the author of the novel* Radiance *and two books of stories,* Oh, My Darling *and* The Falling Woman, *all of which were* Globe and Mail *best books of the year. Her fiction has been published to critical acclaim in Canada, the* UK, *and Germany and has been nominated for the Atwood Gibson Writers' Trust Fiction Prize, the Ethel Wilson Fiction Prize, the Evergreen Award, the Danuta Gleed Award, and the Frank O'Connor Award for the Short Story. Her stories have been chosen four times for* Best Canadian Stories, *and have appeared in many publications, including* The Walrus, Zoetrope: All Story, Ploughshares, The Journey Prize Anthology, *and* Toronto Life. *Lambert lives in Vancouver.*

MONKEY BUSINESS

MY APPRENTICESHIP AS A WRITER

This essay grew out of a series of letters between John Metcalf and me. John asked questions about my early life as a writer, my activism, and my stories and novels, and I puzzled over his questions, always written impeccably in dark ink, and then I would type my responses and send them off. I loved the process dearly, treasure John's inimitable letters, and this essay is the result. I'm tremendously grateful to John Metcalf for championing my stories, and for supporting so many writers in their careers.

TREES AND STUMPS

Barbara Gowdy's book *Helpless* has a scene in which two children play with their dolls. I heard her read it at an event at Bolen's books, in Victoria, and I remember being mesmerized. She caught the tone of the children's voices, the involved murmur, and it reminded me exactly of hearing my own daughter playing with her Barbies in their dollhouse, the intimate sing-song as she spoke in each doll's voice. My daughter was creating a story as she went, and it had rules, yet she was also free to leave off at any second, or take things in a new direction. Kids don't forget where they are, even when absorbed in playing. They hover.

This could be as good a description as any for the brain activity required to write fiction.

I grew up in Horseshoe Bay, an enclave of West Vancouver, and at that time, the mid-sixties, our Italian and Dutch neighbours kept chickens and ducks, while the wooded lots beside our house were full of pathways, "fox lairs" and places for forts. Stumps stood along the pathways, remains of forest giants felled by cross-cut saws a hundred years earlier. The stumps had been notched about a yard above the ground, which gave my two brothers and me footholds to scramble onto the tops. We dug stream beds, built houses out of twigs, that kind of thing.

A huge red cedar grew in that forest next to our house. It had been named Monkey Business by a previous generation of kids.

This tree was my first love.

From the age of six, I would swing hand over hand up the first limb, then climb the branches to a spot thirty feet above the ground where the boughs grew close and made a seat, with back rest, arm rests, and even a footrest. I could see across the woods into the windows of our post-and-beam house and watch my mother moving around the kitchen. Everything in our house looked different from Monkey Business. Smaller, stranger. As I got older I'd climb up there with a book, but it wasn't a great reading spot. It was a place for thinking and watching. I was surrounded by the scent of cedar, the force of the trunk at my back, the arch of limbs, which was so perfect it was almost musical, the dangle of the withes.

It wasn't exactly the same as descending to my desk at six in the morning, coffee cup in hand, but there is a similarity between the two. Some force. Some peacefulness. Climb the trunk. Shut the door. If you are lucky, you will lose yourself slightly, while becoming more deeply yourself.

I became a writer because of my mother.

She came to writing early, quit it for years, and then returned to it in her late forties. I think her gaps influenced me as much as her passionate attachment. Other people have influenced me, but she was the luminous icon. Her struggles to write, her mythic journey, as it seemed to me, made writing seem like something that almost *hurt*.

Yet she made me want it!

My father was a lawyer, and then later a judge on the British Columbia Court of Appeal, and he wrote many well-known judgements—his most famous ones, such as *Delgamuukw v British Columbia*, were landmark cases on Indigenous rights to land, self-government, and to hunting and fishing resources. He had immigrated to Canada from Ardrossan, a village on the Firth of Clyde not far from Glasgow. He missed Scotland and at night he would sometimes play Kenneth McKellar records on the portable record player that sat on a side table in our living room. He'd put on "My Heart's in the Highlands," then he would sit in his brown chair. Pretty soon he would begin to cry. I found this magical and confusing. I could taste Scotland in his grief, and I badly wanted him to know that *my* heart was in the Highlands, too—but what he was going through was too private to interrupt.

My mother also came with myths. The stories of her lonely childhood in the Okanagan Valley—she was an only child for the first eight years of her life—were so wistful and strange. The war was on, and her German family was persecuted. The RCMP searched their house looking for weapons; neighbours accused them of sending signals across the lake; and children at school taunted my mother, calling her a Kraut, refusing to play with her. All of this gave her a sense of having been marked, made to feel different, which stayed with her even as a young mother, when, for instance, she might clear her throat several times before making a phone call. Or seem to need to gather courage to go to a law partner's picnic with my father.

My mother had a long, dark braid, which she wore up in a bun, or let hang down her back. She loved to read to us, and to tell us made-up stories. We'd snuggle beside her in bed, my two brothers on one side and me on the other, and while we looked at the pictures, she would read from *Winnie-the-Pooh*, *The House at Pooh Corner*, or *The Story of Babar*.

She told us Greek myths as we did the dishes at night, stories she had, in turn, been told by her father as he milked the cow: Perseus and Medusa, Jason and his Golden Fleece, Theseus, Ariadne, and Medusa. They were almost like family ancestors. When my first grade teacher, Miss Hills, told us we could draw a picture of anything, I drew Perseus holding up the severed head of Medusa.

Once, after supper, my mother got out Dylan Thomas' "Fern Hill": Standing by the wooden planter (filled with books and toys and the detritus of our lives) she read to us. *As I was young and easy under the apple boughs.* Her voice was sonorous, yet lit up too, as she reached the final words: *Though I sang in my chains like the sea.* We gathered around her. My older brother had a somewhat embarrassed look on his face, but my younger brother and I were bewitched. "But what does it mean? What does it *mean?*" we demanded—but she just shook her head and closed the book on that mystery.

She had had early success as a writer, with stories broadcast on the CBC and anthologized in *Stories with John Drainie*. But how to keep going, how to keep believing in herself, with the stresses of raising three children born within three years, and a demanding and brilliant husband whose career was now in full swing, and who thought of her writing not as a burning ambition to be stoked, but as a charming but unnecessary add-on to her real work as helpmate, housewife, and mother? Not to mention the childhood shadows, which had laid a strip of insecurity into her soul. How, against the force of these counter currents, to fit in the time not just to write, but to dream—because dreaming is just as important as the physical act of composing, or even more important. It was the dreaming time—I can see this now—that was truly missing in her consuming life.

Still, she tried. Even after the death of her mother, which gutted her entirely. She hurried through her morning tasks—dusting, dishes, making beds, vacuuming—then brought out her Underwood typewriter and placed it at the end of the dining room table, and she worked away on that typewriter, with its *t* that stuck, the *a* that flew above the line. She read over what she'd done, erasing with the circular rubber disk, brushing the crumbs away. Or, in extravagant frustration, she ripped the page from the typewriter, balled it up and tossed it in the wastepaper basket—a great show of writerly disgust. I lay on the floor and drummed my feet on the underside of the table in time to her typing. How hard it must have been to concentrate!

There was always the problem of "making it right." Anything "dreadful" had to be thrown away. We were not a family of wasters. (I once threw away a half-eaten piece of chicken leg because I'd seen someone on TV clear their plate into the garbage, and I was chastened by my mother, child of the depression that she was.) But words required the frequent use of the garbage can. They also required luck, daring, breath, and some quality that seemed to need to be called down from the ceiling. A blessing from the gods themselves. Not the Christian god, but the gods, plural, who would eat you as soon as look at you, or demand you fly through the air with wings on your slippers, or come at you in a sparkle of dust.

This was a valuable lesson. More valuable than if she'd gotten it right each time. It taught me the importance of art. But I have also spent a large part of my creative life building workarounds to the problem of demanding and fretful gods.

It's hard to make art while feeling that you are making art. You can't have gods peering over your shoulder. You have to be doing something that pulls you into a place of private involvement and pleasure, sufficient to clear out fierce and watchful eyes.

When I was eight, my mother stopped bringing out the Underwood. That phase ended. Shortly after, she took up other arts, becoming first a batik artist and then a silkscreen printer. She founded Tree House Studios, and had success with fabric art. But writing was in her cells, and separation from it took a toll on her. My parent's marriage had its rocky moments. My mother battled with alcohol. It was only in her late forties that she took up writing again. By the time she was publishing, I was, too—the braids of our writing lives overlapping. Even starting late, my mother had many successes: winning the Danuta Gleed Award for best first story collection, being nominated for the BC book prize, publishing four well-received works of fiction, the last of which, *Wanda*, comes full circle—diving deep into her childhood in the Okanagan Valley.

READING

Shortly after my mother stopped writing, we moved to Barbados for a year, as my father was hired to rewrite the country's tax laws. I remember this time vividly (and later used it for my story "Little Bird"). Everything was so different from misty, forested Horseshoe Bay. The heat was intense, and in rainy season a huge mud hole grew down by the cane field. My parents went out dancing, and to cocktail parties, and they often came home fighting. They both drank too much. I spent a lot of time alone. My school started a month after my brothers' did, and to fill the time I started to really read.

My parents gave me Enid Blyton's books, which were available in Barbados, with its recent British heritage, and I fell right into the stories of Fatty and the Five Find-Outers, children who solved crime. I loved how they went home for "the hols," and ate crumpets; how they made the local policeman look like a fool.

I remember stretching out on the red vinyl couch, reading. My brothers were at school, my mother out, and for some reason it was my father and me at home. My father approached. He seemed nervous, standing by the couch in his Bermuda shorts and short-sleeved shirt. When I looked up he asked, almost diffidently: Did I want to do something? Just him and me. We could go to the beach. We didn't tend to do things just the two of us, and maybe he felt he'd been neglecting me. Anyway, the point of this story is that I didn't think, I just said no, I didn't want to go to the beach, because I was reading.

Why is this memory important to me? I think it meant that books gave me rights. Wholly absorbing sanctuaries, for sure. But also the right—at least in that instant, as I came up for air—to say what I actually thought. Nobody said no to my father. We all—every one of us—appeased him. And yet I had just said no. The memory still has a flare of subversion to it.

Another reading story. We are back from Barbados. I am ten and I hear sobbing coming through the wall from my younger brother's bedroom. (The wall is tongue-and-groove cedar—sounds carry easily.) I push open his door and there he is on the bed, crying as though his heart will break. He gestures to the book beside him. *The Yearling*, by Marjorie Kinnan Rawlings. *The deer dies!* He sobs. *The mother shoots him!* But it isn't just the deer's death that has got to him—the hardscrabble family in the Everglades having to get rid of it because it eats the new corn—it is how the boy, Jody, is forced to grow up. A tiny flutter-mill of twigs he constructs carefully at the book's beginning, gets rebuilt by Jody at the end—but having experienced the deer's death, Jody finds the flutter-mill meaningless, and he smashes it. It is this act—the terrible way that Jody has to abandon his childhood pleasure and join the circle of adulthood—that got right under my brother's skin.

Of course I read the book, too. And I sobbed as well, both for the deer and for the smashed flutter-mill. But it was seeing my brother like that that really stayed with me.

Broken open by a book.

THE BLACK JOURNAL

It was a present from my mother, and it came with trails of that particular mystery only she could impart. She'd written on the inside cover: *May your thoughts flow freely in this book, a liberating stream of consciousness*—words I read over and over, finding them exotic and marvellous.

I became a writer with that journal. Scribbling. Analyzing. Capturing scenes, such as a fight with my father, or being sent to the principal and wrongly accused of skipping math class. I began to learn the *physical* pleasures of writing: the sense of arrival; but also how fun it was to pay attention, to describe things the way *I* saw them, not as other people told me they were. I also spent a huge amount of time—I know this because I still have the journal—writing about "how to be good." And "what life means." I wanted to sort these issues out, possibly once and for all, while at the same time wanting to look pretty, and to turn heads in the school hallway.

I tried out phrases: "Sobbing and shaking, she cupped her dawn-grey face in her hands, as though to catch the rain." "Embarrassed, she looked down at the ground, as though the answer was stuffed between her toes." (After that last entry, I wrote: "Hey—that's pretty good!") But mostly I wrote about how hard it was to have pimples, how much I wanted to try out for *The King and I*, but was afraid to, how Mike Garnett made my stomach "flip" when I saw him in the hallway. Flipping was a real thing for my girlfriends and me. We'd see a boy and then report to each other—oh! I saw x in the hallway—and I flipped!! A thrill greater than anything.

Keeping this journal, I began to feel I had two selves: a writer self, who recorded, and a high school self, who went to parties, or drove with my girlfriends up Cypress Mountain, getting stoned and looking down at the Vancouver lights. These selves were quite separate, a fact I puzzled over in the journal. I wondered about the ethics of having two selves, and if I could bring them together. I began to think of writing as a secret life.

ROMANTIC ME

In grade ten, one wonderful teacher, Mr Clarke, got us to read *Who Has Seen the Wind?* by W O Mitchell. I wrote an in-class essay about the book, and to my astonishment Mr Clarke read my piece aloud to all his English classes. Friends came up to me in the hall, wanting to mock me and praise me. Still, I was proud. This meant something.

Another literary high was Miss Barr's grade twelve literature class. She was tiny and bitter-tongued, and she wore clown-like spots of rouge. If you were caught chewing gum, she rang a cowbell, and then hit you on the knuckles with a ruler. But she loved literature. She had pictures of the greats of English literature tacked above the blackboard, and I remember thinking that Percy Bysshe Shelley was a bit of a babe. He was the only one I fantasized about. The rest—Blake, Milton, Shakespeare—looked pretty uninviting.

I felt transported by the Romantic poets. *A sense sublime of something far more deeply interfused / Whose dwelling is the light of setting suns / And the round ocean, and the living air.* I'd seen an ad for Givenchy perfume in a *Vogue* magazine, a barefoot girl in a diaphanous dress riding a horse. This, plus Wordsworth's words, made me long to be a capital R—Romantic Figure. I listened over and over to *Never on Sunday* (it was in my parents' record collection) and my plans, when I graduated from high school, definitely included going to Greece and dancing in a taverna, under the watchful gaze of sexy, interested men.

I only wrote one successful story during high school. It was about a man who is a typical cog-in-the-wheel kind of business-man, a part of the rat race, yet he longs to be an archeologist. It's his secret dream. In the end he can't stand his routine life and goes crazy and is put in an insane asylum, where—to his delight— he's given a small rusted spoon and told to go dig in the sandbox. I was lying on the shag carpet in our TV room when I came up with that, and I remember the sense of thrill. What had come at me out of the blue? *He wanted to be an archeologist—and in the end he gets to dig in a sand box!* I still remember that moment—"fringed with joy," as Virginia Woolf says in *To the Lighthouse*. I had tasted the joy of "closure." It had come sliding out of the story itself.

THE YOUNG ARE SO NIHILISTIC!

Many parts of my life didn't add much to the writerly journey, so let's skip ahead. Now I'm at university. I'm reading

Aristotle's *Poetics*, because a young man I have a crush on tells me it's interesting. I'm in the library stacks, the smell of books surround me, dusty and enticing, and I feel the top of my head lifting off. This idea that realization and reversal come, in a work of tragedy, at the same time! Holy shit! So let's get this straight: a story climaxes with a recognition of the opposite (reversal) of what you wanted and planned—and you see the entire past in a single, shocking blast that unmasks the workings of fate.

I could almost get my head around it. This was everything I wanted. A guide to writing, a clue to what made a story or novel great. It held the breath of ancient mystery, Greek plays. And best of all, it was a formula of sorts—and I needed to have some formulas for writing.

And while I don't think about Aristotle's *Poetics* often anymore, I do think they helped catapult me into thinking about how people change in fiction, that tremendously important question of action across the face of a book—a novel's hidden inner mechanism, which is also well expressed in a Jungian adage I discovered later: *what we refuse to make conscious, gets re-enacted as fate.* This is a very good way to describe the active arc of many novels: they are full of unconscious impulses, half realized intentions, fumbles in the dark that cause consequences in the light of day.

After some useful flailing—studying theatre, two years of ancient Greek—I enrolled in the Creative Writing Department at UBC. I was most interested in writing plays, and was heavily influenced by reading Samuel Beckett. All that nothingness seriously appealed to me.

What I wrote often involved a person alone on the stage, struggling in vain for a moment of personal authenticity—no proscenium arches and living room sets for me! Just a person surrounded by existential nothingness! Looking back, I think I did this because I was smoking mountains of Marlboro cigarettes, which a theatre friend brought back from Washington state, and drinking too much red wine, so I often woke feeling sick; but also because I hadn't actually experienced very much. Maybe that's why young twenty-somethings do often favour nihilism: nothingness suits a life that hasn't yet been filled with things to care about. I badly needed life experience.

Yet somehow, using the drab and strict formula of Nothingness, I still managed to write one short play I was pleased with, several short stories that didn't really work, and a number of non-fiction essays.

There was almost no focus on revision at UBC at this time, and so I felt what many beginning writers feel: *Why is my work so thin and unsatisfactory?* It would take me years to learn that stories grow naturally through revision from thin and unsatisfactory into something thicker. And that this process takes time. I don't think I revised a single piece of work while at university. Nor was I taught how to do it. When I teach fiction now, I always explain how to re-enter work and retain the first draft feeling of falling, of free flow, into the multiple revision process. I'm a stickler for this point, probably because I never got taught it myself.

THREE MINUTES TO MIDNIGHT

As I finished UBC and tried to write seriously, something else was growing inside me. It was the early 1980s. Reagan was President of the United States. The Pentagon was talking about fighting a limited nuclear war. The Bulletin of Atomic Scientists had set their Doomsday Clock to three minutes to midnight.

I had a job in a diner called The Royal King (nobody seemed to care about the name's redundancy but me!) when one morning a waitress unfolded a newspaper on the counter: "Did you see this? The government's going to test cruise missiles—nuclear missiles!—in Alberta."

After I'd read the article, I kept filling sugar dispensers and ketchup bottles. The sun still filtered through the window, and a set of bikers came in, wearing their leathers. Yet I felt as though I'd stepped onto a geyser that was bearing me into the air. The government was going to test cruise missiles—and I had to do something about it.

In our present age of consuming climate anxiety, we can forget the other age of terror we so recently passed through, the prospect of all-out nuclear war. But it was real. In 1979, when NATO announced plans to place nuclear missiles in West Germany to face Russia's SS-20 missiles, experts feared a battlefield nuclear war, which could escalate, within seconds, to an all-out global confrontation—destroying the world, how many times over? We lost track. Thirty, a hundred? After nuclear war the world, our precious planet, would be unliveable, burnt, full of radioactivity with a half-life of—roughly—eternity.

A million protesters marched in New York; women set up their iconic peace camp in Greenham Commons. In Vancouver, I joined the End the Arms Race Coalition, and soon became one of the main organizers for the immense annual walks for peace—100,000 people streaming over the Burrard Bridge, chanting and singing, carrying banners such as Better Active Today than Radioactive Tomorrow, Stop Cruise Testing or (less commonly) Whores against Wars. When an opportunity came for me to work for the national coalition in Toronto, The Canadian Peace Alliance, I jumped at it.

I remember the smells of the cupboard where we kept all our peace books (over-ordered for fundraising and stacked floor-to-ceiling); the excitement of looking from face to face in the Steering Committee Meetings, seeing delegates from Newfoundland to BC, all ignited by what we were doing together. Also, occasional acts of civil disobedience. When the Gulf War started, for instance, a little group of us, "Mothers and Others against War in the Gulf" occupied a federal cabinet minister's office, along with our babies and toddlers, keeping up the occupation for six or seven hours, changing diapers on the desk, commandeering the phones.

I worked in the peace movement for eight years, as a paid organizer, campaigner, and then as coordinator of the national coalition. During the last part of this period I began to realize, once again, how much I wanted to write.

This time the desire—the *need*—came to me as a feeling of floating above my body, wanting to slow down, and to find a way, no matter how difficult, to speak in my own voice. I was constantly hammering out press releases, or being a spokesperson, or speaking for a group. Much of the time, too, my words tended to follow the same pattern in speeches or opinion pieces: *Everything* (insert terrible thing—cruise missiles, nuclear submarines) *is dreadful, the world is on the brink of destruction, but if we can band together and hurl ourselves against the gates using* (insert useful petition, campaign, or mass demonstration), then *we can and will avert disaster.*

It was rote. Important rote—but rote nonetheless.

I really had no sense, at this point, of a useful pattern to my life. I never thought of the peace movement as part of my writing apprenticeship, and now that I was back with the same unfinished, hungry longing to "become a writer"—so like my mother!—I felt I'd wasted my time. I looked at people I considered young and lucky in their youngness (writers in their mid-twenties, compared to my freighted thirty-two), and I envied them their uninterrupted start.

But actually those years in the peace movement taught me so much. They gave me the seeds of two novels, just to start with—

both *Petra* and *Radiance* grew out of organizing a city-wide peace festival in 1986. We invited Petra Kelly, the iconic leader of the German peace movement and founder of the new Green Party to speak; and she both wowed me with her extraordinary charisma, and puzzled me with her dependence on her lover, a two-star former general with the German army. Why was this iconic feminist and peace diva leaning so heavily on the arm of her general? This was the seed of *Petra*—written years later. But I also caught the seed of *Radiance* at that same festival. We had invited the mayor of Hiroshima to come to Vancouver, and he brought a travelling exhibit of artifacts from the bombing. I had the job of helping unpack them from their wooden boxes, unwrapping the bubble wrap, lifting each item from its bed of straw. Again, this feeling stayed for years, and started *Radiance*, which is about a complex Hiroshima survivor, Keiko Kitigawa, who is brought to New York for reconstructive surgery—and who refuses to act like a victim, or to be the spokesperson everyone wants her to be. The novel is saturated in a sense of radioactive fear—fear and fascination— which was what I felt as I unpacked those items from their boxes: burned tricycle, shadowed brick, melted pocket watch.

Those years in the peace movement also taught me some rules I follow while writing fiction that has a political background and milieu. There is an enormous role for fiction to confront the larger world and its perils—perhaps now more than ever before, with climate change, refugee crises, systemic racial violence, and the rise of neo-fascism—but like any fiction, political fiction needs to be *sunk into* so deeply (into plot, people, the complexity of life) that one is working in a fictional groundwater. This groundwater is more important than any political position. Sunk deeply enough, you can navigate the larger issues, but you can't simplify, grind an axe, or send out a message to readers about your overall rightness. That's fictional death.

A MILLION MILES

When I left the Canadian Peace Alliance, the Steering Committee gave me a fountain pen—to see me on my way as a writer. I remember a colleague from the Prairies taking me aside and saying, rather acidly, that writing was a hard life, and nobody she knew was successful at it. I didn't even try to defend my ambitions. I had no publication credits, except for an occasional piece in the newspaper. I felt what so many writers feel about their most secret dream: that I might be about to make an enormous fool of myself. However, with the help of a Canada Council Explorations Grant, I took the leap and began to write stories.

By this time I was living with my life partner, Bob Penner, and my friend Wendy Wright in a communal house on Marion Street, in Toronto. Wendy and I both had little children, Peter and Colette. Both Bob and Wendy were supportive of my aspirations. Still, as a writer, when you are starting out, you are nobody, and no one really thinks you will succeed. You are ridiculous—or so I felt. At a party, if you say you are a writer, people blush for you. They look away, or say, in a kind way as though to a child, *have you published?*

I was now a mother who writes, which, I began to feel, was a bit like being a spy. (That old double persona, back in a new form.) You make lunches, slice cheese, rinse moulding macaroni from a thermos, yet all the while you inhabit a second world where the stakes feel high; a world that sometimes feels as though it could crush you with the weight of its complexity. What was a story? A good one? How did it work? And why were the ones I was writing so thin? They seemed to go on and on, like pieces of spaghetti. How did writers get the thickness, the excitement that thrilled me in a great story?

I was reading Flannery O'Connor, Bill Gaston, James Baldwin, Eudora Welty, Rick Bass, Joyce Carol Oates, Katherine Mansfield, and William Trevor. And of course—that ever-present genius of the story—Alice Munro.

When *Open Secrets* came out, I studied every story, noticing the precise way that Munro drew her character's faces. I started to realize that no character arrived without their face! Be it monkey-like, as Will's is in "Jackranda Hotel," or soft, supplicating, like Bea's in "Vandals," a story I now think of as Munro's *King Lear*.

The first time I read "Vandals" I thought, *Hmn. I guess. A good Alice Munro story*, and that was that. But the second time I was in Book City, leafing through opening paragraphs of various books to see if they caught me, and I picked up *Open Secrets* and turned to "Vandals." I seem to remember being in a bad mood. I had a kind of "prove you're so great" stance. The story begins with a letter from a late-middle-aged Bea to a young woman of about twenty-one, who has just been out to Bea's home in the woods and found it vandalized. Bea is writing after a few glasses of wine, and quickly the letter segues into a dream—a trip to Canadian Tire, garbage bags that, tossed in the air, seem very light, though they are filled with polished bones, and the question: *did you get the little girl?*—all the jumble of dreams. Suddenly—having read the whole story previously—I felt the shock of what I was reading slither down my arms and back like a live thing. Munro was using this seemingly confused and frivolous dream to signal a final layer of meaning beneath the story, a meaning I had completely missed on my first reading, because you can only "get it" if you read the story twice, as I was now doing.

Bea's dream reveals that Bea actually *knows* (bones—*did you get the little girl?*) about the sexual abuse by her partner of the two neighbour children—one of whom died, the other to whom she is now writing. *Knew*. But what is knowing? She guesses at. Her dreaming self knows. But this knowledge has not reached a sufficient consciousness to be expressed directly by her letter. She is sub-knowledge. Sub-remorse. Bea exists, one might say, in an unconscious relationship with her Vandal nature, in a Vandal hole in her mind, a Vandal lair.

The dream also shows a kind of letting go (those bags of polished bones suddenly light, tossed in the air)—but of what? Of a crime that Bea is still predominantly, in her conscious mind, unable to face. And so her offering of forgiveness—self-forgiveness, love to the girl (who by the way, has actually vandalized the cabin), can only be an unconscious offering—a sort of mute call-out to the healing forces of time and death—forces neither woman will, likely, be able to access in real life.

Only the reader can see the layers! Dear god, how that replicated my understanding of the mind, its obfuscations and yet—its tender root of central knowledge. This was genius.

Meanwhile, my stories were getting longer and longer, and thinner and thinner.

I was adding guns and horses.

Around this time my daughter, Lucy, was born. I was working freelance, writing fundraising letters and political speeches, eking out a living. By now I had a mentor—Peter Carey—and we were working by correspondence through the Humber School for Writers. I was writing what would become the first story in *The Falling Woman*, "Resistance," a story I gloomed over in despair. I would write a draft and send it to Peter Carey. He would send back a typed letter. He was invariably polite and distant and slimly encouraging. He might like the way I'd described a woman's wrist, for instance. I had the impression I exhausted him. I also had the impression, which may not be true, that he thought of me as a certain kind of female writer, with female concerns.

In one version I sent, the husband tries to convince his wife to come out of the locked bathroom. Eventually, rather than trying to bust his way in, he removes the door hinges. Peter Carey responded, rather snippily, that I ought to research the anatomy of doors. How does one *actually* remove a door from its hinges? What are the steps? He asked the same thing about a set of eyeglasses that lose a hinge (lots of hinges in that story). "Make them real," he said, and I remember walking down Bloor Street near Avenue Road while hearing his advice like an admonition, entering a glasses shop and staring at the hinges. *Make. Them. Real.* I didn't yet understand that making things real has to do with the contract of veracity you make with yourself as you go along—a kind of inner listening.

I was looking so hard for clues and guidance. I wrote to Peter Carey and I said, "Tell me. Tell me. How far am I from getting this story right?" I waited, and after a while he wrote back. He said: "A Million Miles."

This was a dark moment.

But then he said, "Ah—but a million miles can sometimes be crossed in a single step, or several steps." I didn't have a clue what he meant! But now I do. What he meant, of course, is that something small but staggering needs to fall into place (for instance, the discovery of a voice) and then you begin to be able *to move sideways* though your material, rather than doggedly moving forward. Most of all it has to do with dropping your "good idea" in favour of things that begin to emerge out of the writing itself. (Hinges might be a fruitful place to start?) It meant learning to have patience, to listen for the shifts that can take you down and in.

I remember the breakthrough I had with the title story, "The Falling Woman." Again it was getting longer and longer, and I was feeling bleak despair as I crossed the Serengeti Plain each morning and added a new scene. After one morning's work, I lay down on my bed and cried, then went upstairs and ate something fatty, then lounged some more in myopic misery. When I finally got up, I headed back to the computer, turned it on and—the draft was missing!

So, after some lamenting and gnashing of teeth, I started again. But this time, out of sheer fury, I began differently. I heard a voice in my head, saying: *some of my dreams feel like memories*—and I followed the voice. I realized, after a couple of paragraphs, that the story was coming. The story was tucked inside the voice, and by following the voice, I could unspool it, covering acres in a paragraph, or even a sentence. At last I was getting at the compact meat and gristle.

This was a breakthrough, and when the story was done, I liked it. It actually had reverberations, echoes inside it. I sent it to *Prism International*, and they accepted and then put it forward for *The Journey Prize Anthology*, and again it was accepted.

Another breakthrough came to me one day at the Toronto Public Library writing a very early version of my story, "The War Between the Men and the Women." I'd hit a wall—I can't remember which wall, there were so many—and I decided to amuse myself by looking up Alice Munro interviews. I found one on a tape reel. She was describing how she wrote stories. "Oh," she said, "and then of course sometimes the surface gets too shiny, and I have to go in and break it up. But this is nothing special," she said. "All writers do this."

What? All writers? I had never heard of this before. I didn't even know that shininess was a problem! But it made sense to me, a kind of dark sense. And after that, I began to try to break up the surface of my stories when they had become too slick.

I created a technique for myself that I still use. I draft in a notebook, get a lot of material flowing, then, at a certain point, transfer it to the computer, then print out this first or second draft and tape it into a scrapbook. I leave the facing page blank, and large margins all around, which gives me room to write questions to myself, follow tangents, add dialogue, new lines, even scenes. Effectively, I am "breaking up the surface," yet all the while retaining—right there in front of me—the original draft, so I don't have the writerly anxiety that my new draft is destroying the old one.

This process was messy, tactile, and deeply satisfying, especially because the scribbled notes and impetuous stabs often had a better tone than the writing I laboured over. Revision began to have some of the pleasure of first-draft doodling. No, it actually had more pleasure. It harkened back to play. Stump play. Doll play. Working quietly in a scrapbook, adding paragraphs, making notes, began to have that same soft, involved *brain feel.*

At this point—as I approached my fortieth birthday—I had about seven finished stories and a very big, messy draft of my novel *Radiance.* The director of the Humber School for Writers, Joe Kertes, was incredibly helpful. (Joe Kertes and Antanas Sileika, who followed him as Humber's Director, were hugely and generously helpful to me and many writers.) Joe took me for lunch and, on the basis of having read three of my stories, said he'd recommend me to his agent.

I remember going to Anne McDermid's then-office in the Annex. I was frozen with nervousness. Anne was signing all the new talent—Andrew Pyper, Russell Smith, Sheila Heti—and to my delight she was enthusiastic about my book of stories. "Finish it up!" she said, in her English accent. "When can you get it to me?" Three months, I told her. Then I went home and promptly broke out in hives. I poured an entire bottle of calamine lotion into the bathtub and rolled around in it.

For some reason, after that windfall of validation, the stories took even longer to gel. I suppose I felt exposed by this lifeline to the business end of writing—too much like the gods watching?—and the book, rather than taking three months, took three years! Anne McDermid had pretty much given up on me by the time I met her again in the lobby of the Vancouver Hotel (we had moved to Vancouver) and I handed her my finished collection of ten stories, in a lucky red file box, held in place by a red elastic.

She was in Vancouver signing up all the bright young things that had graduated with MFAs from UBC—all of them at least ten years my junior, writers I envied for their early start. I was, by now, too old to be in any Best Young Writers anthology! But not them. Still, Anne, even if slightly alarmed to see me, took my carefully wrapped box of stories, and, along with the promise of a novel, sold it within the month to Anne Collins at Random House Canada.

"It's thrilling," Anne McDermid breathed into the telephone as she broke me the news. "Utterly thrilling, my dear." And it was.

THE END OF THE BEGINNING

After that it seemed that my long (long!) apprenticeship might be over. And, in many ways, it was. I had a literary agent, and a wonderful publisher and editor in Anne Collins, who was leading me through the publication of *The Falling Woman*, while Anne McDermid sold the book to Virago Press in the UK and Berlin Verlag in Germany.

I no longer had to look down at my hands at parties, and say—"well, yes, I am a writer, but no, I haven't yet published a book." I got a door into a world of other writers, festivals, readings, and every encounter felt exciting. I liked seeing *The Falling Woman* in stores, being invited to sit on award and grant juries, joining The Writers Union. I liked the feeling, after what had felt like eons in "the cold," of having arrived.

But there were new struggles. Or old ones persisted. The writing was always slow, a case of feeling my way. I often hit snags, dead ends, or places where it seemed a concrete wall had suddenly been built, the Berlin Wall of the Imagination. I couldn't get through or over. And so I learned to put down the piece entirely and write something else. This meant I often had several pieces—a novel, a story, another story—growing simultaneously.

At first I thought I was mad, and kept my lonely jumps to myself. (In fact, I mostly do not talk to people about what I'm working on: I find it can make me self-conscious and slow the work.) But I began to notice how many other writers also did this jumping. Emma Donoghue, for instance, calls this leaping from work to work "cheating on her novel"—it creates all the quiet excitement of an affair.

I remember being lost. I remember working obsessively on *Radiance*—which I had titled, at first, *The Firebird*—and trying to explore how Keiko, a Hiroshima survivor, in the 1950s, might be both incredibly alive to her own imaginative world, and a place for the post-war projections of her hosts.

All the while, I kept writing stories, many of which went into *Oh, My Darling*. After it was published, I circled back to the novel I'd started years before, about the loves, political brilliance, and murder of Petra Kelly, a story which brought in my own lived experiences, coming of age to the beating drum of nuclear Armageddon, and my fascination for the tragic Petra Kelly—complex, narcissistic, irksome, and wholly beguiling.

Each novel or story posed its own internal puzzles. And while craft and knowledge helped, each needed its own visitation of something interesting, some flare of light, or multiple flares, outside of my conscious control, which I had to hope for, wait for, write towards, and kind of attend to. This part of writing is like visiting an empty room, hoping one day to walk in and see Rumpelstiltskin. After a while, you realize that the craft almost guarantees his eventual appearance. But when?

THE MAGIC OF HAMBURGER AND DUST

The story ideas for *Oh, My Darling* came as shards. I wrote them down in a story ideas book, then I had to figure out, often very slowly, how to make use of them. With "Crow Ride" I had a crow shard and a druggy teenager shard, and for a long time these bits sat in my notebook. I didn't know what connected them. Then one day my son walked into the kitchen and said he was going on a crow ride— cycling from west side to east side, to where all the crows in Vancouver fly to roost. As he spoke, I saw my story. Not the whole thing, but the action of it, the trail it could leave on the page. It would be a journey across town, from west to east.

As I started to write the first draft, I set the opening scene in Whole Foods, because that was where I was actually sitting, drinking coffee with my notebook. Whole Foods—where better? Bastion of personal growth and limited self-awareness. The story took on layers, but only after it was completely written did I see how I'd worked in a motif about darkness (the story takes place near the shortest day of the year), and southern light (the peonies at the entrance to Whole Foods are imported). The chase from west to east, then, was also a chase into the underworld, following a dead boy.

I didn't plan Whole Foods to represent anything in the story, certainly not what I just wrote, above—because I don't believe you can write consciously *towards* symbol and have it work out.

I feel powerfully indebted to Flannery O'Connor's notion that surface and detail in fiction are the only access points to symbol (*Mystery and Manners*). All detail in story, O'Connor says, isn't actually detail, per se. If you render it with care, "the dust of the story," as she calls it, becomes imbued with meaning.

Writers are taught the value of sensory detail—"show don't tell"—but it often gets discussed as though it were merely a utilitarian craft issue. *Showing* makes our worlds more believable. But this is a secular way of understanding what is actually more like a magical question. In fiction, anytime you press into the five senses, you will write something specific, something, precisely because of its singularity, which will begin the strange work of becoming freighted with meaning. Things of the earth *want to be doors into something greater.*

Large concepts and symbolic utterances will not open these doors. But the smell of hamburger meat will take you into a kitchen, unlocking meaning. Hamburger meat that is uncooked—for instance—could mean redness and tenderness. It could mean sunburn, but it could also mean corpulence.

Pressed inside its plastic package, the dots of fat could mean sorrow.

Placed on a granite countertop, that sorrow could be laced through a marriage.

John Metcalf, in a letter to me about this essay, quoted from *Walter Pater: Lover of Strange Souls*, which describes how poetry (which Metcalf took to mean short stories, as well) needs to resist intelligence. I wrote back in immediate agreement. Really good fiction moves beyond intelligence, into something that happens on the page that is beyond the writer's conscious construction. It's not entirely emotional either, although it does involve hitting an emotional depth. I think it is a third thing—more like what E M Forster calls "prophesy" in his book *Aspects of the Novel.* He defines this hard-to-describe quality in fiction as a kind of "song of the gods," where the writer's theme widens all at once to the universe. "He proposes to sing—how will song combine with the furniture of common sense?" The melding of song and furniture seems to me to be the thing a fiction writer is doing constantly.

This song is what I often look for, consciously or unconsciously, when I read, and what I am interested in having happen (if possible) when I write. The shock at the end of a story—the way it might open and close simultaneously, (snapping its jaws even, as happens at the end of Henry James' "The Beast in the Jungle," for instance, or Munro's "Vandals"). It is the blast of light from the ceiling. Or the unrolling of something hinted at, yet completely unexpected, which comes with multiple, attendant flashes of understanding, as happens at the end of Virginia Woolf's *To the Lighthouse*.

This part of writing is hard as hell to achieve—and one of the prime reasons that writing never stops being difficult. You have to hold on and let go. Then navigate the high-stakes feeling, because who knows if things will come together or not?

But meanwhile, you have compensations, dark and physical. Like hours of quiet play, hovering involvement, making up voices—and the daily climb into the branches of a tree, which you have been lucky enough all these years to call home.

THE WOLF EXPERT

SHAENA LAMBERT

We can't feed them anymore.
I tell you, husband, we must set the children loose in the woods.

Raj has his laptop open, and he types as Kathy leans towards him, whispering intensely. She catches a glimpse of herself in the cabin's living room window—pale face framed by red pigtails, next to the burgundy orb that is Raj's turban. Beyond the window the bluff forest falls away to a glint of sea.

"Raj."

His long fingers tweak and twiddle at the keyboard. Moon cuticles. He is connected remotely to his boss's laptop in Vancouver. Two hundred miles south, in Kitsilano, a ghost cursor moves through alien files, transferring, saving.

"Maybe we could give the girls walking sticks to carry with them. Or air horns. That's what the parents did after that attack on Whale Island."

"Air horns."

"I was reading online. Apparently just the feel of an air horn in your pocket gives you confidence. Then the wolves read your body signals and stay away."

Raj nods, head bobbing a little longer than necessary to denote agreement.

"What are we talking about, Raj?"

"I know what we're talking about." Click, click. "The wolves."

"What about the wolves? Raj!"

He stops typing and then tilts his head, seeming to retrieve the data of their conversation from the ceiling. "It's not about us. There are no known records of wolves going after adults. It's about the children, and if need be we could give them sticks, or better yet air horns, as the parents did on Whale Island, after the wolf pack surrounded those kids on the beach." He pauses. "Of course we'll be walking them to school and back."

"But what if they get separated from us? Or play in the woods at recess? Or there's a beach excursion?"

"Right."

"More than anything else, we need to get advice from this wolf expert. The one hired by Parks Canada."

"That's what you'll do tomorrow."

"I'm going to get her number from Tracy—the cashier at the Island Grocery. Because for some reason she doesn't list her number on the wolf website."

He presses *send*.

She goes up to check on their twin girls, Suki and June, snuggled in the double loft bed. Glossy hair like Raj's. Plush lips open. Suki's nose is plugged from her cold. Kathy gets a tissue from the bathroom and gives it a gentle wipe. Her dark, sweet babies. Though not babies anymore. They are five, and will start school the very next day.

When she returns downstairs, Raj has poured them wine. They sit on the couch together, admiring the last light on the islands of the remote Sound—a view new to them still. They have only been at the cabin for two weeks. It is a six-month rental hastily arranged through a friend of a friend at the bakery Kathy managed before the kids. A spontaneous decision, meant to spur an act of spontaneous healing—wasn't that the idea? Raj had said yes. Yes to Kathy's impulse. It probably felt good to throw himself into her wake, to give in to the voluptuous sway of her decision making. He planned to work remotely, with a trip to town every ten days.

"It's beautiful," he says.

"We're lucky."

The sea glimmers whitely under a streak of moon.

The next morning, the big school day, Raj makes pancakes, Kathy finds the girls' boots in a rubber box, and then all four of them follow the roughly cleared forest trail toward the Montessori schoolhouse. They pass yellow bracken taller than their heads. Suki and June look into the mossy darkness with big, passionate eyes. They are beautiful, perfect children, and Kathy is sorry to think that one day they will have to die, that life produces such waste, that an unfeeling chaos rules the universe and that nobody—nobody!—is exempted, not even her children splashing through puddles wearing raincoats with duck-head hoods. Raj turns to smile at her, as though to say: *Look at our happy family on our children's first day of school.* But then he sees her face and reaches for her hand. She is still in shock, that's what he must think, shock from the cancer that blasted through their lives like a freight train, but now is gone. His clasping of her hand reminds her of the solicitous gestures of the radiation technicians. *Can you breathe in a little more, Kathy? Okay, just a little more, a little more. How about a tiny bit more?* If she failed to fill her lungs to the maximum would they miss the cancer cells entirely? Radiate her heart? Her lung? The technicians never said, just aimed that pinpoint of burning light at her.

That's it. Hold still.

Now here they are. Everything in the woods smells of fertile decay. They step over a fallen alder log covered in six inches of moss. Raj holds back a branch and Kathy sees the itchy growth on its achingly tender limb.

They cross a little bridge and emerge out of the forest, onto the farm where the schoolhouse stands in the distance. They made a pact in bed that morning. No talking about wolves with the girls, not until Kathy has the information she needs from the wolf expert. This means no falling into excited discussions with other parents. No mention at all about the two attacks, the one on Whale Island, or the other on nearby Bessie's Beach, where an elderly couple beat the wolves away from their Jack Russell Terrier.

Raj opens the robin's-egg-blue door of the schoolhouse. The girls are so shy, they bury their faces against Kathy's legs, but soon they are seated cross-legged on cushions, reading about pigs.

No posing of wolf-related questions to the grim-faced Montessori teacher, who seems soured from her years on this island paradise.

On their way home, Raj and Kathy are silent. First Raj, then Kathy, step over the fallen alder. It seems to Kathy that they might be able to fix things so easily, return to what they had before, if they just stepped off the path, into the moss beside the horsetails and salal. She imagines taking Raj by the pocket of his raincoat, his look of grateful wariness as she leads him through dripping spiders' webs, then lies down, reaching awkwardly under her raincoat to undo the clasps of her corduroy overalls. Then him moving on top of her, complaining about his freezing ass. They made love once under the table in a Chinese banquet hall. He loves her spontaneity, that's what he says, loves it and fears it. Whatever it is that makes her like this (life force? Is it life force?), has pulled him right out of the trajectory laid down by his doting parents. He was meant to marry a nice Sikh girl from Burnaby, and look what he went and did instead. Married a carrot top. The love of his life looks like Anne of Green Gables.

She could grab him now, but it feels like a lot of work, and they'd get cold, and inevitably he would do something careful and kind, like laying down his raincoat. That was the way he was at night now, when he pulled down the straps of her nightgown, and they both looked at her pink nipples. Her breasts so full of heat now, after the radiation—heat, anger, strangeness. When he reached out to touch them, it was with a scientific precision, as though dismantling time bombs.

.

Are the Wolves out of Control? (Or could it be the humans?)
Public Meeting at the Island Co-op with Island Wolf Expert,
Anna Hoffmann.

This is the sign on the bulletin board outside the Island Grocery. Yes. This is what she needs—a public meeting. Unfortunately it took place three days before. Kathy and Raj are strangers here, and nobody thought to alert them. Beneath the headline is a photo of a wolf's face. Its intelligent stare beneath furrowed brows reminds Kathy of her mother-in-law's shrewd glance over her reading glasses.

Setting her groceries beside the till, Kathy asks Tracy how the wolf meeting went.

"Ha!" Tracy has silvered hair but a youthful face. She's swathed in a knitted tunic.

"So, who's out of control? Wolves or humans?"

"Neither—It's Anna Hoffmann. *Calm down, calm down.*" Tracy imitates a Hitler-like accent. "*If you don't know how to relate to wild animals, then don't live next to them.* That's what she said. And you know my dog Martin has gone missing." She shakes her head, temporarily unable to speak, before finding her rage again: "It's fucking ridiculous. We have two out-of-control wolf packs, and another that swims over regularly from the mainland." Tracy repeatedly swipes a barcode. "She said in front of an entire room that Martin shouldn't have been let outside. I said, 'He was on the deck, Anna. Listen to what I'm saying. The deck. The *deck*!' Then she says, 'The wolves were here first.' What the fuck. I'm going to complain to Parks Canada."

"I'm sorry," says Kathy. "Tell me what kind of dog. I'll help look."

"Thank you—I appreciate that. I appreciate human reactions to human problems. He's part Border collie. Short-haired."

"I've been worried about my girls."

"You can expect zero sympathy from Anna Hoffmann."

But she gives Kathy the phone number from the co-op directory.

·

That afternoon Raj leaves on the floatplane for Vancouver. An hour later, Kathy is walking through the woods to pick up the girls when something in the feathered moss catches her eye. She squats innocently enough, but then her blood chills. The thing is three fingers wide, a foot and a half long, feathered at one end, and thickening at the other to a stump of marbled gristle and bone. A tail. With two sticks Kathy picks it up, as though with chopsticks, and tosses it into the woods, where the girls will never see it, and then she runs, slowing only to note scat by the fallen alder. Grey hairs. Cracked bone. More of Martin's remains?

·

"Ja. Hallo?"

"Is this Anna Hoffmann?"

"Yes."

Kathy stammers out her facts. She has small children, twins, younger than the ones attacked on Whale Island.

"That was not an attack."

"I'm sorry. I'd heard—"

"The wolves were on the beach first. Those children recklessly approached them. I don't know how to tell you people. Leave them alone, and they will leave you alone."

"Could we meet? I'd really like to have a briefing. I'm new here, and I'm not sure..."

Heavy Germanic breathing.

"Please," Kathy adds, recklessly.

"I don't like to support the hysteria. Read the website."

"I'm not hysterical," Kathy says staunchly, "and I did read it, but I still have questions. Look, I just want to learn the ropes. Wolf-wise."

It takes Kathy a full half minute, listening for the breathing on the other end, to realize that the woman has hung up.

.

The wolf expert lives up a rutted, washed-out road that is hard for Kathy's city car to manage. Rocks whack the undercarriage, pinging against the pipes. Poor Raj! He loves this car. Tracy at the co-op supplied directions. *Be careful*, she said. *I actually think she might be crazy.* Kathy couldn't bring herself to mention the tail.

The land is flat in this central part of the island: no mossy bluffs or views of the Sound. No purple wistfulness. Just a forest floor with occasional elephantine stumps covered in salal, the remains of an old-growth forest. Between these, columns of cedar and hemlock rise a hundred feet into the air before they put out branches. Kathy unrolls the window and hears the wind. All that action so high up: it feels as though she is moving across the bottom of the sea.

All at once the road opens to a picturesque clearing in the forest. It's as big as a baseball diamond, carpeted in needles, a few rocks showing their cool backs. Across the clearing, a trailer gleams like a refrigerator. This is what Kathy notices, and it disappoints her.

It looks so out of place. (*Cold*, she thinks later.) Why move to the wilderness only to live in a home covered in metal?

When she swings the car door closed, it hits the tongue of the seat belt and bounces open again. Embarrassing entrance, but unnoticed: no face appears at the trailer window.

It is then, as she closes the car door, firmly this time, and turns back towards the clearing, that she sees the little house in the trees. Oh! Kathy gasps out loud. It is so charming, so perfectly nestled at the edge of the clearing, perhaps thirty feet from the trailer. Shingled roof, tin chimney, board-and-batten sides. A window with many little panes, divided by mullions.

And? (She interviews herself months later, lying in bed, going over every detail until they are straight and in order.)

She starts toward that little house. All around she smells pine needles and the loamy scent of mushrooms.

"Hello?" she calls. "Hello?" It is just like that poem, 'The Listeners.' *Is there anybody there, said the Traveller, knocking on the old oak door.* Though this door has a window covered in a square of heavy translucent plastic. The wind snaps at the edge of the sheeting, and rides the tops of the trees. Kathy puts her eye to the plastic, but can't see through it. She raps on the door. Inside, soft as anything, she hears the creak of floorboards.

"Hello?" she calls again.

She steps over to the mullioned window, frames her eyes with her hands and peers in.

And?

That's when I screamed.

Because she sees a system of ropes on the far wall. They feed upwards through a series of metal eyes, and then across to the beam, from which hang three purpled carcasses. With their ribs showing, their muscled shoulders and thighs, they look like the skinned torsos of children.

"How was the wolf expert?"

Raj has come back on the floatplane, picked up the girls, and now he stands over the stove, a piece of mushroom in his beard. He holds a wooden spoon stained with spaghetti sauce. Kathy takes the mushroom from his beard and pops it in her mouth. Portobello.

"Who?"

"The wolf expert."

"She wasn't home. I guess I'll need to go back another time. Or maybe just use the internet to find out more."

"You sound calmer."

"I am calmer."

The compost bucket on the counter needs to be emptied. She puts on the Crocs that came with the cabin and goes outside and around the house. She dumps the contents in the compost bin. On one side of her is the steep rise of the bluff, wind in the trees, the ferns. On the other, the house. Through the kitchen window she sees a square of light, Raj in the centre, like a Renaissance painting, measuring noodles by hand, a quarter inch for each family member.

She lied. The wolf expert was at home.

Kathy stands with the bucket, watching Raj stir the pasta, while from the loft window upstairs comes a blue-white flicker. The girls are watching *The Wonderful World of Bugs*. Something is opening inside her. How she used to feel going out for Halloween, running down the driveway towards the night.

Who lives like that? That's the question she wants answered now. Who lives in a trailer by herself with a workshop set up for skinning deer? The word that comes to her is *loneliness*. The clearing reminds her of a cupboard swept clean of human things. Also: *Poverty, simplicity, pride*. The painful biting down on the inside of your cheek, rather than uttering a word of need, a cry for consolation.

Of course she can't see all this right away. Much of this comes later.

.

Clearing.
Door in seatbelt.
Crossing to house.
Is anyone home?
Eye to window.
Shriek.

Then she is running toward the car, catching her toe, falling, grasping her bloodied knee, pink overalls ripped. A door slams. The wolf expert stands over her, angrily wielding a blowtorch. "Who are you?"

Then laughing as Kathy picks herself up.

"I talked to you on the telephone," Kathy says.

"You're the one who's worried about her babies."

"Not babies. Twin girls. And yes, I'm worried. Why not?"

What nobody has mentioned is that this woman has a face that leads with her cheekbones. Huge Macedonian hair. Coils of it. Tresses. She is perhaps forty, with heavy eyebrows and dark eyes. Olive skin. She wears a red-and-black lumberjack shirt. When she speaks—"So. You saw my deer-skinning station"—her teeth seem small to Kathy, like teeth in a Victorian doll.

She is German on her father's side, but Turkish on her mother's. (Kathy will learn this much later, lying in bed beside Anna, tracing the veins down the pathways of her muscled arms.) This accounts for the German accent, the dark colouring. Also, for the two sides perpetually at war with each other: the German side subjugating the Turkish; the Turkish retaliating at night, with scimitars.

This is one way that Kathy will imagine the furious interior of Anna Hoffmann: insisting almost from the beginning that there is gentleness inside. This will be her job. To come close, name that gentleness, taking the ferocious fending-off that comes from this act of touch. To do this Kathy will have to open herself in ways she never dreamed. For instance, riding home in Anna's truck one day after picking bolete mushrooms, their scent emanating from the willow basket on Kathy's lap, Anna reaches for Kathy's hand, bringing it to her lips. And Kathy says: *I want to be yours.* This is her response, breaking some terrible rule about never showing your heart. She is wide open. How did this happen? *Let me be yours.* This is months before the end, the final banishment, before Kathy kneels in her cotton underwear on the linoleum floor of the trailer with its coffee-coloured swirls, clinging to Anna's knees, pleading, *Look at me, just look at me, please.*

But for now the wolf expert stands with her blowtorch, taking in the red pigtails, the pink overalls. She seems awkward, almost deferential. She offers to show the deer-skinning station, and Kathy notices the blood-softened wood of the floor, the deer carcasses hanging neatly from their beams, heads and hooves cut off. The blowtorch is used to remove hair from a skin spread on a rack beside the door.

Inside the trailer there is a single bed with a patchwork quilt, a tidy loneliness. Kathy sits on the quilt and Anna on a plastic chair. She doesn't seem to know what to do next, and so she asks Kathy if she'd like to see a video of the wolves. She opens her laptop and shows a fuzzy clip of the largest wolf pack swimming to Whale Island. Dark heads, pointed ears. They knew that Anna was filming, she explains. A wolf that doesn't want to be seen is never seen.

"Off to eat the newborn seal pups. So, you see: you don't have to worry about your babies. They're going to eat other mothers' babies."

The video is followed by a series of still shots. Anna has caught one of the packs at dawn, at Stayatuk Bay on the south point of the island. Several photos show a grey wolf the size of a large husky running across the beach, leaving huge footprints, leaping over a tidal pool.

"Joy." Anna's voice is suddenly loud beside her. "You've got to love that. That wolf is leaping for joy—no other reason."

After the last of the still shots, the computer reverts back to its screensaver: Kathy recognizes the furrow-browed stare of the wolf from the poster. Anna says that that's it, the show is over. Still, they stare awkwardly at the computer, Kathy on the bed and the wolf expert in her plastic chair. Kathy isn't sure what will happen next, but then Anna speaks.

"Cute pigtails," she says. "Trust me. No wolf's going to want to eat you."

Kathy is on the verge of saying it's the twins she worries about. But she doesn't. Instead, she hears herself saying that she's been through something recently, doesn't talk about it much, or at all really. It was hard. Anna leans close, a tang of peppermint soap over the darker scent of sweat. "What is this hard thing?" she whispers teasingly, as though nothing Kathy could say could be so serious, not with the pigtails and all. Still she is asking. She is curious, and Kathy finds herself saying that she had cancer recently.

Anna is so close, Kathy feels rather than sees her answering gesture, which is a shrug of the shoulders. Roughly speaking, it means, *What do you expect? Life doesn't spare us.* Then she reaches out and takes hold of one of Kathy's pigtails. Kathy feels the weight of her braid in the other woman's grip, then a slight tug against her scalp, as though Anna is testing a length of rope, or the heft of a knife, or any useful object to be learned by hand.

Home. Compost bucket in hand. Raj calls the children to the kitchen table and Kathy keeps thinking: *In another moment I will go in, in another moment*, but still she doesn't move. The light has spread to the living-room window, the girls sitting cross-legged in their chairs, holding their knives and forks. She can see the soles of their bunny slippers, and hear Raj telling them that they need to wait for their mother.

In another moment Kathy does go inside, but she feels the outside in her eyes, in her hair, and she remembers standing apart from them all in the dark, listening to their voices, familiar, binding. When the children are asleep, she unwinds the wrappings of Raj's turban, and they make love under his hair, as if surrounded by Spanish moss, his body on top of her, heavy and strong, doing everything he can to reach her. There is still time to retreat into the sweet depths of his love.

"You see," he says, when they are done. "Bit by bit."

He leaves it for a long time. She thinks he may have fallen asleep.

"Bit by bit what?" she says.

A pause, then: "Bit by bit we're getting back to normal."

She falls asleep and dreams of the wolf expert, olive hands grasping her earlobes, tilting her head back as though she is a pot to drink from. She wakes to Raj's breathing, his back turned to reveal the knobs of his spine, his hair unbound. And Suki and June are close too, filling the house with their breath. But she is thinking of the wolf running across the sand at Stayatuk Bay.

Stand, Kathy. Go to the window.

See yourself in the glass, and beyond that, the stars, the wind moving the trees. It must never go back to normal. *Say it, Kathy.* Normal is what you now fear. Your job is to destroy normal. Rip it open. Eat the entrails.

ELISE LEVINE

PHOTO: BRITT OLSEN-ECKER

ELISE LEVINE *is the author of* Say This: Two Novellas, *the story collection* This Wicked Tongue, *the novels* Blue Field *and* Requests and Dedications, *and the story collection* Driving Men Mad. *Her work has also appeared or is forthcoming in publications including* The Hopkins Review, The Walrus, Ploughshares, Blackbird, *and* The Gettysburg Review, *and has been included five times in* Best Canadian Stories. *Originally from Toronto, she lives in Baltimore,* MD, *where she teaches in the* MA *in Writing program at Johns Hopkins University.*

THE PROVISIONS

1. WANT NOT

For a few years, starting when I'm around seven, my mother claims my brother and I are lucky my father isn't making us all live on dog food.

My parents grew up poor in and about Saint John, New Brunswick. They never forgot.

My mother was the second youngest of nine, one of three girls. The eldest, Marguerite, died at eleven. In one version of the story, she fell from a hospital bed and her appendix burst. My grandmother Rosina took to her own bed for weeks. She was of English-Anglican stock, a Rockwood born in Heart's Content, Newfoundland. An RN, educated. As a young unmarried woman in December 1917, she'd taken the train from Saint John to Halifax, Nova Scotia, to help nurse survivors of the Halifax Explosion, the devastating maritime accident that cost nearly two thousand lives. But now she missed attending her daughter's funeral and neglected the rest of the family—aside from the two remaining girls, six strapping, hockey-playing boys, bruisers. And Mickey Joe, the alcoholic, combative husband—a Catholic-raised union organizer of Scottish descent working for the Canadian National

Railway, a veteran of WWI's Battle of the Somme wounded and treated for a year in England for shell shock before returning home fiercely atheistic. He revered rye whisky and the books of Bertrand Russell, bemoaned not having people to talk philosophy with, and wrote letters for illiterate co-workers. Likely unsupported and overwhelmed, my grandmother never really recovered from Marguerite's death. Her own health declined. My mother, Betty, and her surviving older sister, Ollie, learned to fend for themselves among the rest of the McPhees.

Hard times. The now-ten of them making do with a single outhouse during the frigid New Brunswick winters. My mother and her youngest brother, with few toys to call their own during the Great Depression, on the back steps of the old house in then-rural Hampton (now a suburb of Saint John), secretly delighting in a fox kit as playmate until the adults find out and, fearing rabies, forbid the pastime. The treat of chicken-bones candy every Christmas, and the warm memory when my mother goes to bed hungry on cold nights.

As for my father's early years: he relished the sight of his grandmother chopping pike and carp on a huge wooden board to make gefilte fish. In his telling, the sole happy experience from his early life—when, as an adult, he was asked about his childhood, he claimed he never had one.

He grew up even poorer than my mother. Or maybe just more of an outsider, born on a kitchen table in Yarmouth, Nova Scotia, to an Orthodox Jewish couple who hailed from the same town in Lithuania. As children my paternal grandparents, Max and Jennie (née Benjamin), fled the murderous pogroms in the Pale of Settlement with their families, travelling by steamship from Kiev to Liverpool and then to eastern Canada—the Levine side saved, family lore has it, by my father's hustling Uncle Meyer, who at thirteen years of age made friends with the ship's cook, who set aside extra food for the boy to share with his people among the sick and dying in steerage. My father's parents, along with his paternal grandparents, eventually resettled among the small Jewish-Lithuanian community of Saint John, as the Benjamins did, when he was an infant. Apparently it was fairly common for Jewish families from the same area in the old world to revive their communities in the new. My father's parents struggled to provide, and when my father was three or four they farmed him out, the second youngest of five, to his paternal grandparents to raise.

My father's father was a tailor, strictly observant. Strict period, ungenerous toward children. His interests lay elsewhere: he played violin and loved classical music and was an avid photographer. My father's grandfather was a peddler of pots and pans, in those early years by foot, and later—once most citizens travelled the city streets by motorized vehicles—by horse-drawn cart. As with many Lithuanian-born-and-raised Jews of the time, Samuel Levine was something of a Rabbinic-style intellectual, an expert in the Talmud—a near birthright that nation's once-powerful yeshiva tradition, with its emphasis on learning, on close textual analysis, on logic instead of on the emotion and mysticism associated with the competing Judaism of Hasidism.

Yet he was also an exorcist, in the tradition of the Eastern European shtetls. For a fee he'd take away your fright—a manifestation of a ghostly possession by a dybbuk, a malevolent spirit—by beheading a chicken and swinging the body by its feet while reciting a prayer in Hebrew and then Yiddish.

His enterprising spirit extended to the third business he conducted, as a small-time bootlegger, running a still in the backyard and occasionally getting busted for it. This was the Prohibition era. My father on more than one occasion came home from school to the tumult and shame of policemen at the door.

One strand of the story of my becoming a writer is that my mother never outs her father as an alcoholic. I learn the truth at age fourteen from a much-older cousin, a former New Brunswick beauty queen, visiting our suburban Toronto-area house from New Zealand. By way of illustrating why *her* father was so easily wounded and swift to rage, my cousin recounts how, among numerous inciting incidents, our grandfather liked to turn up at the local hockey rink and humiliate his athletic sons by shambling drunk onto the ice to bellow instructions on how to play.

My mother goes silent and the subject drops. A week later my cousin leaves and I ask my mother about her father's drinking. She quits with her habitual nervous flitting and picking—at the living room curtains, the dining-chair cushions, her sweater, on occasion mine while I'm wearing it and which elicits terrific fights—and melts into a chair. I wanted, she says, to protect you and your brother. For your own good.

Protect me and my younger brother, I take it, from shame, from shouldering and internalizing a sense of disgrace. Prevent us from growing contemptuous of our family history and by extension a part of ourselves. Or keep us from adopting a normalized view of addiction, a perspective that might cause the disease to rub off on us? Or is that she simply can't let go of wanting to protect her father, to for some reason cover for him?

Whether for any or all of the above reasons, in my mother's calculus she has decided it best to lie by omission—especially since my grandfather's dependency has rubbed off on her. Our family doctor has a lucrative side practice as a pharmacist and, like so many women of her era, my mother's corrosive unhappiness—isolated and trapped in what has turned out to be a toxic, miserable marriage to my father, a short-fused, verbally abusive philanderer—is sunnily treated with pharmacological interventions that addict and further dismantle her. And strengthen the damaging, inchoherent-seeming circuit of wreckage within our family. Who knows what trials she faced growing up and fester unrelieved in her? What I do know is this: for years while my two-years-younger brother and I are growing up, her daily use of a variety of prescription anti-depressants and painkillers, mixed with possibly unnecessary hormone and thyroid therapies—to the point of severe impairment—terrorizes us. Best to deny this too.

But now, in the wake of my cousin's visit, the cat's out of the bag, or semi out: the revelation about my mother's father recalibrates my world. Affords me headway in making sense of my, at times, caring and uniquely perceptive, and other times unpredictable, angry, violent mother—herself raised on the shattering vagaries of a war-traumatized, alcoholic father, a mother unable to mother—and yields another related truth. One I've by this point long suspected and which runs counter to official family doctrine, according to which so many of the battles at home are my stubborn, spiteful fault.

All the bullshit? Maybe not my fault.

Maybe, it occurs to me at age fourteen, there's another story here: my own. Divergent, as yet unannounced, and already hard fought for.

·

If it's telling that my mother lies by omission about her alcoholic father, it's equally revealing that my father never shares the story of his given name or reveals the truth about his bootlegging grandfather.

Even more illuminating, for its convolutions and contradictions, is that it's my mother who comes clean about the secrets of my father's early life.

I'm fifteen. On a rain-blurry March afternoon, I've been locked in my room reading, as I usually am when I lucklessly find myself at our volatile home instead of at a friend's. I emerge for a glass of water, and from a chair in the living room my mother greets me in what I've come to recognize as the strangely milky voice she uses for her rare confessions. Her big asks for forgiveness.

At this age, I'm still lured by that voice. I lean against the doorframe, ears pricked while she picks at some lint on her pants leg, takes a drag off her cigarette.

I might be curious but I'm also untrusting. Her peaceable interludes, when she's not raging about my father or some infraction I've supposedly committed or *You and your father both*— or when she's not making maniacal, scary fun out of her own freakishly childish impulses—increasingly repulse me. I know the flip side of these confidences too well.

Worse, such moments feel squishy, overly intimate. As if she's brushing her hands over my body, including places she shouldn't. Which she has sometimes done during the preceding years, and still tries—even though at fifteen I'm beyond old enough to know how shitty these violations are. And to fight them tooth and nail. Which only refuels her sense of hurt and rejection, and her venom.

I can't wait to escape this cycle, among others. To remove myself physically, psychically. Cut myself loose.

In significant ways I already have. My teenaged self has learned, is still learning, to distrust and disavow any closeness between us. Same goes with my father, given his casual verbal abuse, his occasional violence toward my brother and I, his over-sexualizing of me. Chafed raw by their grasping oversensitivities, their lashing out when emotionally wounded, the savagery passed off as love and affection, at this point I can hardly stand either of them. When they're out grocery shopping on Saturday afternoons, I lie on my bed and pray—calling upon my own learned savagery—that they'll die. A car crash would be nice. Cancer in a pinch. Anything to be free of them.

.

Even as, in certain significant ways, they've given me the world— whole worlds.

Before I learn to read, my mother drops whatever she's doing to read to my brother and me. Mostly Dr Seuss or nursery rhymes that conjure careening, thrilling realms ultimately rescued from the horrors of sheer chaos by not only the plots but also by the orderliness of the rhythmical language, the way it resolves into sentences and rhymes. In both form and subject, zaniness unleashed and then safely contained.

Once I can read—between kindergarten and first grade—my father, who is a big reader of thrillers and the like, takes me to Memorial Public Library every Sunday morning. We stroll hand in hand through the parking lot and, once beyond the front doors, he unleashes me. Over the next few years, unsupervised I pluck up *Ferdinand the Bull*. Anything about horses, including an abridged version of *Black Beauty* that I read over and over. Collections of ancient Greek and Roman and Norse mythology, German and French and Russian fairy tales. At home I obsessively write my own stories and poems. Wildly attracted to the abracadabra of words, horse manes fly in the wind and hooves piston over snowy plains and high chaparral, usually depicted from the equine perspective.

My parents treat books and reading with reverence, regard learning as paramount in gaining social and economic mobility. But the deprivations of their own childhoods and subsequent educations have left them short on knowing how to direct and shape my reading habits. At home we don't have *Charlotte's Web* or *The Secret Garden*, *Peter Pan*, or *Winnie-the-Pooh*. I'll chance upon the children's classics at friends' houses. Spend late afternoons curled on their bedroom floors reading while they try to enlist me, to no avail, in Barbie games.

My family does somehow proudly possess a massive *Webster's Unabridged*. My little brother and I lie on our stomachs for hours at a time fingering the onionskin pages. We cover our eyes with one hand and with the other point to words whose definitions we then read aloud. The words strike me as keys to the secrets of the universe and also as powerful, tangible objects my mind can possess, all of them.

As they possess me. As do the stories and tales I read. And the ones I write.

.

At fifteen there's a part of me that still leans into my mother when her voice softens and she yields what I yearn for: words and stories, however bafflingly conveyed, that help chart the origins and departure points of my miserable family.

.

Two tales on this cold spring day. The first relates my paternal great-grandfather's bootlegging, his arrests and the shame and fear my father experienced as a result. The second concerns my father's given name, and involves his tough-guy Uncle Abe, part-owner of a taxi fleet and a racehorse, a small-time bookie. He'd helped raise my father, and oversaw legally transforming my father from Isidore—too Jewish, too womanish-sounding—to the much Waspier Edward. The change spared my father further schoolyard bullying and taunts.

Don't tell your father I told you, my mother says.

Don't tell him that she's accounting for my father's unpredictable and violent temper. His shouting, the foul meltdown insults.

The way he theatrically, pompously undoes his belt to threaten strappings. Don't let on that she's trying to excuse some of his worst behaviours and generate sympathy for him.

Her gesture is especially rich—or pitiable, gut-wrenching, this evidence of her co-dependency—given how septic their fights. How verbally abusive my father is toward her. Including that he tells her the details of his extensive philandering. A miserable fact that she tells me: a woeful case of oversharing, to say the least.

Their marriage has come of age, for the most part, during the 1960s, an unfortunate by-product of a cultural shift touting freewheeling sexual experiences that benefits men in particular, with women often bearing the damaging, misogynist brunt. Which, given the virulence of my parents' relationship, might account for at least a sliver of another possible motivation for my mother's spilling the beans: payback. Bringing me into the fold of knowledge of my father as weak, frail, harmed. A counter to a narrative he clearly favours of himself as respected, powerful, and powerfully desirable.

Like so much in my family history, it's complicated. Really complicated: in this case, even more so, as my mother's truth-speaking ends with her entreating me not to tell my father what she's revealed. She's offering me the role of accomplice. Anointing me a standard-bearer of the myth—the lie—of us as a happy family. Attempting to draw me back into that fold.

Does she think she's protecting me in this way? In enlisting my help in keeping this lie from unravelling—and calling on me to feel compassion for my father, no matter what harms he's visited upon us, upon me—she seems to believe I'll be smoothed over too. Redeemed, tamed. Rendered inviolable as the official accounts of us as a loving, caring household.

As if I'm the one in need of redemption.

My parents' omissions, deceits, complications and coercions, strike me these many years later as examples of self-invention. Wishful thinking. Such brainchildren also leave me with a larger question. Does it go without saying how provisionally I'm exhuming details of my parents' pasts? Given how they shaped their own stories, disregarding and refashioning what happened or didn't in order to effect a future they desired. Lying through silence and alternative tales in order to go on, manufacture better lives. For themselves, and especially for my brother and I.

They only wanted more for us. More for the future. As people do. As one does.

Am I being overly harsh here? As a fiction writer, an inventor of selves. And of myself. And of them.

My parents in this telling summon a larger truth. In fabricating elements of their pasts, clinging desperately to the splintering fiction of our family as whole and loving—as normal, according to the times and place, 1960s and '70s suburban Toronto—they shape a parallel story. One of erasure and illusion that represents a desire to forget. But as Chilean writer Nona Fernandez notes, "What we forget takes up space just as surely as what we remember." This parallel story—this otherwise blank yet profoundly potent, charged space—holds a truth about the obsessive and, in this case, destructive power of hopes and dreams sublimated, channelled through unwitting and eventually resentful, dazed offspring.

To this day my head whirls just thinking about it.

Here is what I do understand: this troubling of their story is part of mine. My story of making stories.

.

More beginnings—inciting incidents, in the language of traditional narrative structure, which adult me teaches aspiring writers. More complication—rising action, in the same narrative-structure parlance, that which drives the story forward—except in this case, my case here in writing of this, ever more circling around and back.

By the time my parents meet, at the wedding of a mutual friend, they're ripe for abandoning what to them are the old ways of family and Saint John, repositories of privation and small-mindedness. Hunger, fracture. Nothing stable, nothing to count on but a chaos of dire distrust. What we might nowadays, in the 2020s, call the effects of intergenerational trauma. My father feels, as well, that he's never been encouraged—was never considered worth encouraging—in his education. Or encouraged to succeed at anything much.

In escaping their hometown, which is how my parents view leaving, they re-enact a central driver of the time-worn immigrant experience: the hope they can offer their own children greater opportunities. But my parents' aspirations for economic and social mobility—which in short order they'll project onto my brother and I to the extent that they don't seem to have their own lives, seem instead to try to possess ours—will seem heavily inflected by a toxic dread, a holdover from their early lives that they never escape. It haunts and stains and sustains them, as the pasts from which their families hoped to liberate themselves must also have upheld and shadowed them.

This ancient story of leaving.

In my parents' story, for Montreal and then Toronto.

But first, more fracture, back east, what my parents would in the coming years always refer to as *down home*.

My father, who'd completed high school and a one-year business program, is by the time he meets my mother working as a manager in the steamship business and living in Montreal, where once they marry my mother will join him. They want a Saint John wedding though, as most of the relatives can't afford to travel. The problem is that Saint John's sole synagogue refuses to marry them at first—despite my mother studying with a visiting American rabbi in order to convert. To this traditionalist community, Judaism can only be transmitted matrilineally.

Until my father's Uncle Abe—a valued annual financial donor to the shul, despite his sometimes semi-legal and maybe illegal wheelings and dealings—again intervenes in my father's life, this time on my mother's behalf.

My mother must feel very determined, audacious even, in carrying through with the conversion. And vulnerable. My father's strict orthodox father disapproves of her. Her immediate family, and presumably the culture at large, is casually, hurtfully anti-Semitic. In ways difficult now for me to take the measure of—given the emotionally tortured and equally abusive woman I would come to know, who somehow could also inhabit the body and mind of someone capable of being enchantingly raucous, crazy as fuck fun during games with her kids—here she is in her late twenties, a woman who'd never completed high school, now learning Hebrew. Marrying a Jew and embracing his faith during the 1950s, despite opposition from Jew and non-Jew alike.

As a young mother and on until she dies in 2006 at the age of seventy-six, she will never feel accepted by those in her chosen creed. Unable to find her way to more welcoming communities—especially in the pre-internet era, with no idea where to start, and eventually fearful of what she feels keenly as her own ignorance and lack of confidence—she will always have her back up around other Jews. Her own natal, latent anti-Semitism will emerge with shocking vigour, in spirited, often profane ways around my young brother and me. When she complains about my father during their frequent fights. Or when he's away on business trips, catting around, as she puts it, and later bragging to her about his exploits. Her robust slurs, which she must have learned growing up, also surface around her perceived mistreatment by those Jewish by birth. Who might refuse to recognize her conversion and view my mother's lack of shared experience with the ancient customs and language as an incontrovertible sign of not belonging.

More Jewish Jews. Who might also regard my father as a traitor. And both my parents as hapless in their severing of significant roots.

.

If they hadn't already, in getting married my parents come to occupy a social and cultural space of betweenness. They leave Saint John and settle where they're mostly isolated from family and old friends. Likely mindful and fearful of class distinctions, they also lack social connections, and are tentative at making fresh ones. Their fears magnify their isolation and play out in how pridefully and self-damagingly they regard certain new acquaintances as not good enough and others as too good, too *full of themselves.* The dynamic is especially the case for my non-working mother, who lacks even the chatter of co-workers to support her and tease her out of her shell.

As a result, my parents' migration swiftly culminates in an echo chamber of inflamed disjunctions. Into which my brother and I are born.

After a year in Montreal, my father gets a better-paying job and my parents relocate. My brother and I, Toronto-area born and raised, enjoy tremendous privileges by comparison with our parents when they were kids.

You're lucky you don't know what it's like to go to bed hungry.

Lucky you don't know what real winter feels like. If I go away, your father will send you to live with your aunts and uncles down east. See how you like that.

My mother's angry outbursts, her towering menace, sudden and explosive, likely reflect her exhaustion. How overwhelmed and lonely she is—and how bored, locked up with the brats day in and day out while my father works. And plays around with whatever women he can get his hands on. Further pressuring her must be the conflicting sense that she too is now lucky, living the life my father affords, compared to what she came from.

Lucky we're not eating dog food.

Lucky, I guess: as a kid I'm spoiled in certain ways, eating chocolate cake for breakfast and daily turning my nose up at milk, fruit—in my defense, the latter usually takes the form of some canned thing, the former usually soured—and the frozen peas and carrots my mother boils until they taste like nothing at all. I mostly subsist on varieties of sugary junk, of which we always have ample stores. Shades of the chicken-bones candy my mother nostalgically raptures on about? What her sweet tooth—diabetes rampant on her side—craved as a kid and can now indulge daily. But I also bear my father's admonishments concerning my appearance, usually passed to me via my mother. He prefers slim. He dislikes big-bottomed.

In a number of other common-sense matters my parents are the children. Bedtimes, for example, involve my brother and I staying up as late as we want. In deferring to our untutored likes and dislikes, it's as if my parents believe that such nestling and imperfect comprehension can guide and nurture us all. Pave the way to the great remakings of wealth, respect, self-respect. Belonging. Ideals for which no recipes exist that my parents can confidently follow on their own.

.

To this day, as an adult, the smell of wet dog food nauseates me—and I say this as a devoted dog parent. I'm also hyper-sensitive to the sounds of chewing and swallowing, slurping, lip-smacking, even heavy breathing, especially at table—where every day as I grew up my father, birthed to scarcity, heartily and imperiously indulged such behaviours.

My gustatory reactiveness has a clinical name: misophonia. Part of my heritage, is how I think of it—a response to the loaded tensions and fractiousness that marked home life. A combustible atmosphere begat by psyches and relationships generationally freighted with the dramas of baseline survival and by a pursuit of mobility that translates to uprootedness, cracks large and small. Fragments of truth mixed with figments of wishful thinking. A trail of crumbs in a fairy tale.

.

Don't get lippy with me. Don't be a spoiler.
My father, in response to my back-talk—forcefully rejecting his sticky, reaching hands and crooning sexualized innuendo.

Getting lippy, being a spoiler can mean the belt, a punch, a kick.

Listen to the mouth on her.
Dad again, speaking to my brother and I, noting the spectacle of cursing, agonized Mom.

This woman willingly separated from her family and friends.

Who birthed me, her first-born, out of a body even in her pregnancy my father lay claims to, already referring to me as his little girlfriend, according to the intimacies my mother will come to confide in me over the years. My mother doubly abused and molested: by his cruel and divisive words while *trying to get cute* with her, as she primly puts it, and also violated by me in utero: fetal me transformed by my father into not only a beloved and wanted first child but confusingly into a previously unimagined enemy within, a competitor—a role ascribed to me that she will also come to enforce.

These many years later, years following her death, I see her rages, her profanity, *her* verbal abuse, as acts of defiance. The only way she knew to speak up and resist.

How many times growing up do I hear my father try to silence her?

Shut up, stupid. You dummy.

My father's minatory mouth. But also my mother's and mine, for him to feel so threatened that he needs to deride, attempt to shut off what erupts from mouths that have swallowed down their truths until they can't anymore, just can't.

Look what you've made me do.

How could you?

My father genuinely seems to believe he's the victim. And as with my mother's case, I don't find it hard to imagine he once was.

Not hard to imagine him strangling inside. Sense him choking on old wounds.

Not hard to feel for him, feel for all of us. Hard as it is to speak it.

.

How can I?

I'm in my early thirties, three years before my first book will come out—though I don't know it at the time, as the sole participant at a writers' program in the Canadian Rockies who has yet to be published or even have a single short story accepted for publication. It's the day before we're to read from our work at a public event. Anxiety, stage fright: although I've read from my writing publicly a few times previously, such terms do little to convey my terror at the prospect of crossing the threshold from what I hope are my meticulously constructed, near-endlessly revised, and now highly polished words on the page to those same words— hopefully polished to convey an intentional, raw precision— issuing from this mouth on me.

My fear—these many years later I might say my awe at what I'm about to do—acquires subterranean, oneiric proportions. I'm eating lunch in the cafeteria with the other writers, listening to them chatting and cracking jokes while my vision turns X-ray, hazing to a grey and black tunnel, distress narrowing my perception. As hyperbolic as it might sound, I feel like my life is on the line.

I slow-hike a mountain trail to clear my head and shake myself out of myself in the cool thin air. Manage to sleep briefly that night. And dream so vividly that when I wake, for a few moments it seems real: the gargling and struggling to magic a long, jagged shard of glass up my throat and pass it through my lips, followed by the sparkling and expansive relief, my boundless pride, when I succeed. Here it is! I proclaim in the dream, as if with a tremendous flourish I've pulled a rabbit out of my hat.

Abracadabra: of the several folk etymologies for the term are phrases in Hebrew that mean *I will create as I speak*. From the Aramaic: *I create like the word.*

.

These fragments circle around. Vicious circles, they feel like, for which—on behalf of clarity and forthrightness and orderliness—

I feel I should apologize. Say sorry for the hoops I jump through as I try to figure what to take and what refuse for my own portion.

According to the German writer Jenny Erpenbeck, "Every text is, fundamentally, an attempt at a text." I feel this keenly as I attempt to take stock, to reckon, translate from old stories sourced from confounding gaps and misdirections, from slippery tenses and sprawling, spiralling enigmas. In recursions and recessions I work here through a heady absence of stories—slim pickings, pitiful tales with tongues removed, compacts sealed by mute suffering. Longings pressured beyond polite language and tidy narrative.

I arrive at this: a sharp awareness that the feints and absences—the presence of them—form counter-narratives that have distinctly informed the how and why of writing for me. Provisioned me with an understanding of writing as taxonomy of peril and dislocation. An aesthetic of itinerancy that values the broken, the hybrid, and prioritizes range and transport, however unhallowed, across emotional and psychic territories beyond the pale.

2. PRIVACY

I trace more breadcrumbs back.

The first house is a modest townhome on Talara Drive, in Willowdale, a near-suburb of Toronto. My brother is born when I'm two. Eventually I go to kindergarten and one day my teacher asks a question and right away I know the answer. Nothing unusual there. My classmates chirp and hands shoot up around me, but I keep mine down. Seated cross-legged on the floor with the other kids, I rock side to side with happiness, keep what I know to myself.

It's like my not-saying glows. I nurse, exult in the feeling, which seems to enlarge me. Inside me: a place suddenly powerful with knowledge and self-possession. All mine.

.

In sharp contrast to what happens at home, where little of my emotional and psychic landscape goes uncontested. I am not mine. I am my parents'. They hang on my every word, facial expression. They defer when their personal stakes seem low—who cares what I consume for breakfast?—and roar when they feel personally slighted, their fantasies seemingly threatened when in their minds I veer off course.

Spoiler. You spoil everything with your ugly moods.
What happened to my bright and bubbly girl?
Look at the ugly puss on her.
I'll give you something to be unhappy about.

For what? I'm *five*. My worst and most actionable expressions of independence take the form of not smiling all the time, the offence of looking sad or unhappy.

Nothing is ever one single, simple thing. Instability rules as any situation or feeling can change in a heartbeat, as my parents' over-involvement rockets from pleased to displeased.

Long ago appointed daddy's little girlfriend, a role enforced by my mother, I'm also his antagonist. A demon who with evil intent shreds reason and stomps on our special attachment, which he seems to interpret as an act of willful abandon, and an abandoning of him, his desires, his enshrined goals.

You should know better..

Then he jabs with his fist.

My mother who drops her housework at a second's notice to

read to me and my brother from Mother Goose—and, our favourite, tell us stories from when she was a girl, tales of overturning neighbour's outhouses on Halloween or the time a farmer in muddy gumboots asked to dance with her at party—also slaps me with alacrity, scrabbles at my chest with her nails. For what, again? Not laughing and playing along when she alarms me with one of my dolls, speaking in a scary-doll voice that claims it's out to get me. She calls me a *dirty little bitch* when I forget to put on my underwear one day, which she discovers by sticking her hand down my pants at the park in front of other kids and whomping me hard. She accuses me over and over of taking sides against her during her frequent fights with my father.

You and your father both.

Though it's not as if such a side actually exists. Not with the numbing punch to the jaw from good old Dad or Daddy's belt on my bare butt. For my over-exuberant five-year-old's babbling at my brother's birthday party. Or my absorption in watching a game of older girls skipping on the sidewalk in front of our house, which causes me to miss hearing the call to supper.

I'm in *kindergarten.*

My parent's fragility speaks volumes about their anger and frustration over their own fraught upbringings, given the extent to which their dreams collide and smash at the drop of a hat. Hope itself must seem at stake for them.

·

At this young age I'm learning above all that my parents' love for me must be boundless. Their intense fear and rage at the mildest insurrection—that they perceive the slightest infraction as such—is a measure of absolute devotedness. Of which I must ultimately be worthy.

In other words, despite and somehow because of the upsets,

as if they're proof, I'm convinced they love me beyond all reason. My understanding is in part due to their reassurances once they've calmed, worked the toxins out of their systems enough to apologize for their behaviour.

We punish you because we love you so much.

This is their most-told tale.

.

Which I will come over time to understand as meaning that some words, certain proclamations, don't mean shit. Except maybe coercion. Manipulation. I'll gain double vision: there are official versions, especially those that arise from fantasies of mastery and compulsion. And something altogether else. My own ideas, for example.

I'll come to layer my earliest intuitions about multiple truths, about how there are stories written in silence beneath stories, into my developing sense of the writing of others, and my own.

.

By some miraculous alchemy on this regular day in kindergarten, lips glued shut against the answer to my teacher's question, I've glimpsed what self-possession might entail. I've discovered the wondrous presence of an internal realm shaped by language, knowledge. A self I own. That I in secret make.

A potential strategy, not in so many words at the time, but the gist is: if I extinct my external self, muffle how I present to the world, I can defy that world's unjust pressures. And turn inward toward an expansive interiority.

This self-erasure is the opposite of the mechanism by which my father erases and replaces me, transforming me into Daddy's little girlfriend. The process is more akin to how he chose to, at least in theory, erase his past by changing (with his uncle's help) his name and by leaving Saint John to begin a new and better life. As his parents and grandparents before him sought in leaving Lithuania. This kind of hoped for self-effacement is also the opposite of the narrowing transformation I experience when my mother calls me a dirty little bitch.

At age five—again, not in such terms at the time—I intuit that practicing a selective mutism, a form of disordered communication, will allow me to enact erasure on *my* terms and yield a freeing latitude.

.

A near-disastrous cost to my newfound and resolute silence in kindergarten: at the end of the school year, when the rest of my classmates are sent on visits to what will be their first grade classroom, I'm separated from the pack and sent to another room, to sit among those who are labelled as slow learners. I observe as they labour through a reading sample, learn a song. They seem swampy, alien to me. I'm not like them. I suddenly feel as if my head is too big for my body. A feeling of sheer wrongness clamps down and my throat, chest, what else, shrink. I'm physically small for my age, but this extreme sense of contraction and constriction, unlike how I ever felt in my kindergarten class, suffocates. It's a feeling I recognize as one I sometimes feel at home.

The sensation will spring at me in various guises innumerable times over the coming years. A force generated externally and also sometimes purely internally—and destructive rather than conducive to the generative, creative urges I first experienced in silencing myself at age five, when I first become aware of my interior self. A force, or forces, against which time and again I'll claw back.

3. GRANDIOSITY

The second house, a little bigger than the first, is on Hillcrest Avenue, also in Willowdale, though in a different neighbourhood. It's also in a different school zone, where I begin first grade. I'm placed with the regular kids, including the popular ones, who quickly become my friends. I'm popular, normal.

Better than normal, as language continues to evolve in me and evolve me. Fairy tales and nursery rhymes are spells, spellbinding. In their repetitions and recursions, their stabilizing shapes and forms of beginning, middle, end, they take apart and remake—violence and misery conjured, deflected, surmounted by cleverness and righteous force of will. I'm thrilled by their trade in deeper truths, ones I recognize: how dangerous it is to be a child, to come upon dangerous strangers, to have parents maybe more dangerous than strangers. As I lose myself in reading, I find not only the self I might become but who I am at the time, a someone distinct from my parents' version. Thus the act of reading feels like self-invention, as does writing about all those horses and that giant black cat that narrates a trip through our neighbourhood, my brother and I lording around on its back. At school I excel in reading and writing, well advanced for my age. I have a gift, my first- and then second- and third- and so on teachers tell my parents.

My parents are beyond proud. In their eyes, education is their kids' ticket toward economic and social mobility. They also fear the stigma of official labels and diagnoses, believing—perhaps rightly—that they can be used against my brother and me, employed to keep us from achieving. So when I underperform in arithmetic, confused and preferring instead to daydream, my advanced skills in reading and writing allow my parents to vigorously offer their own diagnosis and vehemently make their case at each parent-teacher meeting they attend: instead of needing help I'm merely selectively lazy.

There's nothing wrong with her. She just needs a good swift kick in the ass.

.

I often wonder now, more than a half century later: where did they get some of their language? John Wayne movies. Jackie Gleason in *The Honeymooners*. Rat Packers my father venerated. A language of belittlement, usually spoken by men at the expense of women.

What could I do growing up but hunker down with my brother on afterschool afternoons and worship gutsy, anarchic Lucille Ball in *I Love Lucy* reruns? Deem Ricky an insignificant drip for trying to take her down a notch.

.

During these early years, my brother and I continue to lie on our stomachs on the living room carpet and pore over the bulky hardcover treasure that is the *Unabridged Webster's*—I wish now I could figure out where it came from. I continue with my library hauls: Russian and Celtic fairy tales, Grimm and Perrault. *Bullfinch's Mythology*—popularized Greek and Roman myths—plus children's versions of Arthurian legends and medieval romances. My brother and I pool our weekly allowances and buy horror and *Archie* comics, and stay up exquisitely late on Friday nights to watch scary movies.

By sixth grade I've read Tolkien's *The Hobbit* and *Lord of the Rings*, twice, and plow into Isaac Asimov and Arthur C Clarke, Ray Bradbury. I copy out the lyrics to pop songs I listen to on my tiny transistor radio—a gift from my parents, I'm so lucky to have it. "Joy to the World" by Hoyt Axton and made famous by Three Dog Night. "Timothy" by The Buoys, a narrative about cannibalism that I adore—so much tension, so macabre. I pore over the printed Tim Rice lyrics that come with the album for the musical *Jesus Christ Superstar*. I groom through my father's thrillers for the sexy bits, very eye opening, and race through his *Reader's Digest* and *Time* magazines. I devour the steamy *Valley of the Dolls* and *The Love Machine* that my parents hide beneath the sofa cushions and which I secretly retrieve, combing through the pages for sex scenes I don't fully understand. These latter books especially fascinate me. I'm drawn by what I would now call their frank treatment of fallen women, their cautionary troubling of the conventional narratives of women's lives.

Other reading material that interests me: copies of the business letters my father writes and brings home to share, well-pleased with his *Reader's-Digest*-enhanced vocabulary, his verbal flair.

Each year my teachers praise my stories and poems. When my class visits the Honeybee Honey factory or Pioneer Village, I'm the one who writes a thank-you letter on behalf of my peers.

The honey was delicious, I say of the small tubs each child receives as samples. *We couldn't wait to get home so we ate them on the bus.*

Our favourite part was milking Emily the cow. We also liked it when Mrs Ruth spun the yarn.

.

I also love to tear through our suburban outdoors. Like many of the other kids in this lower-middle-class neighbourhood, outside of school hours I tomboy it in an idyll of unstructured, unsupervised play that results in frequent cuts and bruises, barely noticed. Except for when I anger my mother, having ripped the knees out of my pants or she beholds my mud-coated hair and torn sneakers, which will necessitate extra work for her and dent the family's tight budget. Even so I never miss a day. I skate and toboggan in winter. Swim at the nearby public pool in summer—like most of the parents in our neighbourhood, mine can't afford summer camp. We kids are impervious little gods, mouthy and seemingly invulnerable with joy, in all seasons roaming the deep culverts of the local creek, flushing out muskrat, breaking through the ice and getting soakers, miraculously declining to drown.

·

Like my outdoors pursuits, my sense of inner expansion in these years has a propulsive dimension, and parallels an external imaginary. I picture flying my body to crest among the treetops. I'm increasingly obsessed with horses—like many girls, taken by their meaty power and grace—and envision riding them, jumping every fence in the then-open tracts of suburbia. I crave the feeling of suspension, a simultaneous experience of acceleration and deceleration, presence and absence.

Ecstasy, euphoria, self-abandon: I find these too when I'm writing my stories and poems. Transport straight from the desk, where the mundane—the surface with its ugly narrowness, its restrictions—falls away, replaced by a more intense, vivid world.

In retrospect I'd categorize these experiences as states of self-lessness, a transcendent coming out of oneself. A yearning for union with the unbounded. A desire that's key in spiritual devotion and which, from my secular standpoint, reflects creative energy, a freeing, generative possibility, panoramic and encompassing. And which also arises from an erasure, in which the boundaries of the self dissolve and fall away.

Which my parents' early erosions of such boundaries—their attempts at disappearing my developing autonomous self—primed me for.

·

Gift or curse? During my late teens and twenties I'll abandon myself. Nothing major: just the somewhat usual excess of drink and indiscriminate sex and not particularly addictive drugs. More major are a couple of miserably obsessive, overly juicy love affairs—crazy stories in and of themselves. I'll also move a lot. Have no money. Inconsistently attend my classes at the University of Toronto. By my late twenties, beginning to get a handle on my life, I'll throw myself with equal abandon into the excessive demands of an exploitive job—at least it's an editorial position, in educational publishing, and I learn boatloads more about the possibilities of language, and how to put large-scale projects together, and what the publishing process entails, knowledge that will serve me well later. Even so, throughout this decade, while I remain a dedicated reader I neglect my own writing and torture myself over the delinquency, often feel near paralyzed with depression, believing that my life is drastically off track. Not until the beginning of my thirties will I begin to seriously harness myself to, and make manifest, my own words and ideas.

I will, however, continue, until I'm thirty-five—the year my first book, a story collection, is published—to explore the contours of obliteration by obsessively taking up technical diving. Far exceeding the limits of recreational scuba diving, my activities will include forays in underwater caves and far inside shipwrecks. I'll eagerly submit to a euphoria brought on by weightlessness—a state of suspension—and by the chemistry of breathing various gas mixes at deep depths, inducing nitrogen narcosis, the zing of endorphins, and the sharp and nearly otherworldly effect of the pineal gland stoked awake by the need, my need, to come close enough to dying to prove to myself I'm alive. The elation of hauling butt back on the dive boat, having survived—also another story. Pertinent here is that, all through the writing of my first book, I'll nearly pulse with the belief that the rigours of meticulous mental planning, the honing and re-finement of skills and technique, and the steely mindset of utter commitment to the dive needed for these endeavours beat with the same heart as my stories. That with both, I'm pushing back the darkness to lay bare the hidden, the secretive, to witness what's there. And live to tell the tale.

Tales: as in my experiences of technical diving, I'm trying with my writing—in terms of both character and the techniques I use—to hold the impulses of presence and absence in a creative suspension, a chiming contradiction.

Gift, curse: not until my first book comes out do I start to untangle the literalness of this dynamic. Recognize I don't need to actually put my life on the line.

.

Other, early perils abound—centralizing, centripetally focusing my perceptions and forming axes around which much of my preoccupations concerning writing will take shape.

For all the years I'm growing up, mine is the sole Jewish family in the area. We're not particularly observant. Starting when I'm around ten we begin eating bacon and, while my brother will eventually attend after-school Hebrew lessons to prepare for his bar mitzvah, as a family we only make it to services once a year, for the High Holy Days.

The sole Catholic family lives down the street. Five or six kids and a working mom abandoned by the dad, which also sets them apart from the neighbours. The eldest kid—a girl, big and brute for her age, often picking fights with boys, in retrospect likely urgently in need of therapy—bullies my brother the fall and winter that I'm in fourth grade and he's in second. Despite my mother's phone calls to the girl's mother, to the principal, this tough act knocks my little brother into snowdrifts and rubs his face with snow. She pelts him with stones and gravel. Tells him his people killed Jesus.

Sad to say now: at the time I'm preoccupied with my friends and activities, my reading. I don't pay much attention to this torment. Until one bright spring day when I'm walking home on our quiet streets from a friend's and this wounded girl comes for me, furiously pedalling a boys' bike much too small for her size. Stolen? She pulls alongside me and drops her wheels on the ground, balls her fists. I back off the sidewalk and onto the grass. Behind me, a tall chain-link fence, the deserted high-school football field. Leave me alone, I tell her.

Or what? You going to have your puny Jew dad come after me?

I hesitate for a second then let go. I say, At least I have a dad.

The second the words fly out of my mouth, before she even reacts, I feel guilty. I realize I've used unnecessary force—know in a profound way that I've mortally wounded her. It's a moment of radical empathy. The first I remember experiencing and which I'll never forget, feeling for her as she freezes, face flushed, jaw clenched.

I understand for the first time that my words can protect, and harm.

She drags up the bike, slings her leg over the bar and takes off. Never bothers my brother or me again.

·

This is all of a time—the sixties and on into the seventies—in which it's considered appropriate for parents to spank kids. For kids to roam on their own with little or no adult supervision, and bumps and scrapes and barbed altercations and much worse, the worst happen. Two younger kids from our school are killed by a car that mounts the sidewalk as they're walking home at lunchtime. Our next-door neighbours, better off than most in the area, have a young nanny who is brutally murdered by an ex-boyfriend.

A teenaged girl who lives a few blocks away is spirited into the car of a stranger and is murdered, probably sexually assaulted too, judging by the strained tone and elisions my mother employs in discussing the incident with me, clumsily aiming at what we now call child-proofing—unmistakably the same clumsiness and ellipses she uses in explaining the mechanics of sex to me one sunny summer afternoon at a Holiday Inn swimming pool near the Montreal airport, surrounded by smiling, encouraging Lufthansa stewardesses while I want to die of embarrassment and an even deeper discomfort, all while my father and brother take in an Expos game at Jarry Park.

At the age of seven, I'm beginning to recognize the more gendered nuances of violence. What is for many females—in later years I'll recognize this as the case too for many LGBTQ and BIPOC people—the near-ubiquitous Venn diagram of sex and violence, the easy proximity of violence to sex.

How to keep from becoming a dead girl?

Wrapped in my hotel-room towel at the Holiday Inn, wringing chlorinated water from my hair—and already aware of my father's widespread sexist denigrations of women in general, myself subject to his grimy appraisals of my growing body and his claims that he's my boyfriend, and witness to his cruel insults directed at my mother—I puzzle over the great conundrum. How can, how does, a female boldly go forth?

The question will gain greater transparency and urgency for me as the years unfold. And elicit greater nuance, further questions. How does a female, or gender nonconforming person, say? What is she, what are they, allowed to say?

·

While these questions bristle at me for years—and still do, forming a baseline in my writing, and in my sense of what is considered most available to women and nonconforming writers in terms of subject and style and how those writing outside the norms are received by critics—most of us kids in our neighbourhood do make it home again. More or less in one piece, as far as I or presumably most of us can tell, given the entrenched codes of discretion and denial of the time.

Home again, home, here we are, paused for a moment, an eternal time-out: whooping and hollering, splashing up a storm at Memorial Public Swimming Pool, cutting perfect spirals with our skates on the rink at Mitchell Field. Sheroes and heroes all.

4. LOVE (TEARS US APART)

Home again, home: in my household, love is the greatest violence. In addition to the strap and the occasional punch or kick, verbal abuse is the norm.

Dummy.

What are you, a pig? Yes she is, she's a pig.

What's wrong with you? We're just kibbitzing. Why do you have to spoil everything?

Onward into my teens. Ever more comments about my body, usually framed, by both my father and mother, in terms of daddy's preferences for the slender, the busty, leggy, a tidy butt. Attempted gropings—mock slaps and swipes—at my breasts and rear, from both parents, though especially my father, who seems to believe that all women within his purview exist for his purposes. Of female strangers he finds unattractive—too fat or masculine—he routinely gives a theatrical shudder of disgust, shakes his head, says, *I shouldn't have to look at that.* (I'm reminded of my father when I read, in a September 2020 *Atlantic Monthly* article reported by Jeffrey Goldberg, that then-US President Trump, who loves staging military parades, had asked a 2018 parade-planning committee to exclude wounded veterans. Referring to amputees, he said, *Nobody wants to see that*.)

My self-defenses include cutting back-talk and slammed doors, the time-proven arsenal at so many teens' disposal, and my aloofness, my attention absorbed by books, my own attempts at writing when I'm not escaping to friends' places, a freedom I'm fortunately granted. My parents take to calling me Daughter instead of by name. I call them by their first names, Betty and Ed, rather than Mom or Dad.

Fear of not fitting in, fear of rejection: these seem to increasingly set them off. Their fears isolate and imprison them. They never once entertain friends or neighbours, only the occasional and to me little-known relative up from down east on a business or medical trip. Our cozy Ontario family is all chiasmus, a cage. All four of us: we shrink ourselves in self-defense and out of a lifelong sense of betrayal and emotional abandonment. Armed with rage, we fight back at what's most vulnerable and close at hand. Ourselves. My brother and I fight savagely. My parents have always practiced a divide and conquer routine with us, despite their disavowals of doing so. One of us deserves the belt, the other a favourite dessert. No hope for forming an alliance in this situation.

I really do want my parents to die. Often, I want to die. *Spiteful. Ingrate.*

.

What heightens the atmosphere of near-annihilation is the drama over attempts at carving out private space. Quietly shutting my bedroom door can elicit a rabid response. The bathroom? My mother storms in while I'm in the tub the day after my ninth-grade prom and flails at me for having a hickey on my neck. Many times my father whips off his belt when I tell him to leave me alone, to stop staring at or reaching for me—and I take to the bathroom, wedge myself between the toilet and door with the broken lock while my father shouts outside, rattling the knob, lunging against the door as if to splinter it, until his anger works itself out of him.

From my parents I learn that one can be not only powerful with rage but rendered powerless by rage. Made even more powerless over one's children and one's life as a whole. Powerless with and captive to a rage that pushes those one loves away and one's family apart.

Whatever mechanisms originally engendered my parents' behaviour, what corrosive disappointments, I'm learning that damage breeds damage.

Weekends are the worst, if I don't make it to a friend's. I can hardly begin to describe the feeling of desolation. My father home all day, school out, my parents fighting, picking on and blaming my brother and me, the two of us fighting each other as we try to claim back some kind of power, however dirty, for our isolated selves. The texture of daily life greyed and withered. Reflecting a bleak, unspeakable inner landscape, sealed from the outside to the extent that speaking itself feels like a violent act.

Outside the home, I never say a word about any of this to my friends. Can't possibly reveal the piercing sense of shame I experience when, for example, my father presses himself to me in our narrow first-floor hallway. His livid reaction to my sharp pushback: the too-literal kick in the ass I receive when he angrily lunges at me on the basement stairs. My scrambling escape out the back door to stand shaking in the neighbour's driveway.

Shaken and confused, wondering: How can I be so small?

Where are the good times in my version, here, of our story? We have a fox terrier I love. My father grows a vegetable garden every year and bountiful marigolds and pink petunias in planters. I can usually talk him into supplementing my allowance so I can buy books or student tickets plus subway fare to go with a musically inclined friend to hear the Toronto Symphony. In my later teens, there are season tickets, and I take with me a friend, or my father who, charmingly, I believe, tends to fall asleep and snore softly through the performance. My mother and I see the international dance contemporary dance troupes perform, and I willingly suffer through her remarks about how beautiful the dancers are, their physical beauty apparently the only element of note for which she has language. To my parents, such interests are cultural markers of socio-economic mobility, and they support them in hopes I'll one day ascend to the class of doctor or lawyer. My rising cultural passions are reminders, too, for my father, that though he hadn't felt encouraged growing up, it's important for him to encourage his kids. Also: my mother makes amazing fudge I bring to school bake sales and which always swiftly sells out, and when lucid she counsels me to follow my own path and make my own money when I'm older.

Never be dependent on some man.

Over my earlier years my parents make financial sacrifices and spoil me with horseback riding lessons, though I'm terrible at it, tending more often than not to fall off rather than soar over jumps. Beginning in tenth grade I take private double-bass lessons from a musician in the Toronto Symphony. I'm terrible at this too but I also love it, acquiring a feel for the discipline required in acts of creation. To this day I can score-read Schubert, Beethoven, Mozart, Monteverdi—standard repertoire—and hear in my head what I see on the page. I can even manage with some of the more complex New Music composers whose work I love, Iannis

Xenakis, Kaija Saariaho, Unsuk Chin. Texture, methods of development and shaping time: music provided and still provides me with a revealing analogue to the literary arts.

.

Throughout these early years, my parents believe in me: I believe this to the hilt. In a deformed, contorted way, the intimate, closed circuit formed through these staunchest of sentiments allows me to feel that despite everything I'm special. That I have a destiny to fulfill.

For these beliefs—in retrospect as warranted or not as they might be—I'm grateful to this day.

.

Where are the others in all this? The friends.

People will always let you down.

Based on this foundational principle, my mother—chewing over some past bitterness, consistently and daily undermined and shamed by my father, and fearing a future of soul-crushing separation that she herself will painfully, tragically hasten—pushes her two closest friends away. By the time I'm thirteen, fourteen, she's mostly retreated from the world at large. She further pushes me away by engaging me as her sole confidante, a cringe-worthy paradox if there ever was one, revealing that my father tells her the sordid details of his sexual escapades with other women.

More to the point: why doesn't she leave?

She has no job and no decent prospects for one, or for surviving if she leaves. She's mostly estranged from her family. And while it's easy for me to wonder now about my father's narcissism, or if my mother was bipolar and suffered from manic depression—easy for me to attempt to pathologize them—what I can say with certainty is that by the time I'm in seventh grade, my mother is heavily dependent on her buffet of prescription drugs. Her speech routinely slurs. Her behaviour is increasingly erratic. Heart-sick, heart-struck, she further weakens and at age forty-six has the first of two cardiac surgeries and more drugs thrown at her. She hallucinates like crazy. Dinner with the Chinese ambassador. Grown-up me in a baby bonnet, perched on the ledge outside her hospital-room window, threatening to jump.

How can she leave? Where would she go?

.

Good times? For now, my lips are sealed.

Spoiler.

Ingrate.

5. FORTHNESS

I go to my friends' houses, when I'm not reading or writing or skating or swimming or riding a horse or my bike or messing around down at the ravine or creek. Or, as I get older, smoking weed, roaming downtown.

From the time I'm six until I finish high school, I have two best pals, switching back and forth, I'm not proud to say now, between them—friendship something I conduct intensively and serially in those years. In their homes I find replacements for my own—theirs are also fraught with dramas, mostly absent dads, and moms frequently harried and unhappy but surrogates who by comparison with my parents seem reasonable and kind.

Years later I sometimes wonder how much my friends' parents knew of or guessed at my situation. This was a time when people minded their own business, never dreamed of interfering. I like to think now that their silence was circumspection, a graciousness expressed through gentle offers of shelter that didn't threaten to utterly rip my world.

.

The family of my musically gifted friend belongs to a church in downtown Toronto with a celebrated choir, in which her parents sing. I sometimes attend with her family, revelling in the gorgeous sounds and uplifting beauty of the High Church of England service. Beginning in seventh grade, in addition to occupying the cheap seats for symphony concerts at Massey Hall, my friend and I get high and wander our suburban streets, splitting single chocolate bars, all we can afford. Bored and hankering, we roam the aisles of the nearby Dominion grocery store, dreaming of foods we might someday be able to buy. Or we practice the instruments we sign out of school and take home with us—improbably (given I'm five-foot-two), that double bass for me, cello for her. For a few summers, on afternoons we convene with her talented violist older sister and our equally talented violinist friend and play along to recordings in the family collection of Hayden and Mozart quartets and Beethoven symphonies, my friend's father checking out scores for us from the downtown music library. Though I sight-read music well, and can transpose the cello parts for bass as needed, when playing at tempo I often only manage the first note of every bar, and usually warp that note so out of tune it's a sweet wonder my cohort manage to hide how much I must make their teeth ache.

.

I don't date during my high school years. Instead I have my other best friend.

Her father is the literature and film officer for the Ontario Arts Council, separated from her mother when my friend is maybe in third grade. By high school this friend and I are skipping classes to hang out downtown at the Royal Ontario Museum, the Art Gallery of Ontario. We peruse books at the grungy, dimly lit former Central Toronto Public Library on College Street—where late one winter afternoon I pull a copy of Samuel Beckett's prose trilogy off the shelf and read the first few pages of *Molloy*, skip to the opening of *Malone Dies* and the first page or so of *The Unnamable*. The top of my head catches fire and blows off.

I've already been reading George Orwell, Aldous Huxley, browsing the Penguin Classics at the Coles bookstore in my neighbourhood. I adore Mervyn Peake's *Gormenghast* gothic fantasy novels. At fourteen I'd read Tom Wolfe's performative, strutting *The Electric Kool-Aid Acid Test*, discovered it at another friend's house, something her older sister had to read for a class and hated and donated to me when I pawed the cover and admiringly scanned a few pages.

But oh, Beckett: I sign the book out and in its highly pressured, precise language, its elliptical, disintegrative approach to narrative, its treatment of character psychologically *in extremis* and ultra-compressed interiority, I truly uncover a path. Techniques, methods. I read his plays and attend productions of them by tiny Toronto theatre companies who offer student tickets for a song. In his works I find a means with which to capture the psychic and emotional states of betweenness, constraint, defiance, the craft involved in giving shape to the tension between the abjection of self-exile and the unyielding human voice. I grasp how what is not said on the page can speak volumes: how silence itself can render an eloquent and moving subtext, and wrenchingly convey the unspeakable. I locate the effects of a dark humour, with its underlying austere pathos and compassion. I discover a deeply immersive technique that functions as a possibility space.

Each time I crack the spine of his prose trilogy, especially, I feel I'm holding self-knowledge, an eerie sense of the future, in my hands. *This* is it. What I want to do.

.

I'm lucky to spend weeks of many summers at this friend's lovely, modest family cottage at Balm Beach on Georgian Bay, near Midland and Penetanguishene, Ontario. The place was built by her grandfather, and I borrow a welcome sense of lineage, of stability and ease from this. At fifteen I lie in my bottom berth in the tiny bunkhouse near the main cabin that my friend and I commandeer and read Virginia Woolf's *To the Lighthouse* and *The Waves* to the swaying birch and pine outside the window. Woolf *orchestrates*, it strikes me, using the instruments of language and narrative, image and sound. She profoundly and unapologetically foregrounds interiority, the psychological and emotional at the expense of plot. Her Lily Briscoe's *I have had my vision* slays me (still does). As does the killer use of white space to convey the unspeakable weight of loss and grief the characters experience at the death of Mrs Ramsey. At sixteen I read *Moby-Dick*, that encyclopedia, swallowing it whole in an intense four days mostly prostrate in my bunk, forbidden the beach following the first of the three concussions I'll go on to sustain so far in my life—having fallen backward off a chair while horsing around and banged my head on a concrete flower planter and knocked myself out. (Can I say here—I can—that I'm writing this now while recovering from my third and fortunately mild concussion? With any luck, my last.)

At one point partway through Melville's epic, lapsing into near sleep, I experience an unforgettable hypnagogic hallucination (common to those with sleep apnea, which many years later I'll learn I have). In my white sundress, I *am* the whale. Most likely the experience only lasts a few seconds. Or a lifetime: here in my sequestered bunk inside the sheltering cabin, trees outside the window inhaling and exhaling like tides, time slips loose, my future itself some kind of book I can glimpse—not as a whale, of course, but as a person who slips the bounds of self in books I read and in the fictions I might myself come to write. Me and not me. Me in this real life of mine that lies ahead, waiting for me to catch up.

Back home in the neighbourhood, I sometimes access similar states. Rounding the corner of Princess Street onto Empress Avenue—their actual names, I kid not—blocks from my parents' house at winter dusk, an unlatching inside me, a sense of the future, while in my head I recite lines from my own poems and stories.

·

Throughout this time—not until, when? my late twenties?—I don't know any fiction writers or poets in person. I don't know the first thing in a formal way about craft or criticism except in a budding, intuitive sense I pick up on my own from books I read. Nor do I have the faintest about how to live a writer's life, how to get by. I only know there are more books to read, plays to see, art galleries and museums to visit, music to listen to. So many books. Nearly all the rest of Woolf. Margaret Atwood's 1968 poetry collection *The Animals in that Country*—the first book of poetry I ever purchase—and her 1969 novel *The Edible Woman*, which speak worlds to me about women's experience, and that this is a significant, lit-worthy lens. As is the Toronto setting, places I know. I discover other writers invested in giving voice to a newfound, and 1970s, sense of Canadian cultural nation-alism—and that Canada has a literature. That one needn't live in or write about anywhere else in order to be a writer. In terms of formal and psychological possibilities, Michael Ondaatje's shape-shifting *Coming through Slaughter* offers an unforgettable primer in hybridity, in prising open the borders separating genre and rejecting compartmentalizations in favour of rich psychic ecotones—and in writing with a spikey urgency about lives not traditionally centred in narratives, foregrounding the gaps and distortions of the multiple stories through which people might live their lives.

From my school library's copy of Northrop Frye's *Fools of Time*, his brief study of Shakespeare's tragedies—a book I never return—I begin to acquire a nascent critical vocabulary and framework. At my local Coles bookstore I buy his *The Bush Garden*, a critical study of CanLit. I read the book reviews in the *Toronto Star*, and in the Sunday *New York Times* at my friend's house. Every week I read the *New Yorker*, cut out poems from it and tape them to my bedroom walls.

I see productions of Ionesco and Pinter plays. On weekend nights, cheap triple-bills of Bergman and Fellini and Antonioni at an art-house movie theatre. I borrow jazz recordings from my excellent local library or from my friend's older brother's record collection—Charlie Parker, especially, and Lester Young, John Coltrane, Ornette Coleman, Billie Holiday, and the blues of Robert Johnson and Bessie Smith. My friend and I pool allowances and buy albums by Joni Mitchell, Bruce Cockburn, Neil Young. We listen to her brother's John Cale, Velvet Underground. My little brother represents too: I'm no fan of his AC/DC, but The Sex Pistols? I can hardly believe my ears—an experience I'm more than okay with—and in later years will try to incorporate into my writing some of the punk ethos of the female adherents of the genre.

Also from the public library during my teen years: a precious red vinyl LP of Allen Ginsberg declaiming his book-length, crazy-glorious poem *Howl*, seemingly aflame on the turntable, spinning the very picture of outrage and ecstasy. I commit the opening to memory, as I will at seventeen the Prologue to Chaucer's *The Canterbury Tales*, which we'll read for English class.

Also at the library, and through some of the occasionally more adventurous programming of the Toronto Symphony, I discover the pleasures of atonality and its kin, advancing the project of rewiring my aural receptivity through works by the composers Arnold Schoenberg, Béla Bartók, Igor Stravinsky. One Sunday afternoon my friend and I sit on the splintery floor of the now-defunct A Space Gallery for a performance of the Art Ensemble of Chicago's ferocious experimental improv. I clearly remember wondering at such times: how to translate into writing? Without resorting to reductive, ham-handed description.

My friend and I attend a viewing of films by Joyce Wieland and Michael Snow at Toronto's newly opened Harbourfront. Their ten-minute collaborative *Dripping Water* is another possibility space. Its trance-adjacent, prayer-like focus, demanding a reciprocal sustained attention on the part of the viewer, echoes what I'm finding in the practice of close-reading complex literary works.

Wieland's art in general will eventually take on a touchstone status for me. It fires my interest in conceptual works, including so-called experimental writing. In my late twenties, I'll see the 1987 Wieland retrospective at the Art Gallery of Ontario, where her painting *Wrestling with the Paint Demon* will shock me. Here is the very picture of my relationship to writing. At the age of fifty-seven, I will experience a similar shock when, in Toronto for the launch of my third book, I'll notice an historical plaque affixed to a house on Queen Street East near Parliament Street and realize that during my early twenties—in the eighties, when the neighbourhood was rough, not yet gentrified—I'd lived only a few houses from her. Probably passed her countless times on the street or waited beside her for the streetcar. The upper-floor apartment I lived in at the time, shared with a friend in the early stages of gender transitioning, was where at the age of twenty-four I wrote the first work, a couple of poems, that I dared send out in hopes of publication. A year after this belated discovery, when I'm fifty-eight, and thanks to the internet, I'll also realize that the two poems had, unknown to me at the time, been accepted and published. In *Bad Attitude*: a wonderfully in-your-face, political-to-the-eye-teeth lesbian s&m porn mag out of San Francisco. Thirty-five years following my poems' publication, I'll find myself thrilled to make the discovery online, and purchase a rare collector's copy of the issue. Anyway, whatever. Except to say that in late retrospect, this will all feel oddly constellated to me. Strange, early-on clues to the writer I will become.

.

Throughout my mid-teens: I also inhale Baudelaire and Rimbaud and Verlaine, Kafka and Borges. I find a poetry of witness in Osip Mandelstam and Anna Akhmatova. In the European symbolists and American Beats, extremes of thought and feeling, an inflamed ecstatic and gritty swagger, the puckish over the pious. Faulkner wallops me.

I'm responding to the bent and twisty. Rewired fables and parables and allegories. Expressionist techniques and the technique of repetition in high modernism which, I'll realize not many years later, will influence minimalism. I'm taken with the grim visions and bold departures from the niceties of realism. From there it's a half-step to the social critiques implicit in the magic realism of Gabriel García Márquez, Julio Cortázar, Octavio Paz, whom I'll come to at seventeen. I'll recognize that pushing the boundaries of writing's realist traditions is consonant with a socially or politically engaged literature. I'll also see fictions and poems as art objects, akin to music and sculpture. A budding formalist, I'll also understand that such objects can still engage at the deepest, most political levels in their ability to model and witness human experience. Also at seventeen, for English class I'll read and love Thomas Hardy's dread-drenched *Jude the Obscure*, the high drama of parts of Milton's *Paradise Lost*. Keenly desire absorbing as much as I can of the multitudinous literary traditions.

Regrettably it will take me until my early twenties and beyond to encounter the booming wealth of books written by women and people of colour, works outside the traditional canon. In my undergrad English lit classes and on my own, among the seductions of Edmund Spenser and Laurence Sterne and George Sand and Jane Austen, Walt Whitman and Emily Dickinson, I'll discover Angela Carter and Toni Morrison, Adrienne Rich, Audre Lorde, Joy Williams, Dionne Brand. Ben Okri's beautiful and nightmarish *Stars of the New Curfew*. These and many others will twist my head around and allow me to see everything anew. See how so many stories, not only my own, exist parallel to those enshrined in the canon.

Meanwhile in my mid- to later teens I haunt the (now-closed) Bob Miller Book Room, a capacious basement bookstore on downtown's Bloor Street, across from the Royal Ontario Museum, which I visit with my friend on days when we skip school. I read on the subway, and sometimes roam the city streets solo for hours, looking, listening, imagine myself a flâneuse-in-waiting. Dreamer. When home, locked in my bedroom, I play Bach's cello suites on my cheap stereo, listen to them over and over—transfixed by the counterpoint and voice leading, the glories of form and variation, the pulsating sense of a living, organic entity manifesting a complex and singular vision using a precise and highly evolved language. A refined technique and skill.

I'm early-stages grasping the rudiments of an understanding that will remain crucial for me. That there is no binary between polished and raw—the opposition a false notion I'll come by the time I write my first book to reject, recognizing the idea as one that's been historically applied to women writers and writers of colour. Often couched in terms of excess, too much: *too polished* or *too raw*. Sometimes in nearly the same breath.

Instead there are these words of Charlie Parker's that I take to heart. "You've got to learn your instrument. Then, you practice, practice, practice. And then, when you finally get up there on the bandstand, forget all that and just wail."

Years of books and music and art. And also, at the same time, years of sexual coercion on my arty friend's part. It begins when we're in fourth grade, ebbing sporadically only to crest again when we're fifteen, sixteen, seventeen and I'm nearly graduated from high school. She polices her coercion with suicide threats and one attempt that results in a psychiatric hospitalization. Plainly put: if I don't let her lick and fondle and fuck me, and often hurt me physically in the process, not only will I lose her and the escape I believe she offers—believing her to be an active agent in my ability to make myself into something—but the whole world will lose her too. The whole freaking world: it too will suffer the loss of her genius, never see her realize her ambitions of becoming a theatre director or a filmmaker. Her instability a measure of that genius, she likes to remind me. Just as she reminds me we're in love. Of a superior kind. A measure of *our* genius.

Her manipulations dazzle and her threats terrorize me. Without her I'll never write. Never magically transform into who I'm meant to be. I'll amount to nothing. She *clothes* me, for god's sake. Decides I should convince my parents to buy me this coat, that shirt. Sews me outfits she dreams up. Including one based on her idea of what Orlando from Woolf's novel might have worn: forest-green velvet breeches with green satin edging at the knees, pearl buttons, a "poet"-style cream-coloured blouse. My friend is also a fabulous cook who easily whips up cheese soufflés and crêpes suzette, which I scarf, vastly preferring such offerings to my mother's burnt steaks and potatoes boiled until they disintegrate. I also beyond all reason, or perhaps reasonably, prefer my friend's predations to the chaos I dread at my own house. Prefer her chasing me around her living room. The shots of ice-cold tequila she pushes to loosen me up—and which I'll invariably puke up later—as prelude to stupefying me when she oranges her nipples with Bonne Bell lip gloss as prologue to an afternoon's forced sex.

When we're sixteen she keeps me around as she also gets very close to a new student at school. He's already getting acting gigs in commercials, he's smart and, like me, he can write—which my friend can't. She directs him in plays and eventually they have sex together, but on the down-low since he has another, more official girlfriend. I get to hear about it all though, lucky me, hear how great he is, how bright his genius burns, and years later he will in fact become a celebrated actor and playwright and screenwriter. His nickname for me in back in the day: *the viper*. Another erasure. A role assigned me by someone else, based on other people's terms of engagement.

.

During these years my mother refers to my friend as a dirty little bitch, the same phrase she has sometimes applied to me.

You two dirty little bitches.

She knows, sort of knows, what's up. But my girlfriend is my *friend* and I'll resist my mother on this to the death. She offers no way out.

Given the atmosphere in which I've grown up, raised on the notion of an exceptionalism that goes hand in hand with and is enforced by abuse, by an indifference to my bodily and emotional autonomy—made to feel at once special and small, shrunken, not deserving of space—I'm in the dark about love. Like my mother, I'm also isolated, with no one to speak to—certainly no one in my family, and no other friends at the time—about what's going on.

What *is* going on? I hardly know. And with no way to confide in anyone, an effect too of my friend having isolated us by deeming other people our age unworthy of our company, I have no chance of understanding that love is not the same as denigration or coercion. I'm meat in her mouth. Especially since I don't even remotely, as far as I'm aware, know any lesbians or gays, so I'm ignorant of what queer love might look like. It's possible that the first queers I am cognizant of meeting, so to speak, are Woolf, Ginsberg, Jean Genet, Gertrude Stein.

This tainted, tortured love—familiar to me in some respects from my early home life and new in significant other ways—frightens as it purports to elevate me. In retrospect, I see that our teenage relationship enacts the now-worn and damaging trope of doomed queer relationships, an internalization I'll fight as an adult, thankful to have friends and colleagues who model more positive connections. But at ages sixteen and seventeen and younger, I'm faced with choosing my poisons.

.

During all these years I mostly hide my writing. In keeping with my old instinct toward privacy and silence, I show no one the stories and poems I write and rewrite by hand, unless I can submit them as work for English classes whenever appropriate, which is not often—creative writing having little curricular value at the time. I copy 'final' versions into mini collections I file in folders and place inconspicuously on my bedroom bookshelves next to paperbacks and geography textbooks and school notebooks chockfull of not much to do with me—I excel only in English and history and music and fuck everything else. My writing allows me to extend my practice of self-erasure and abandon—not to self-extinction but toward a discipline and a host of literary traditions, although beginning in my twenties I'll eye the traditional Western canon with great suspicion. At the same time, at that age, I'm discovering that writing allows me to translate, through the ensorcellments of language, my experiences onto the page—and attempt to transform them into literary objects, to reach into and join with the traditions and innovations of literature. This work, this project: me, not me.

On some high school nights, when I'm well into the small hours trying to write an essay for English or history—when my post-op and highly drugged mother is in the living room, which is next to my first-floor bedroom, and she's swearing, crying out, moaning, taunting me—I pack up my pencils and pens and papers and books and leave. Cross our high school's football field in the dark and half-run the few deserted, spooky blocks to my friend's house. I let myself in and take up residence at the kitchen table. Where her mother or older brother find me polishing my last paragraphs when they get up in the morning. Surprised by my presence, they thoughtfully don't say a word. Except to offer cereal, juice, tea.

.

When I'm a teen, to write—a concentrated form of speech—is thus even more acutely tied to danger. The risk of having torn from me the safety and quiet I'm able to carve out for myself—the necessary room to think and mentally explore—always looms large. The risk of at the most fundamental level being unsafe.

It's a lesson I've learned well from an early age.

When I'm maybe eight, my brother six, my father out of town on one of his frequent business trips, Montreal or NYC, my mother operatically flips out one night. She's caught or only imagined him cheating on her while she's stuck at home with her increasingly moody, wary kids. Especially me, his number one girlfriend. Which she reminds herself of out loud to add insult to the injury of his cheating ways, and to punish someone, anyone—my being at hand, in the house, unlike my father at the moment.

It's dinnertime but there's no dinner and it's as if my mother is speaking in tongues, guttural obscenities and insults streaming from the living room and kitchen. My brother and I take refuge in my first-floor bedroom and cower, contemplating—as my mother throws pots and pans and a dining-table chair down the hallway to bash against the locked door—her notion that every shitty thing is our fault.

On numerous occasions over the years but especially that evening I think she might really kill us. Something mothers sometimes do, don't they? I get the idea from the stories on the TV news my mother likes to remind us of, about parents who kill their young. Drive them off cliffs or into lakes, poison or shoot them. Stories my mother relates with relish. As if she's trying the idea on for size.

6. MORE ANIMALS IN THAT COUNTRY

I also get the idea from the fairy tales I continue to love throughout my teen years, and still do as an adult. No wonder I'm drawn to them, these often grisly stories—arising from histories of starvation and social unrest—involving fragile, destructive parents and exposed yet resourceful children. Mute women killed by husbands. Parents who kill or attempt to kill their offspring.

But for all the terrors these tales encapsulate, as a kid and teen they strike me as somehow reparative—as do the works of Beckett, Woolf et al. That there exists a short-hand language—one of syncope and near-collapse and eloquent, powerful caesura—to capture the multiple truths that make up the brokenness of life heartens me. To my mind at the time, a truth told, however painful, wins over a lie.

I still believe what I was just grasping way back when: that language and the forms it takes can re-story, can remake and revise falsehoods. Re-wild conventions and assumptions that have outgrown their ability to name experience—or subvert rather than reinforce the dogma propping up an unjust status quo, reality that's real only for a privileged, powerful few.

Teenage me is onto this: that the ability to capture the pressured, destabilized self in an unstable world, through words as with other art forms—what I first consciously notice in the tricksters of high modernism—is a kind of power. The power to accurately name, to say: *this* is what things feel like, *this* is what happened. And over my teen years, my awareness of the need for precision and skill at the techniques involved in shaping meaning grows. This awareness goes hand in hand with my developing sense of the materiality of writing, that writing is fundamentally rooted in the inverse tools of language—of words and sentences—and silence, what is not said, intentionally withheld. That an aesthetics of *foregrounding* language can be consonant with witness and disruption, can be called into service in questioning received notions and distortions. That such disruptions can serve as an antidote to what is cruel and tyrannical.

In brokenness, the restorative.

As a teen my burgeoning sense of writing and of art in general gives me hope. I sorely need it.

I'll need this hope later too, when in my early thirties—beginning to undertake the many drafts of what will become my first book—I'll need to believe that if I work hard enough, I can thrift my own writing out of what feels like lost, shitty time.

.

As a teen I translate, on my own terms, my parents' belief in me and my abusive friend's belief in me into believing I might become, might already be, a writer. I take the act of committing words to paper seriously, as much as I know how, given that I have no in-person models or mentors. The hyper-vigilance I've acquired as a survival strategy also aids my powers of observation.

In writing myself, I'm centering my own very fucked-up experience. And I'm also not. I'm writing beyond me. This involves movement: from an obliteration of the self to something greater than. To word objects, language machines. To a sense of connection to multiple traditions and contexts and other voices. Other people, the lives and experiences of those other than myself. Me and not me.

By age sixteen I begin to see all art forms as expressions of pressured, heightened speech and believe I'm undertaking a project. One that's not mine alone. One that's ripe with contradiction and a potentially fruitful contestation. Hard won, to this day.

7. DESK JOB; OR, TALE OF THE DESK

For my sixteenth birthday, I talk my parents into buying me a high quality and, for them, costly desk from a high-end Swedish furniture store. I cannily sell the idea as an investment in my education. The desk is pine and handsomely crafted, topped with blue slate. An elegant and longer, narrower-than-usual, adjustable drafting table I can easily customize to fit my petite frame.

My mother plans a party for my sixteenth. *Sweet sixteen*, she calls this milestone. We invite both my best friends and my mother bakes a cake. Not long before my friends are due to arrive, my mother and I argue over something—I can no longer recall what about—and she snaps. Stung to a fury, she phones my friends and informs them the party is off, due to what she calls my *brattiness*. I hole up in my bedroom. I hate my mother. I hate myself, my life. I listen as both friends, sounding sheepish, come to the kitchen door to drop off their presents. Alone, I open them. Gratitude. Then I sit at my desk and get to work.

My desk: did I say it's beautiful? One gift of many bestowed by my parents that create a path leading me away from them. From their hurts. Their high hopes for me.

Or toward their hopes. Toward my parents.

This desk at which nearly half a century later I am writing this now.

So many times during my teenage years I undertake frequent nightly passages, kitty corner from my family's house to a friend's. Or across the high-school football field on my way to my other friend's house. On a direct bearing toward degrees of sanctuary with lines from my own writing in my head and a copy of *To the Lighthouse* or *Our Lady of the Flowers* in my coat pocket. The latter novel written in the solitude of a prison cell—a corollary, I think now and might have intuited then, to my experience of the paradoxical dualism yoking externally imposed states of confinement to inner expansion.

Like my parents, I imagine now, on my crossings I both suffocate and dream.

I survive those years by shutting doors inside myself and
sometimes unlatching them a merciful, merciless crack. Listening,
looking, trying to translate complexity and nuance into words—at
risk of skirting the edges of legibility, the known world. Sometimes, while I'm working and reworking a paragraph or stanza
or reading a voltaic passage in a form-breaking book while my
parents watch TV upstairs, the doors inside me blaze wide.

.

Many later years I'll cross from one peril to another. Out of habit,
necessity. Sometimes with little I can trust except books, music,
visual art. Even when I feel I've abandoned them, given myself
over to the exigencies of numbing work and other fuckery, they
never cease to call me. These beasts. And my own words, scribbled or typed in private but, I hope, bold on the page where I've
learned and keep relearning to raise my voice. This light in my
head a map of the suburban-Toronto stars above the football
field at night and which at fourteen, fifteen, sixteen I have no
choice but to believe in. A calling. Surging and sometimes mon-
strous-seeming energies I'll come to meet, inside myself and outside too, along the way. This drive to harness the learned chaos
and disruptions inside me and consider these another gift. This
need to try to find language for stories that have none. To take
charge of the narrative. To raze and revise, to rise. Whatever it
is that shapes the urge to make.

.

I no longer believe wholesale in the redemptive power of art. I
don't think it necessarily saves or instructs, though it may in the
political and social realm help disallow machinations based on

secrecy and manipulation. I also no longer of necessity believe in destiny or fate. Or I do. As I do.

Here's what I can say: I'd originally set out to title these pages "The Extinctions," to heighten their focus on damage and loss. They never seem far away. While what does seem to remain distant is a totalizing, liberating endpoint.

What can I do? I think, rethinking things a little more. Except to try to view precariousness as backhanded opportunity and to remain faithful to the task of inflection and nuance. Try to face what feels abyssal and to mine, envision it. Electrify it. Light the fucker up.

I know this much: on the page I can't seem to quit moving. It's my gift.

I have many other questions, large ones, as I believe any reasonable person might—or perhaps should, given the mess so much of our world is in—about the nature of justice and forgiveness and compassion and art as a restorative force. What does it mean to name something? Who gets to tell certain stories, as opposed to having stories told about them? Or not told at all. Simply erased, the end. The French memoirist Annie Ernaux—2022's Nobelist for literature—speaks of the loneliness in not having words. The American poet Aracelis Girmay of language and the act of naming as forces of estrangement. Both conceptions make sense to me and don't seem mutually exclusive. They're about writing to make strange the world, the self, so we might more clearly see it. And know we're not alone.

How to human? And animal, which is ultimately what we are.

I try to carry such questions with me into daily life and onto the page. Questions for which I have no answers. Which suits me fine.

I keep trying to say. I keep trying to make. This.

ARMADA

ELISE LEVINE

The first Jesus from my father's mouth, the Rabbi startled, then he rolled—*Baruch* this, *Adonai* that, what a pro. Soon my father looked like he was boiling, curses bubbling into the December air. Twice I tried to take him by the arm, get him to settle, maybe coax him along the shovelled path and put him in the car and lock the door on him. But no go. Each time I plucked the sleeve of his old duffel jacket he shook free, swore like a stevedore, some of which tribe he'd once known personally—before retirement many years ago, he'd been the general manager of a shipping company, contending with layoffs, strikes, Ukrainian stowaways, the city in those days still a major port.

Jesus all through Kaddish. All through my brother, soft in youth but now stiff as a sword in his black overcoat, occasionally flicking a drop or two from his face. Beside him his stick-thin AnnaMaria, shivering in her tiny wrap, un-gloriously underdressed for a Hanukkah burial—Jesus, hard to believe. Apparently her only dress coat was red. Apparently not even she had the nerve to pull that off.

At least the freaking cold was working in my favour, since beneath my parka was a pantsuit that used to fit but was now tighter than drying rope. Earlier that morning, dressing in my mother's disorderly bathroom, dizzied by thoughts of what to keep, what to toss—useless for the final journey her dull manicure scissors, eye cream, four nearly finished jars of Vaseline, what the fuck?—I'd handled my belly fat then sucked it in and yanked the zipper, tortured in private places.

I was thinking though that the cold could be even colder. I imagined a rent-lung clarity, vapour, a vacuum-packed nothing. Freedom through freeze drying. Rebirth as astronaut-drift in an unblinking beyond. Escape.

Instead there was the snow. Was it ever coming down, fogging the surrounding hills. Leaving not much to look at except each other, the hole in the ground, and the lilac-coloured coffin, dainty, impractical, pre-selected by Mom herself and about to be wholly surrendered while we blinked, unfathoming. We were fudged, smuzzy. Something we weren't before.

For one thing, we were in a section of the cemetery reserved for the deceased of a local Labour Zionist congregation. My father, who hadn't attended a service since my brother's bar mitzvah, and counted himself no member of any group, had purchased the double plot here because it was by far the cheapest available, in his books a moral victory of sorts. Making small talk with the Rabbi pre-service, my father had make-believed about synagogue so-and-sos there was no way he knew, holy days he'd last celebrated in the Antediluvian Era. When the Rabbi asked how many years my father and mother had been married, the answer was fifty, a fantastical beast, in his telling, of the best creation had ever bestowed.

A creature called Dummy, I'd immediately thought—what my father used to call my mother when, during their frequent fights, he broke a lot of furniture trying to break her warrior silence. Hearing my father's lies, I'd wanted to call him out. Of all times, I'd fumed, re-tightening my thick scarf. Of all places.

But with the Rabbi reciting and my brother mumbling along, my father totally lost it. Jesus, he shouted, tears streaming his cheeks. Jesus! I steadied my gaze on the shovels spiked like spears in the hard dirt heaped around the grave's perimeter. There was scaffolding too, and wide straps, some kind of gizmo for lowering the box and conducting the business at hand.

I kept my back turned on pretty much everything else. I'd already seen there weren't many mourners hanging around for any of this. Only AnnaMaria managing, despite her shaking and quaking, to leaf her hands through her thick hair. Only a few unimportant relatives—an aunt and uncle, childless people my mother had never cared much for. No friends.

My mother had been embarrassed to have lung cancer. Years of smoking, what she'd openly referred to as her filthy habit, had caught up to her. When she'd received her diagnosis eight months ago, I'd worked to convince her not to say she had breast cancer instead—which she thought might gain her greater sympathy, pink ribbons, stuffed toys, balloons. Some prize. The whole thing made me realize how much my mother must have lived confused in her head. My own head swam just thinking.

So when my father began racing the wooden plank alongside the grave, backing and forthing over the now-descending casket with its cargo of emaciated sheet-wrapped body, I let him be.

.

The purity of that sheet had been important, evidently. Keeping it that way had caused some consternation.

I'd driven all night and part of the early morning to arrive at my parents' apartment crammed with a riot of meds and a ripe cat-litter box, my father exhausted and possibly incorrectly, dangerously drugged into brief acquiescence accepting coffee, a buttered roll— the bread not too far past its use-by date. And—the phone call. This from some clown at the funeral home. There was a problem. In accordance with custom, they'd wrapped my mother—what was left of her—in a white sheet, but as sometimes happened with the dead, the guy explained, inside she was a cauldron of stomach acids and bile emitting a staining fluid at the mouth.

Took me a moment to comprehend. The only way to keep the sheet pure was to sew her lips shut. Permission was being sought. My father, too out of it to deal, passed on the matter.

I didn't hesitate.

All those times I'd begged. Eat, please. Anything, especially toward the end. Mushy pasta with bottled, over-salted sauce. Simulac by the teaspoonful. In those last months I'd desperately tried to ark as many calories as I could into her. Get her to pack some on. Get her to live.

She hadn't wanted any of it.

Yes, I told the funeral guy. Yeah. Go right ahead. You do what you need to do. Do it!

He seemed taken aback, stammering a few words before cutting short the call.

I hadn't cared. Here was some news. All along my mother had been full. On her surface, mute suffering, blankety-blank. Inside, a delicacy of churning eels and lobster claws click-clacking—*tref*, impure, an unbridled unclean. In death she was well provisioned. The proof—just some foam breach-burping the surface.

.

But here now was my teetering, imprecating father, here was the snow curling like the crests of waves over the leagues of the dead. While I was taking my magic carpet ride into the past. Please, the Rabbi was saying. I'm afraid. Your father could fall.

My brother started and the Rabbi shrugged apologetically and peered at his shoes. Hefty numbers, scuffed and salt-soured, clearly they'd seen better days. Like his face, the flesh listing, skin pouchy and pocked. He was not an attractive man. Tell

AnnaMaria that though. Unmoored from my brother's side, she hove closer to the Rabbi and was cocking her hip, maneuvering her trembling bits and pieces. Now the Rabbi looked really scared. Worse, instead of directly retrieving my father, my brother dallied, selecting the best shovel for the job to soon come. This lawyer in his fine cashmere blend, former brat who, from the ages of four to twelve, my best friend and I picked on mercilessly, before he transformed into an untouchable teenaged Doobie Central, all torn jean jackets and Lynyrd Skynyrd black armbands—I had to admit, watching him now as he hefted the shovel, he'd manned up nicely over the years.

Jesus, Jesus, my father called.

The Rabbi shot me a pleading look. Like I was the one prolonging things indefinitely.

.

I walked. I'd done it before, a lot. The second I'd turned eighteen. Cities, provinces, countries, whole emotional territories shipped and skipped. Good riddance. So I walked forth to collect my father and possibly dodge my brother, thinking: Big deal. Soon I'd return from whence I'd newly arrived, to my bullshit job tallying columns of numbers for a questionable nonprofit and my squamous low-rent apartment squirming with learned bullshit papers—though I certainly couldn't be said to have sailed through school, I had over the years amassed degrees this, degrees that until I was an impoverished pack rat of esoteric knowledge, with murderers and thieves for neighbours. Someone with places to go, people to see. Including a new young guy—the young dudes getting younger while I got on—who I was secretly entertaining designs for, and even more covertly not.

.

I went. This time toward what was left of my family. The wooden board nearly bestride the grave was soaked and slippery and I inched toward my father minus my mother—my father chuffing and capering bareheaded since, moments before, a flapping gust had disappeared his yarmulke. At the opposite end of the pitching plank, my possibly pre-pre-divorce and probably very fed-up brother was walking too.

Took a death grip to halt my father's wind-milling right arm. Just in time, as my brother now bore straight toward us with his shovel. Jesus—who and what were we anyway? Uncivilized, bereft of dignity, sure. Otherwise, I had no idea.

Not that I was beyond imagining some other life. Desire like melt, river runs throating deep-cut banks. A cock-salty, scorched-caramel scent to the stirring breeze. Not that everything had to be about sex, but.

I was so there.

Until I remembered. On my way here, gripping my device with one hand while steering with the other—scudding between ruts and potholes, mind trammelling apparitions of black ice—I'd called my oldest best friend from the road. This after speaking with my brother, father, weeping, scratching and gouging, packing, cancelling meetings at the office.

My cell was for once getting brilliant reception.

Becca, she rasped into the phone—before she'd found what she called her spiritual centre as a born-again, she'd been a shit-disturber of epic proportions. Becca, she gravelled a second time in her semi-destroyed voice. I'm so, so sorry.

And then, before I could so much as get a sniffle in sideways, she went off on her sister, Kitty. There was a John involved. Or a Shawn, or Sean. Cast of thousands.

But Jen, I managed to get in, choking back a plug of snot. How's Doug?

Surprised me, for sure. Doug was her recent ex-ex who, for a not-so-recent while, had been mine. Why ask about him now? I swear sometimes, my brain!

Doug? Jen said, then paused long enough for me to think the connection was a wash.

I stayed on. I thought I could detect a sinking, rising sound, an aqueous sub-throb, a forked-tail flick. I wished.

Then Jennifer's voice, shark-skinned and unlovely, resurfaced. She said, Doug is Doug.

I got off fast as seemed polite under the circumstances.

I'd been surprised to still be there, in the car, north-easting I-94 and so on, so forth—December, the billboards of once-fant-abulous Michigan. Eat Here, Eat This.

.

What there was of my family rocked, our rent-a-Rabbi rolled. Father, brother—who were they and what was I to them? Around us, the tall pines waved their arms hello, goodbye—maybe in their language these were the same word. If I squinted, instead of wet snow I saw apple blossoms. I opened my mouth. I closed it. I didn't want to think what might be in those flecks, the dreck of dead, cold-kissed stars. I didn't want to think. And yet hold on, I thought, unsure of what I meant while amid the bare trees, across the snow-swept swales, the winter sparrows dervished like dreidels. Like there was so much to cease to know.

KATHY PAGE

KATHY PAGE's *fiction ranges widely in terms of subject matter and form, but always features complex and compelling characters. She is the author of eight novels, including* Dear Evelyn, *winner of the 2018 Rogers Writers' Trust Award for Fiction and the Butler Book Prize;* The Story of My Face, *nominated for the (Orange) Women's Prize;* The Find, *a ReLit finalist; and* Alphabet, *a Governor General's Award finalist.*

Her short fiction has appeared in The Walrus, TNQ, Fiddlehead, New Writing, Best Short Stories, *and* Best Canadian Stories. *Her fabulist short-fiction collection,* Paradise & Elsewhere, *2014, and subsequent collection,* The Two of Us, *2016, were both nominated for the Scotiabank Giller Prize.* Paradise & Elsewhere *was also an Ethel Wilson finalist. Page, according to Amy Bloom, "embraces the creepy, the odd, the other and the rest of us. Her unforgettable prose is moody, shape-shifting and always compelling as a strong light at the end of a road you hesitate to walk down, but will."*

She has written for radio and TV *and her personal essays have appeared in a variety of journals and anthologies, including* Best Canadian Essays 2023.

She has taught writing in academic and other settings in the UK, *Finland, and Canada, most recently at Vancouver Island University. Born in the* UK, *she moved with her family to Salt Spring Island in British Columbia in 2001.*

DO WE BITE?

I was born in 1958 in Bromley, Kent, effectively a suburb of London. My father, after serving in the artillery in ww2, took night-school courses and eventually qualified as a quantity surveyor. My mother kept house. As a young woman she had worked briefly as a secretary in the bbc, but they fired her when she got married, a normal practice at the time.

My parents were both "upwardly mobile." They had made the transition from working to middle class. They'd each done well at school, changed the way they spoke, liked to go to the theatre, and since their move to the suburbs before I was born, they now owned (were paying for) their own house and garden, designed by my father: a huge achievement. Both sets of grandparents, still encamped in their grim rented Wandsworth terraces, were rather over-awed by it all.

My maternal grandfather was an alcoholic who worked as a casual labourer and died young, and my maternal grandmother was a charlady. On the other side, things were a little better with my paternal grandfather sober and working a lathe. My mother was an only child and my father one of two.

My father gained a scholarship to Emanuel School, effectively a ticket to white collar work, though the war intervened (it also meant you started out as an officer after all those hours of drill with the OTC after school). My mother went to the grammar school and learned to type. In school, both of my parents excelled and were introduced to theatre, art, and so on, and both learned to drop their "sowth" London accents and speak just like the radio. A vital skill!

After the war, Dad trained in night school as a quantity surveyor: it was a well-paying profession in demand. Mum did not work out of the home. My parents bought a house turned into two flats with a sitting tenant in one of them and made a substantial profit on it when they sold it a few years later and moved to the suburbs. Dad worked for the Greater London Council (at that time there was still a lot of municipal building: housing estates and civic buildings) and eventually became the head of quantity surveying for the entire Greater London area. By the time I came around, they were comfortably off, solidly middle class, members of the National Trust and so on.

I was the third of three daughters born at long intervals and each of us into a very different world and emotional atmosphere. My oldest sister was born at the beginning of the war. She had a young mother and hardly saw our father until he returned. As a small child she endured the Blitz, evacuations, Mum's anxieties and so on. My middle sister was born shortly after the war in much more optimistic circumstances, and then I arrived ten years after that. My oldest sister was old enough to be my mother, and very wary of being seen as such if she had to push my pram around. I remember her mainly as a visitor, bringing her fiancée to Sunday lunch and so on, and after their marriage she and her husband emigrated to the USA: I didn't really get to know her well.

My middle sister was feisty and defiant and rather glamorous in a sixties kind of way; I admired her very much. I remember her with great gratitude as the one who taught me to read, though I'm sure it was really a family effort. My mother used to get me to spell out road and shop signs when we were out and about, and my father would bring home children's books for me. But my middle sister soon left for university, marriage, etc., so I was much of the time effectively an only child. Visits to this sister and her artist husband were always exciting, especially for the late-night conversation and the spectacular arguments they had

All three of us were relentlessly drilled in correct speech and punished if we picked up the "wrong" pronunciation at school. We absorbed in the womb that school was extremely important, that we must do well there and continue onwards and upwards (these were pre-feminist times, and not so many girls received that kind of message). Visiting our grandparents, who dropped their aitches and went to bingo, was like going to another world.

I attended St George's C of E primary school, about a mile's walk from home. There was a huge variation in income and circumstances at the school, but everyone was Caucasian, until, about half-way through, a lone Black girl arrived.

I have very vivid memories of the sights and smells of the place, of the terrifying headmistress about whom I later told stories to my children, and the cast of teachers, friends, and other kids. I always found school—the combination of whatever they were teaching us, the people themselves and the daily dramas they created—totally absorbing. I'd learned to read before I got there and soon I was writing a great deal, filling whole notebooks with my stories. In the primary school I think I was often set to write a story because I was ahead with reading and it kept me from being bored. There was another girl like me and we shuttled things back and forth between us.

I liked writing because of the feeling of doing it, of being absorbed in the thing I was inventing. I liked art, too, for similar reasons. I think I did have aesthetic ambitions of a sort even then: I would have a vision for the story or the picture and be to varying degrees pleased or not with the outcome, but the feeling of commitment and engagement, of doing just this one thing and living in it and devoting myself to it for the duration, was a very big part of the attraction for me. I am still a terrible multi-tasker.

I've said that my writing sprang "from my father's love of books and my mother's habit of exaggeration." It's true that these were both very formative influences. I remember Dad, on his birthday, giving me Beatrix Potter's *The Tale of Peter Rabbit*, and how my desperation to unlock the words it contained, combined with my middle sister's patience, drove me to learn how to read. This was well before school began. Later, at the end of the day, I used to go and meet Dad from work. Looking downhill towards the railway station, I could see the other men, smartly buttoned up, stride homewards, their briefcases clutched rigidly in one hand, their eyes looking forward to their destinations. Dad, his coat or jacket open, was always right at the back of the group, increasingly left behind as the main group poured up the hill. He did not stride, but ambled towards me, the book he had been reading on the train still open in his right hand, reading as he walked. It was almost a shame to greet him.

On holiday he and I haunted second-hand bookstands, and shared the same books: thrillers (Alistair Maclean), sea stories (C S Forester's Hornblower books were a favourite), as well as classics. I remember sitting up past my bedtime while Dad consulted a slim volume called The 100 *Best Books* and marked the titles he thought I'd enjoy: the Brontës, Dickens, Jane Austen … I read these far too young, missing much, but I think they helped to give me an ear for voice, and the music of sentences. Periodically Mum would decide that what I was reading was unsuitable and we would have to go underground for a while. She also had a rule about the number of books kept downstairs (one bookcase only) so we recycled a lot of our trashier reading materials.

From all this, it might sound as if my father was the main influence on my writing, reading. But my mother was also important, and perhaps more so: she died a decade ago and, as is the way when someone is lost, I sometimes think quite intensely about her and the role she played in my life, and in particular my writing life. Her habit of exaggeration, as I put it, was indeed vital. She knew how to make a story better by knocking out the distractions and upping the ante, and she had a way of tinting whatever she said with emotional subtext that I'm sure has seeped deeply into me. She knew how to make you notice her words, which were rarely bland, but often suggested a drama of some kind. If one of us was late for a meal, we had vanished, or absconded. It never merely rained—there would be a tempest or a deluge. My bedroom with the curtains closed was like a mausoleum. These words came alive, and nothing in our house happened by halves.

As well as modelling this vital skill, my mother continually encouraged us (and in turn, our children) to imagine and pretend. Looking at the family photographs and slides she kept is a powerful reminder of this apprenticeship in the extended kind of pretending that I undertake as a novelist. I was encouraged to talk to statues, animals, and imaginary beings of many kinds, and sometimes she would join in with this too. My friends and I dressed up, made houses in trees and under tables, and for the duration of the story we took our meals in role. We were allowed to play out our fantasies until they finally bored us or turned into something new. I think Mum encouraged imagination partly because it kept us out of her way and partly because she enjoyed it herself. What would it be like to have musical genius in the family? To fly first class? To live in a mansion?

She was also extremely good at evaluating the truthfulness of what was told to her, and trying to beat this inner bullshit-detector of hers was a very useful challenge for me. You could say her child-rearing methods backfired on her, for all the exercise she provided for my imagination made me quite a good liar, too. Once, I convinced her of the existence of a school play, for which she duly made my costume and in which she believed until the day of the performance was upon us. Later, as a teenager, I set off with a backpack saying I was going to volunteer on an archaeological dig (and did, briefly, appear at the site) but spent the rest of the week in a tent with my boyfriend.

Between these two were a thousand small deceptions, but I hasten to say that this mendaciousness only came out in the family home context, and in my real life, now, I much prefer to be honest.

Mum never wrote herself, but when I was a child she was my first reader, and always appreciative of my efforts; her suggestions for improvements were often excellent. She was a good typist, keen to add a professional touch, and also prepared to push me into action when she saw the need.

When the school sent around a flyer encouraging all pupils to enter a national children's writing competition sponsored by Barclay's Bank, she was determined that I should try. The assignment was to write a short story *set in a bank.*

"You should do this," she told me. "Nothing to lose. Look at the money you could win!" In principle I was willing. The year before, there had been a story contest sponsored by The Royal Missions to Seamen, for a science fiction story. I had enjoyed writing my brooding piece about Cody, an astronaut who slipped out of the spacecraft and launched himself into outer space (and certain death) in order to experience something I called "freedom." J G Ballard had picked my story, and signed his book *Vermillion Sands* for me (this introduced me to a writer whose work I admire to this day), and I had been awarded an educational Adriatic cruise with a group of other precocious children. However, outer space was one thing and banks quite another: set in a bank?

Had I been politically aware, I might have come up with something to do with apartheid, given that Barclays was, at the time, heavily criticized for trading in South Africa. But as it was, the only potential I could see was in bank-robbery, which everyone would do. (Years later, it was with great pleasure that I read what must be the best banking/bank-robbing story in the world, Tobias Wolff's story "Bullet in the Brain.")

"Have you started it yet?" Mum kept asking; she had a fair bit of time on her hands with just the one rather self-sufficient child to look after.

"Banks are so boring," I told her—and as the words slipped out, a story came to me: two male bank employees, one in London, one in a place I rather vaguely called *Africa*, both bored, bored, bored. A memo comes around, offering the opportunity to exchange posts. Both bored employees jump at the chance, only to discover, once they have made the break and taken over each other's lives, that they are bored, bored, bored, the food is dreadful and they miss their friends! I got it down as quickly as I could, and handed the scrawled sheets to Mum.

"They won't like this," she said. "I mean, suppose you were them." All the same, she typed it out at 70 wpm and, to give the bank credit where it is due, some months later a congratulatory letter and a cheque arrived. My "career" has never been so simple or so successful since . . .

·

It was not all dressing up in a sun-dappled garden. We tend to simplify and idolize the dead, and in doing so we do both them and ourselves a disservice. My mother was a powerful woman, a vivid, magnetic personality, and also a fighter, not at all inclined to doubt.

Her feelings were strong and she was incapable of concealing or questioning them. She could be overwhelming, and as well as all the wonderful things I mention above, there were huge power-struggles, long periods of difficulty and conflict in our relationship, especially as I moved into my teen years. During that time, there was a great deal of overt conflict in our by then shrunken household, and that in itself, whilst unpleasant for all of us to live through, was very formative in terms of writing: for example, I have never been in danger of writing passages of friendly chit-chat instead of dialogue.

My relationship with my mother deteriorated as I emerged from early childhood, started to make my own independent judgements, and have feelings, opinions, and desires. All her life, Mum found it physically impossible to simply accept a difference, let alone be curious or interested to explore it, and as I grew up this rigidity became increasingly problematic. Whether it was that someone had made a different choice to hers, or a different way of living, or that they entertained another belief system, or simply wished to articulate a feeling she did not share or deem them entitled to (the latter she especially disliked), her approach was to verbally batter such aberrations into submission, using argument, sarcasm, mockery, humiliation, and so on. She was quite articulate and very persistent. It made no difference whether the point at issue was trivial or immense. Once it had raised its head, she would bring her full artillery to bear on it and fight to the point of victory or mutual exhaustion. Modifying her point of view (= defeat) or apology were not options. Add to this that although Mum was intolerant of others' feelings—especially if they involved vulnerability and could be seen as signs of weakness—her own rages were seismic and ruled our lives.

An argument with my father in the car would result in her dragging me out of it at the next traffic light and the pair of us setting off on a rainy six-mile walk home. Earning a parking ticket, when she had parked illegally to do her shopping, she withheld payment, fought it to the highest level and ended up in custody until my father slunk into the police station and secretly paid her debt. During an argument one breakfast time she hurled the butter dish (stainless steel, sharp-edged) at me as I was leaving the table. I fled, and it was only later as I removed my school hat, that I realised I had a very sore head and a large lump of melting butter stuck in my hair.

Mum had a difficult menopause and doubtless this played a part in how extreme everything became, but from my point of view at the time the reason was immaterial. Everyone suffered from my mother's fixed ideas, bullying, and awful rages, but the others spent less time with her, and as the last child at home I think I bore the brunt of it. Since it rapidly came to seem that almost everything about me incited disapproval, I began to feel as if I had nothing to lose. I remember reading R D Laing's *Knots*, *The Divided Self*, etc. as a teenager and finding much of it very recognizable (Laing, it has since been revealed, was a terrible father and presided over a train-wreck of a family).

A wiser person might have found a way to deflect Mum with grace and humour, or to develop a façade and keep her thoughts and feelings to herself, and I do remember a kindly neighbour reminding me that I would eventually leave and advising me to do this. But I felt compelled to defend myself, particularly in respect of what I felt and what I did with my own body. Neither of these, in any context but ours, were unusual or extreme; both seemed vital. For years, then, my mother and I struggled, emotionally, verbally, sometimes physically. We were each utterly obsessed with the other. The situation was unhealthy—I knew that—but had no idea how to stop it (and it would in any case have taken two to do so). On one occasion, when my mother was trying to push me up the stairs into my bedroom, and I, body locked, refusing to go, was pushing her back down, I became suddenly aware of both of us grunting as we pushed, our hands buried in each other's flesh, and was flooded with shame. I remember thinking, what next, then? Do we bite? But nonetheless I pushed on.

On top of this, it gradually became clear that I was not just picky, but anorexic. Doubtless Mum was horribly worried as well as upset by my rejection of the food she made; she was also contemptuous, ashamed, angrier still, and determined to root it out of me. Meals became another thing we fought about; they served as a kind of symbol of everything, and then, later, all this was the source of another everlasting (several decades long) argument: Why had I developed an eating disorder in the first place? Mum believed this to be genetically derived: I must have the same crazy chromosomes as Mad Aunt Flo (whom I had never met). I took a more psychological/sociological approach.

At one point the GP sent us to a family therapist. Our inter-actions were observed by students through a two-way mirror. The therapist, who had long hair and wore a leather jacket, gave us homework to do; he was quite strict. I liked him and found having another person involved very useful and interesting too, but Mum and Dad felt stigmatized and blamed, and they hated going, so soon there were arguments about that, too.

So it was very grim. Yet despite all that was going on at home, I was also fortunate too. I had other important and absorbing re-lationships nothing like the embattled one with my mother, and many passionate interests. There were many things that I wanted to do and so I was not in the end going to starve myself into non-existence, which, even as I veered towards it, I knew to be a tedious pursuit. I had long conversations and correspondences;

I drew and painted, read poems and wrote in my notebook to articulate what I made of the chaos and wonder around me. Painting and writing, coupled with the kindness of my teachers, saved my sanity and possibly my life.

If you survive a difficult relationship, it eventually becomes an asset. I've understood since that, horrible as those battles with my mother were, they left me with a deep appreciation of the value of conflict, and of how riven with contradiction people are. This may not sound like a great prize, but I'm immensely glad of it, not just because I prefer reality to illusion but also because it makes for interest and possibility. The same person can be both nurturing and crushing, manipulative and selfless. Most of us contain opposites (or multitudes, as Whitman would have it) and it's possible for a personal attribute, such as honesty or curiosity, to have either or both wonderful and appalling consequences: you can't be certain how things will turn out. Another legacy is a lifelong openness to and interest in difficult people, an active fondness for them. I think my mother probably made me into a novelist, and that the fight on the stairs had as much to do with it as the sunny garden and the games of let's pretend.

During my stormy teenage years, school became a refuge. I moved from St George's to the rather grim and driven Bromley Grammar School for Girls on Nightingale Lane, where we were told on day one that our childhoods were over and that now we, the intellectual elite, must start preparing for our very important exams in four years' time. Thereafter many of my classmates went on to have nervous breakdowns, do far too many drugs, or get pregnant.

Again, the daily dramas were interesting, and I did well, but had no real love for the place and at sixteen when many others fled to the local sixth-form college, I changed to a wonderful, much freer school called Bullers Wood School for Girls. This was housed in a William Morris house in acres of woodland. It was at the time a regular state school, but run on very enlightened principles: there were few rules except 1) No smoking (impossible to enforce, given the woodland) and 2) No noisy shoes to be worn when walking up the oak stairs past the headmistress's office. (We removed our platform shoes at the bottom of the stairs and put them on again at the top). It had a secretarial school attached, and lower academic aspirations than the grammar school, but was much more creative and personal in its approach.

The grammar school's zealousness had been such that for the first year I had pretty much nothing to do, and I was allowed to attend or not attend classes as I chose (mostly I did choose, as I liked them), and to spend as much time as I wanted in the art room, a wonderful place lit by huge windows and bristling with easels, art supplies, dried crocodiles, interesting pieces of abandoned machinery, and assorted still-lives (sometimes mouldy), all presided over by a prematurely white-haired teacher called Brenda Pye.

The UK system specializes early and so for those two years, I studied only English, French, and art, resisting all urgings to add in an extra academic subject to compensate for the perceived uselessness of art. This was something I would never have got away with in the other school, though they did insist on me doing not just A but also S (scholarship) level exams. It was a wonderful, university-like experience, and I became very close to Brenda and all my teachers there and very interested in painting and visual art in general.

I remember reading D H Lawrence and Camus at school, and Shakespeare, of course; at home the usual omnivorous and totally unsystematic literary diet: Solzhenitsyn, Doris Lessing, Joyce Cary, Kingsley Amis, Mikhail Bulgakov, Edna O'Brien. Poetry, too. I was increasingly interested in twentieth-century writing.

In the last year, I moved out of my parents' home and lived in a spare room in my art teacher's house. Brenda Pye, a woman of the same age as my parents, was both my art and form teacher at Bullers Wood. Due to the freedoms I had at that school, I spent a lot of time in the art room with her, and it must have been obvious that things were not going well at home. She, like all the teachers at that school, took an interest in me, and, with the permission of the headmistress, eventually offered to take me off my parents' hands. "You drove her to me," she told my mother, many years later.

It was an extraordinary solution but I think that by this point, everyone was desperate and knew that we could not continue as we were. Before I moved to Bullers Wood, Mum had been trying without success to send me to a posh boarding school in the country, a fantasy of hers. She wanted me out of the way, but in a contained situation with regular meals. The school, which emphasized discipline, was expensive and I needed a scholarship to go there. Together we marched around the classrooms and manicured grounds, she deeply impressed, I horrified by the overwhelming snobbery, ridiculous rules, and lack of access to the outside world. When it came to the interview:

"Would you like to tell us about why you want to be a student here?" I burst into tears and said, "Actually, I don't."

Despite that I had officially brought all this upon myself, I felt rejected. I was devastated about the way things were between my mother and me, by the way our family had turned out, and that they wanted to send me away. I yearned for her approval but would not pay the price. My father was helpless, if sympathetic, and took to working late. In this context I leapt at the chance to move in with Brenda, and Mum at least saw the sense of it as a respite.

Brenda's term-time house was in Nightingale Lane in New Cross, a multi-ethnic area next to the railway lines, and the bathroom looked out over an auto repair yard. This ordinary, down-at-heel terrace house, crammed with mainly modern art, was the opposite of the clean lines of our suburban house, just as Brenda herself was in many ways the opposite of my mother. She was routinely gentle, very tolerant, and, I gradually came to realize, tended to neglect her own needs, though she was quite capable of taking a stand on behalf of others when she felt it justified. She trusted me completely, let me do anything I wanted, and believed that children should be let to grow into their own shape, whatever that might be. The love of her life had been a married man. She'd not married herself and had no child of her own; I was not the last young person she rescued.

I moved out in the course of a few days, taking my things in carrier bags to school for Brenda to put in her car. Once I was there my parents were invited to tea.

"What a murky, cluttered little place," Mum told me on the way out, "I don't see the attraction."

During term time, Brenda drove us in to school, where we passed a fair amount of the day together in the art room, and then, if we were both in, we shared supper at the end of the day. She knitted; we both drew. My boyfriend was free to visit at will. There were parties on the weekends, with artists and teachers in attendance; Brenda had many very loyal friends. In summer, she returned to Cornwall, leaving me to look after the house, which in the past had been burgled when it was left empty. Eventually, I visited her in St Mawes too, and did so until she died in her nineties. Her many-windowed home there gazed out over the bay, its walls graced with works by Cornish artists such as Terry Frost, Peter Lanyon, and Barbara Hepworth hung side by side with canvasses painted by lesser-known friends of hers, her own work, and even a few paintings and sketches by her own students, including me. Pretty much every inch of the walls was covered with art, the shelves likewise with pieces of pottery and glassware, small sculptures, and framed photographs.

We spent a lot of time talking about these pictures and objects, simply pointing out what we each liked: the way colours and shapes related, the movement of a line.

Her influence on me was not so much about particular artists (though she did show me a lot in that respect) or things she said, but more about a way of life: her assumption that the artistic way of life was a valid one, that spending all day looking at something, sketching, or for that matter, by extension, writing, with no thought of reward other than the thing itself, was of huge value. Giving yourself over to the work in progress is the most fundamental skill in any artistic discipline, and to be quietly shown this was hugely important.

In contrast, my mother was encouraging of writing and art during my childhood, and later open to the idea of an artist or a writer in the family: she quite liked the glamour she felt was attached to such professions. But once I became one, she was very impatient with the process itself, with what it "cost": the hours of work, the reading, being preoccupied, the moods, the financial uncertainty … Why would anyone in their right mind go through all that? Very late in life, when she was living on her own and found it boring, she told me, "I've been reduced to drawing to pass the time."

More important still was that Brenda provided a home and was a kind of surrogate and alternate mother. Quite apart from me needing some nurturing at the time, I do think having two so very different, virtually opposite mother figures was a positive experience from a writing point of view.

I spent many years immersed in painting and looking at pictures and for a long time felt torn between literature and visual art. In the end, when this finally played out and, in my late twenties I realised that I was becoming a writer, I worried that by not painting, or even keeping it up as a hobby, I had let Brenda down. When (later still) I asked her about this, she merely said, "Well, it was refreshing to teach someone who actually looked at things." So I think she might have been a little disappointed, but at the same time, she appreciated writers, too. She always read my books and enjoyed them. And I still fantasize about painting again, one day, when I have time.

It's a long time since I painted, but visual art remains very important to me. I'm still drawn to landscape in art, to bold colourists and to abstraction. But I also like the work of psychologically explorative artists such as Paula Rego and Louise Bourgeois, whose work has a strong storytelling element. A painting or sculpture can move me as just as powerfully as good writing can. Not long ago, I sat down in front of one of Hockney's hawthorn blossom paintings and wept because it was so beautiful and I could feel, somehow, how he got to it. How he took a lifetime to get to it.

I didn't at this time think of what I would become or how I would support myself. I had worked at various weekend jobs since the age of twelve and could see that for many people work was difficult, boring, and sometimes absurd. I actively resisted thinking about what I would do, and repelled others' attempts to engage me with the topic.

One evening I was sitting on the thick, tan-coloured carpet of my bedroom sketching my own foot when my father appeared in the doorway. I was by then a skinny, argumentative girl of fifteen with an odd haircut, a serious reading habit, ill-informed but strongly held political views, and no interest in sports. If not reading, preferably contemporary writing by that point (I was a great fan of John Berger, especially his novel *G*) I would be drawing, or day-dreaming. It was unusual for Dad to venture into my room; we normally talked while we ate and the subject we had settled on as most productive and least controversial was what we were both reading.

"Umph. Hmm. I wonder." He fiddled with his ear, squinted at

the drawing, sighed heavily. Perhaps, I thought, he was going to tell me the facts of life? It was much too late, but still I was curious to see how he would approach it. "I wonder," he said again, "have you any idea what you want to do after school?" Read? I thought. Draw. Travel. But I knew this wasn't what he meant.

"No."

"A career. It's something you should think about." He took a tentative step into my room, and stood there, rubbing his hands together. I added some shading to my drawing, considered the result. There was a long pause. "What I thought," he said, "was that you might go in for architecture. There's definitely an artistic element in it, you see, which I think you might like." How hard, I see now, he must have thought about this line, how to make the idea as attractive as possible. At the time, however, a negative aura clung to the word architect: It suggested rigid lines, oppressive accuracy, and concrete. Dad himself frequently complained about the prima donna-ish airs and general lack of good sense of the architects he was forced to work with. It was a time of much controversy about hideous modernist office blocks being built in the midst of historical or natural sites. So, when he suggested a visit to his place of work to see what the architects actually did, I had no compunction about turning him down flat.

"Come on!" he said. "Why not look?"

"No thanks. I'll probably go to art school. Or to university," I told him.

"But what for? What afterwards? What does it lead to?"

I had no idea; I liked to read, I liked to draw, that was all I knew.

I returned to the drawing of my foot, and blotted out the sound of my father (a man who had never had the choices I would have) descending the stairs.

To the best of my memory, this was the only piece of careers advice I have ever received, either at school or subsequently when I did in fact attend a university. I see now that it was pretty good advice; I'm touched that my father tried to look after me this way, and awarded me a more interesting job than he himself had settled for. *It might have worked*, I think on days when I wish I was not what I am (every decade or so, I try quite hard to be something else but I never quite manage to jump ship).

Art school or university? This seemed like an impossible choice, and then it seemed simply impossible, because Mum and I were still at such loggerheads that there was no chance of any parental support (parental or state support was the expectation in those days, when many UK students still received means-tested grants to cover the cost of their education. One way or another, you were supposed to concentrate on your studies during the term time, not have to work three minimum-wage jobs just to be there and somehow stay awake, as is the case for the students I now teach).

My school was baffled by my mother's insistence in repeated interviews that she and my father, who were by then quite affluent, would not help with the cost of university. The rationale was that I had already left home and, so far as Mum could see, was headed for the gutter or an early death from starvation, all due to bad genes that were however nothing to do with her, so it would be a waste of money. This was sad and ridiculous, but true to form she took up a position and held it. I don't think my father agreed with her on this, but the marriage would have been on the line if he'd made a stand. And financial arrangements were such that he earned the money and my mother managed it.

During this time, our family was a war zone, shall I say *very dysfunctional*. It was clear to outsiders that something was wrong: Mum clearly off the rails, me stick-thin and very emotional but on the other hand bright and motivated, not doing drugs, loving school. Back then in that kind of middle-class suburb there probably weren't the mechanisms to deal with such things (working-class families were the ones supposed to have problems). Teachers, neighbours, and friends' parents made up a kind of informal support system. When it came to university, I was in a difficult situation and the school wanted to help. They thought it was a travesty for me not to go and they fixed the problem.

The headmistress advised me that there might be a solution if I took an academic degree, so to go ahead and apply in any case, which I dutifully did. Eventually I was told that some funding was available but the source would not be revealed (and it never was). Because of the insistence on academics, I knew it was not Brenda, who in any case did not have much money. I thought it might be Miss Drake, the headmistress, who often had me in her study for chats, but never had this confirmed. I forget the exact figure now, but it was a substantial amount, such that I got through during the term time without working, provided I worked and saved up during the holidays.

I was hurt that my father didn't to my knowledge make a stand, and the abject goodbye scene with the banknote in an envelope was painful and mutually embarrassing. However, the way things happened was far, far better for me in the end, since my parents had no stake in what I did for the next three years or thereafter. I was completely free.

Out of reverse snobbery I refused to apply to Oxford or Cambridge and went for several interviews to universities a long way from home, including one for a very interesting theatre studies/stage design combo at Hull, to which I somehow carried a scale model of my set for *Anthony and Cleopatra*. But it was so cold! I nearly died waiting on the station platform and knew I'd not survive there. At each interview, which was normally a matter of two or three academics asking what you liked to read, and why, I ran into the same red-haired, very serious girl who had also left home early and started work in her local library. We both ended up choosing English and Related Literature at York and our lives have run in a sort of parallel fashion ever since.

.

At York, I threw myself into my classes in Shakespeare, French, learning Anglo-Saxon etc., but I was not yet done with visual art and painted my way through my university years. After driving the cleaning lady in the halls of residence wild with my messiness in the first term, I moved out and eventually had the use of a studio in Walmgate Bar.

But was I any good? I loved Matisse and Rothko and Brenda's Cornish painters but in my own work, I was fascinated by texture and pattern. I remember one painting, abstract, based on a photograph of the skin of a stuffed alligator (!) that Brenda had kept in the art room ... I went in close on part of the body where leg and belly joined and painted every darned scale in great detail. It had a rippling effect from a distance, and then, when you came close up you could lose yourself in the patterns. I sold this to Denise Hooker, a post-grad student at York who went on to become a curator and art critic.

At York, and partly in response to Richard Verdi's art history class, I made a series of paintings that were a critique of Mondrian. I scaled down and copied his grids and colours, but interrupted them in various ways: a plant growing through the middle of the canvas, a single-stemmed rose laid across it (there's a story about this), water rippling over the top, and other more radical interventions. An American wanted to buy just two of the series and I refused: it was all or nothing, and so I ended up with no sale. I had a certain amount of success, but looking back it's clear that I would have needed training to really make something of whatever miniscule gift I had. What happened was that I did apply to art school after university, and got a place at Chichester to study painting. I was allowed to skip the foundation year, but even so, it was inevitable that reality set in: I did the math and knew that even with a theoretical menial job at the hospital I couldn't afford the fees and living expenses.

I was pleased, however, to have been accepted. I thought I would just continue in my own way, but when I moved to London I soon realized that the gallery system was not welcoming of the unschooled, that I needed to learn to work in new media and to a bigger scale, and that there was much that I really did need to learn, just technically, let alone in terms of ideas and vision and how to get along in a very rarefied and competitive world. Conceptual art was beginning to be the hot thing, too, and with a few exceptions this is something which I found (and find) tedious. I began attending a writing class at the City Literary Institute and given I also had to work, there was only so much time for other pursuits. Gradually writing took over and the dream of painting faded away.

Was all this a distraction/waste of time? Certainly not. There's some cross over, in terms of looking and seeing, and the discipline of making and remaking something is a very transferable skill. And my interest in painting has seeped into my writing, via artist characters such as Tuomas Envall in *The Story of My Face* (the novel which features a Protestant sect that bans all visual representation) and Anna's mother in *The Find*. And then of course, in *Alphabet*, there's Simon's first correspondent, the alcoholic art historian and the invented painter she and he discuss. And there's that story, "I Like to Look."

I still love painting and sculpture. I think I'm a better writer than I would have been a painter. I feel the two activities are very different. For me, painting comes from a physical, celebratory response to the world. Writing is more exploratory, more analytical, darker perhaps. Writing is more about people, painting is more about the landscape/world (I must stress I'm just speaking personally here). And so in that sense I do very much miss making visual art.

I had arrived at York having lived away from home for two years, and many of the exciting freedoms other students were exploring for the first time had become routine for me. The friend I had made during my round of interviews felt the same way, and we banded together: there for the education, rather than the lifestyle. Since I loved reading, I looked forward to three years of it but had no thought of becoming a writer.

The draw of my chosen degree course was that it insisted on a certain amount of non-English literature to be read in the original language, and I exceeded that quota by taking both French and Anglo-Saxon. As I recall Shakespeare was mandatory and possibly Mediaeval/Chaucer too, but other than that you could skip around and cluster topics as you wished; there was no historical timeline. This allowed a kind of magpie approach which suited me very well. I liked to collect odd things from all over the place, rather than acquire deep knowledge of one limited area, and still do (at the moment I'm reading an Icelandic writer called Sjón, a novel called *From the Mouth of the Whale*, which is set in 1635 and concerns a scholar forced into exile on a small island, first-person narration. You're right inside the culture and history of the time, looking out. It's a bit like *Riddley Walker*). More than anything (I understand now) I like to see possibilities, the range of what can be done in terms of both form and subject matter.

The French elements in the degree included a module on translation. I really loved this because it was oddly creative. I avoided Molière, etc. I'd read Flaubert's *Trois Contes* at school but now encountered *Madame Bovary* for the first time, and read more from and about the man himself, how he laboured over a sentence or two for hours, even days on end. Mainly, I focussed on twentieth-century writing (much Sartre and Camus) and was for a while very interested in the "nouveau roman": Nathalie Sarraute, Alain Robbe-Grillet. For one "essay" I colour-coded the different motifs in Robbe-Grillet's novel *La Jalousie* and then measured the duration of each occurrence; I then used poster paints to create an enormously long set of vertical stripes of varying widths on several sheets of art paper joined together (it was rather like a giant coloured barcode, except that they did not exist then). You'd probably have to read the book to see how this worked out, but it did...My aim was to visualize the structure of the book, and also to suggest its musicality by making the repetitions and patterns visible. I've no musical abilities, but I do often have this sense of literary works as potential symphonies, songs, etc., a feeling for both prose and overall structure which is a physical rather than a verbal thing: sound, colour, rhythm. Most writing has more than one structure and this physical structuring is important to me. There's a kind of synaesthesia involved... I do visualize or even draw my novels in progress: not as pictures, but abstractly. And I sometimes suggest to my writing students that they do this too, and most of them think I'm barmy then draw a sunset or a sword or something. But some of them get it.

.

I learned about feminism second-hand from my friend Sally who was studying in the Social Sciences Department, and very much aware of the legal situation of women and involved in campaigns and so on. Of course, Simone de Beauvoir was buried in the margins of the Twentieth Century French syllabus (though actually alive at that point); I still admire her and recently reread her memoir about the end of her mother's life, *A Very Easy Death*. So this was one way that I began to see the world and relationships in a new, not pleasant, but true-seeming way. Feminism continues to engage me and certainly inspired my first two novels, written some years after university, both of which are concerned with how the law deals with women and both of which were published by the feminist press Virago. They were agitprop, really, and I've not written that way since, but feminism (the point of which is to unpick what seems like a pervasive misogyny and create more freedom and possibility for both women and men) remains very much a part of my way of looking at the world, and still informs my fiction. *Alphabet*, for example, is told from a man's point of view, but it deals with masculinity and men's fear of women and is in a way the counterpart to my first novel, *Back in the First Person*, which told the story of a rape trial from the female victim's point of view. That said, I feel *Alphabet* is a much better novel.

Tara Murphy, my editor in the UK, recently drew my attention to the way I explore power imbalances between characters in my fiction, and how unexpected and unstable those dynamics can be, and I agree, it really is a speciality of mine. I like to see how a disadvantage can become a strength, and vice versa, how things can, gradually or suddenly, change between people. And I think that interest comes partly from feminism, and partly from growing up the way I did.

There were two very interesting feminist academics at York, Hermione Lee, who specialized in Virginia Woolf, and went on to put together *The Secret Self*, an excellent anthology of C20 short fiction by women, and Nicole Ward-Jouve, who taught courses about French feminism and had an interest in visual art. Nicole was/is also a fiction writer: at that time she wrote short stories in French, and criticism in English.

What else about York stands out? Visual things: Derek Pearsall's lavishly illustrated lectures on medieval literature. Richard

Verdi's course on twentieth-century art, which fitted with my interest in painting and connected with much of my reading, curricular and extra-curricular. He was very charismatic, and gave impassioned lectures, concentrating on a particular work but drawing out its connections to others. He could do a whole hour on one canvas. He had a strong sense of how the ideas, art, and literature of an era affected each other, and conveyed this as an evolving and hugely exciting thing. He was also a fascinating character: both charming and very intolerant of the less able or inarticulate, utterly caustic, to the point of viciousness.

As for Anglo-Saxon...It was an unpopular subject and hence a very small class, led by Sid Bradley, a man completely immersed and obsessed with the texts and the history, who hardly seemed to inhabit the contemporary world at all (one of those difficult people I oddly enjoy). There was something rather humourless about him, yet at the same time he and the whole enterprise caught my imagination: his sheer dedication and the huge struggle he was engaged in as he attempted to reach back into past events and a past mindset via a dead if not entirely alien language. He was looking back at an era of religious transition and it was a huge effort of the imagination; I see now that this kind of historical re-creation from small remnants of the past is similar to what novelists do. Another benefit of this course was that it involved us in field trips to Scotland, Cumbria, and Northumbria where we viewed monasteries, manuscripts, churches, Saxon stone crosses etc. I like these Northern landscapes a great deal and enjoyed the course.

Creative writing was not really taught in Britain at that time, certainly not at undergraduate level, but at York you were allowed to submit a certain amount of creative writing for credit. I don't think there was any teaching: it was just something you could do if you felt like taking the risk. Towards the end of my time there I did this and my first short story appeared in a university magazine; a few years later another version of it was published with another piece in a magazine called *Writing Women*: my first real publication.

I can see now how all this gradually inched me towards writing, but it was not a deliberate path and I had no idea where any of it was leading me. I simply drew and painted and read and read, often going way beyond what was required, and in my magpie way found much to love and to think about: Beckett, Cary, Calvino, Marquez (men, mainly, but that's how it was; Fay Weldon, Angela Carter, Isabel Allende, Edna O'Brien et al. were waiting in the wings). University was good for my confidence. The main skills required were being perceptive and articulate and I was lucky to have these so did well. The faculty were a tolerant lot and I liked writing my somewhat unconventional essays and arguing in seminars. I worked hard and enjoyed it. I'd always felt at home in school and this was not very different, though at the end of the three years I felt it really was time to do something else. When I received a note suggesting that an application for post-graduate studies would be treated sympathetically, I decided against it.

York was also a time during which my long-suffering boyfriend and I gradually let go of each other (we'd been an item since the end of high school), and all the troubles at home began to fade into the background.

.

Once I had graduated from York and put the art school idea aside, I drifted to London, still painting and drawing much of the time. I worked as a shop assistant, art class model, and actor in a touring community theatre group. Even back then, housing in the capital was inordinately expensive. Squatting empty property made a lot of sense, but the council high rise my older artist boyfriend (a relationship that didn't last) and I moved into was a depressing place. We relocated to Carlton Mansions, on Coldharbour Lane in Brixton, where I lived between circa 1980 and 1987.

I always enjoyed telling people my address. There was a piquant contrast between its two parts, one suggesting luxury, the other austerity, and an equally delicious friction between the state-ly-sounding Mansions and the reality of the initially squalid accommodation. The long, thin block of sixteen flats had been derelict and was at that time called "short-life housing." This meant that the property was lent to the tenants by the council on the condition that we fixed it up, managed it, and eventually left when the authorities were ready to re-possess or demolish…The building had an ornate façade, decorated with columns, impres-sive lintels and such, behind which it stretched back along the side of the railway line, so close that commuters could see right into some of the flats. It had the original shuddering, draughty, sash windows, rotten joists, a colander-like flat roof, lead pipe-work and was home to far too many cats. Those who lived there or wanted to had to put in the time to fix it up. We had to learn plumbing, brickwork, carpentry, window-glazing, plaster work, or whatever was required at the time. Most of the materials we used were reclaimed from skips. Until others were installed, there was just one communal kitchen, supplied with cast-off vegetables collected at dawn every day from Covent Garden market.

The hard work was one thing; the interminable and excruciat-ing house meetings another, but the point was, you ended up with somewhere to live. Those who put up with the downsides of the place were people who either wanted or had to live out-side the box: artists, activists, and vulnerable people of various kinds. The flat I ended up with was one of the big ones at the front, opposite the old steam laundry building. Huge windows looked out over the street and the market arcades on the other side. Despite the incessant traffic, the sirens; despite the yelling and pulsing music from the street, and the way the passing trains shook the building at least three times an hour, day and night, I felt at home. I knew all my neighbours. If something went wrong, I had to fix it myself, but the affordable rent meant I could take time to work out what I was going to be and do.

These were the Thatcher years, the beginning of the end of civilized life in the UK. Thatcher famously declared that there was "no such thing as society" and actively promoted a greedy, self-centred kind of individualism. Her government was squaring up to the unions, facilitating the selling of council (affordable, not-for-profit) housing stock and privatizing everything it could see. Brixton, in Lambeth, where I lived, was a site of radicalism and resistance, and certainly that suited me. But also, through my own fault/laziness/instinct to keep some mental space for myself, I had not set out to forge a secure career path, and so had few options in terms of housing: a room in a shared house or flat with people not of my choosing. In the Mansions, for a fraction of the price, I had an entire apartment with a spare room ("of one's own") to work in, and interesting neighbours with whom I was not forced to share a bathroom.

There are two ways to think about the day job: Is it best do something completely different to writing that won't use up the verbal part of you, or should the aim be something connected such as teaching or journalism which could either be a drain in terms of creativity or might in some way (perhaps) support it? I have tried both kinds of work and unfortunately there is no simple answer, though I have discovered that I tend to be more productive as a writer when I have some kind of part-time employment that limits money worries and takes me out into the world (so long as it is not the living-hell kind of job).

At this time, I felt that something physical could be preferable to office work and leave me free to write in the evenings. As a result of the situation in the Mansions, I had already done a lot of unskilled manual work and taken an introductory class in woodwork for women. Lambeth council was offering apprentice-ships in a bid to encourage women into the trades. The pay was good, and the idea of developing a skill and being able to make something useful appealed to me. About eight women signed up as electricians, bricklayers, and carpenters. Many of us had university educations; all were feminists to some degree. The rest of the workforce was, bar a couple of secretaries, male, and despite the union's equal-opportunity talk, not pleased to have us with them. One major concern, frequently expressed, was the inhibiting effect we would have on their ability to curse. Another, which had some truth in it to begin with, was how weak and inept we would be, adding to their burdens.

I struck lucky. My foreman, Tony, presented with the decision as to which member of his team he would inflict me upon, chose Walter, aka Wally, an elderly, old-fashioned stickler whose refus-al to cut corners drove Tony wild. Perhaps Tony hoped we would reduce each other to a pulp, or perhaps he knew it would all work out just fine. In any case, Wally, thin, bespectacled, famous for his grumpiness, was appalled. On receiving the news, he hissed his breath out between his teeth, shook his head and actually stamped his foot. I was standing just feet away. He refused to speak to me the first day and for a long time did not progress beyond brief commands such as "Like this, see," "Latimer Road next," or "That's it, then."

The team I worked in repaired housing stock, mainly Victorian council housing that due to lack of maintenance—persistent leaking pipes, roofs, and window seals, condensation etc.—had developed woodworm or dry rot. The work involved removing and replacing wooden sash windows, flooring, wall studs, and joists, which on upper levels meant supporting the building with expanding steel props while we removed its skeleton. It was exciting to see a house this way, stripped down to its fundamentals. A van would drop off supplies, including noxious chemicals. Wally did not possess a car and cycled very slowly from one venue to the next, pulling behind him a huge home-made trailer containing a full hand-tool kit; I followed suit with a smaller kit stuffed into my saddle bags. Armed with crowbars and chisels we would tear out old, rotten wood, spray the brickwork, and then reconstruct the wooden elements. Various electricians, plasterers etc. joined us as required. The tenants, rarely offered alternative accommodation, watched appalled from the sidelines.

I have a good tolerance for, a fondness even, for awkward characters, so I did not take Wally's moods too personally, and he did eventually thaw. On the other hand, I found the skills very hard to acquire, was on a daily basis reduced to near despair at my own ineptness. I had to be very persistent, another quality that is an asset for a writer. The turning point in our relationship came when Wally returned from eating his lunch in the garden to find me practising my hand-cut mitres on scraps of skirting board. These boards were foot-deep, elaborate Victorian mouldings which would not fit in a mitre box even had Wally approved of such things. You had to measure ("Measure twice and cut once!" Once?) and mark out the forty-five-degree angle, prop the thing up somewhere and then saw through it by hand without departing from the line. Then you had to do the same for the other half of the corner, so that they met perfectly with a knife-like edge. Inside corners involved "scribing" and were even worse. Fitting to the wall was a further nightmare, since the walls and floors were never plumb or flat, and it was hard to get a strong fix into the century-old brickwork. Various tweaks and adjustments had to be made to accommodate reality. Everything you did in one place affected some other part; patience was essential. I won't draw too strong an analogy with writing and revision but there was some common ground.

Seeing me on my knees amidst my litter of cast-offs, Wally decided that I was a "tryer" and "knew how to work." His explanations improved and I shunted suddenly into his good books. The taciturnity vanished. He was never articulate but it got to the point where we could talk about most things as, clad in identical filthy navy-blue coveralls, we pedalled slowly around the borough. Many of the other women were at loggerheads with their colleagues, embroiled in harassment cases, or constantly being transferred. I knew I'd struck gold. In due course I was invited home to Wally's dark, ground-floor maisonette to meet his wife: an immensely fat woman who refused to cook the green beans he'd somehow managed to grow in his virtually sunless back yard and served canned ones instead. They had no children and did not seem to like each other one bit.

I think Wally was one of the loneliest people I've ever met. At the end of my tour of duty with the depot he invited me to go "to a show" (musical theatre) in the West End. This was a first for him and I got to see him in a suit. Emerging from the underground afterwards, I thanked him for the evening and for everything he'd done and he choked up. I promised to keep in touch, but I'm afraid to say I failed. My next stop was the joinery shop, where we made the more complicated items such as boxed sash windows and staircases.

This was difficult work. The mouldings were made in-house to various sizes by machinists. We also had a machine to chop mortices but there was still a terrible amount of accurate measurement required and lot of hand work involved. One of my seniors there was a huge, fearsome-looking biker who was a very skilled joiner. He used to arrive at the last moment on his thunderous machine, sweating in studded leathers, clock-in, vanish, then reappear fifteen minutes later in jeans and a t-shirt. He was having relationship troubles and with increasing frequency would cry as he worked. He seemed grateful of a minimal kind of acknowledgement of this but did not want to confide, or not in me. Eventually he went on extended sick leave. Another man was sent on an anger management course. The manager of the shop wore a white coat, like a doctor. All in all, the apprenticeship was very instructive as to the working and emotional lives of men and I think this, along with the year I spent as writer in residence in a male prison, has been very useful to me as a writer.

We women all went to college once a week to learn technical drawing and other skills. There we worked alongside young men in their late teens, many of whom had poor literacy and numeracy, but (in contrast to us) excellent craft skills. They had been living physical rather than intellectual lives, had handled materials, tools, and equipment from a very young age. We had not, and everything from banging in a nail in three simple blows to lifting a joist without breaking our backs had to be learned. Gaining at least some of this kind of physical confidence was a revelation to me. Quite unfairly, I thought, the women all aced the exam at the end, simply because we could read and knew how to study. To my mind, carpentry (skilled, not bodging!) is just as mentally demanding as academic work.

Once qualified, I worked for the council on a half-time job-share, and during all this completed two novels. For reasons I can't recall, I went into business on my own. This proved difficult to control: either there would be too much work or not enough, and there were other problems. I remember working for a doctor couple who went on holiday, leaving a group of women tradespersons (chosen in the belief that they would be cheaper) to renovate their home. I was pleased with the work I'd done, but on their return the man summoned me to vent his complaints. The antique kitchen faucet they had chosen leaked copiously, so the plumber had taken the liberty of obtaining a modern near-replica: he was furious about that, and also outraged that his wife (whom I had never met) could not, he said, reach the sink because the surround I had set it in was far too deep. Surprised, I nonetheless agreed to slim it down, understanding only when I met the blob-shaped wife on a subsequent visit why the problem had arisen: her stomach protruded to such a degree that every inch counted in terms of reaching the sink. This incident, and the theft of some of my tools, seemed to sum up the freelance carpentry experience and, in the wake of the publication of my novel, I started to teach writing instead.

I did not become part of the literary scene in London. I don't think I really knew that there was one, and I would have felt intimidated by it if I had. So I don't have stories to tell about that. My time was split between writing, my carpentry job, and gardening in one of the temporary allotments nearby. I visited my university friend Ricky in Spain. I had various relationships, each important in its own way, and eventually fell in love with the man with whom I was to have an on-off, tortuous, and sometimes long-distance relationship for the best part of a decade.

House meetings continued to be both hilarious and frustrating: not surprising when you consider that the cast of characters included a troubled Polish man who wore rubber gloves on his feet, an under-employed actress, an alcoholic council employee with aristocratic background, and a manic-depressive art student. The artists knew they had a good deal, and were among the more functional tenants. Right above me lived a puppet-maker who chipped away at blocks of wood into the small hours. Across the way was a photographer whose sideline, enormous chandeliers made of recycled glassware, propelled her work into the pages of glossy magazines. The Mansions, haven and eyesore, madhouse and sanctuary, was in many ways a perfect place to be. Yet it was also a kind of trap, and I sometimes wondered if I'd ever be able to leave.

The publication of my first novel, *Back in the First Person*, had a huge and transformative effect on me. I had received a letter from an editor at Virago Press inviting me to come in for a talk—and was fully expecting and quite content to have the book turned down but in an encouraging way. By that point I was halfway through the next manuscript and more hopeful of that than of the first book. But as it turned out, the editor, Ruth Petrie, after some friendly small-talk, made an offer for the novel and made it clear she wanted the next one, too. I floated out of the office, realizing as I bent to unlock my bicycle from the railings that I was not fit to ride home. I felt that I had suddenly become part of an enormous conversation, or a giant orchestra playing on, and that I belonged there.

Back in the First Person came out in 1986. The book was well-received, perhaps in a large part because of the subject matter, and I was approached for film rights and hired to help develop the script, which I did. The film was never made. I wasn't surprised, since it is very much an interior story, albeit partly set in a courtroom. All the same, I learned a lot from adapting it and working in a team to discuss the possibilities. Until that point I had written purely by instinct, but I began to absorb some useful notions about dramatic structure.

Teaching various writing and literature courses began to take over from carpentry. My second novel, *The Unborn Dreams of Clara Riley*, was inspired by the history of infanticide. Cheerful stuff, I know! What fascinated me, though, was the way the law came to soften in this respect during the nineteenth century as juries began to refuse to automatically convict women who, out of poverty, shame, desperation, anguish, and inability to cope, killed their babies. The book came out with Virago in 1987, and my sister did the illustration for the cover. I had started my third, *Island Paradise* when I read about the MA in Creative Writing at the University of East Anglia in Norwich. It seemed like an excellent way to focus my attention on my writing. I was also drawn to it because Angela Carter, whom I much admired, was teaching there alongside Malcolm Bradbury. I contacted her about the course and she advised me that it was worth doing so long as I obtained a grant and did not have to pay. My first-degree result qualified me for funding so I went ahead with the application and was accepted. I let go of my Mansions flat, packed my things into the back of my ancient Ford Fiesta, and set off back to school.

.

Some creative writing MAS require students to work in several genres, but that was not the case at UEA, where students were simply streamed into prose or poetry (I think other genres have been added since). This was a pioneering course, the first to have dared to show its face in the UK, where creative writing was viewed as a flaky, self-indulgent American invention, and it is still the most prestigious and successful writing MA in the country. Alumni include Ian McEwan, Kazuo Ishiguro, Anne Enright, and countless other highly accomplished, prize-winning and well-published writers, many of whom came to read and speak at the university.

We were required to take a few courses in contemporary literature, but other than that, we simply wrote, discussed, and revised. We were a small group of about six writers producing substantial novel extracts and stories on a regular schedule. Malcolm Bradbury, who presided over the workshop, was the author of many novels including *Eating People Is Wrong* and *The History Man*, as well as screenplays and TV scripts. He was also a serious academic who published widely on Evelyn Waugh, American fiction, modernism, post modernism, and so on. His wife, Elizabeth, worked for the BBC, adapting books for radio. Witty and urbane, Bradbury had an enormous gift in teaching: an ability to sum up the semi-coherent responses of the workshop into a clear philosophical, aesthetic, or craft issue for the writer concerned to consider. He was generous with his time and every year gave a huge party to which literary agents and editors were invited.

I did meet Angela Carter at the interview but sadly, before classes began, she was diagnosed with lung cancer and withdrew from teaching; she died in 1992. Rose Tremain, who replaced her, did a perfectly good job but still, this was both sad and disappointing.

I was revising my third novel, *Island Paradise*, at UEA, but it was a troublesome book and between drafts I returned to writing short fiction and found great pleasure in this, not the least because it offered me a chance to play around with my ideas and with the form without investing years of work into the process. I read a huge amount of short fiction, discovering, for example, Raymond Carver—in many ways the polar opposite of Angela Carter—yet equally influential and inspirational. I became interested in magic realism and in literary writers such as Peter Carey and Margaret Atwood, who sometimes go beyond the merely realistic and integrate an element of the uncanny, magical, or speculative into a short story. J G Ballard continued to interest me and *Empire of the Sun* came out around this time. To the despair of my then publisher, Methuen, I assembled my own short fiction collection. Stories were seen as a waste of time in commercial terms. The continuous "reorganization" that has beset publishing for the past thirty years was then just beginning, with mergers, firings, and "rationalization." Editors, deprived of their autonomy, were fleeing their sinking ships to become literary agents: this was the beginning of the commercially driven industry focussed on internationally marketable product that we have now.

At least two others in the class of '88 went on to publish extensively: Fadir Faquir, and David Flusfeder (even so, I don't feel it was a particularly outstanding group). MA students tended to linger around the university after they graduated, adding to the local literary social life, and I found myself doing the same. I picked up some interesting writer's residencies in schools in East Anglia. At the prompting of a writer friend, I wrote my first screenplay, *Paint*, a ten-minute short story that was produced and broadcast on BBC TV. Starring Ray Winstone, it featured a paint salesman who ends up stripping to show off his tattoos. It had an outrageous, magical element to it and I recognize it now as one the first of my stories to overtly focus on the idea of transformation. At the same time, I was working on my fourth novel, *Frankie Styne and the Silver Man*, which is much concerned with our fascination with horror, and also features a pivotal transformation scene. I was beginning to sense a tension between realism and a more fantastical element in my work and to find my way to a place where seemingly archetypical or magical figures could be part of an essentially realistic storyline.

All in all, I'd say that the MA at UEA ('87–88) was a useful, if not transformative experience. It was perhaps tainted by my disappointment that I did not get to work with Angela Carter, who had been for me very much the main attraction. Living in Norwich was another matter. I liked the city, and loved the surrounding country and eventual coast. I had an intense if complicated love-life. And I was, relatively speaking, prosperous. I had been awarded a grant based on my first degree, and was hired for a series of contracts as a writer in residence at schools in Suffolk and Norfolk. On the strength of all this I moved out of my rented room and got a mortgage on a tiny terraced house on Melrose Street. My carpentry skills came in very useful.

In the three or so years I spent in that house I earned my MA, completed *Island Paradise* (with difficulty and relief), assembled a collection of stories, *As in Music* (1990), and wrote *Frankie Styne and the Silver Man*, which was somewhat inspired by neighbours on the street where I lived. The latter two earned excellent reviews, including a comparison to J G Ballard that particularly warmed my heart; however, I was disappointed to learn that neither had sold well enough to go into paperback. The frustration I felt at being marooned in hardback and the pressure to produce something more commercial was at least part of why I did not publish another novel until 2001.

I have a strong visual sense as well as good dramatic instincts and writing that short script, *Paint*, in response to a call for submissions from the BBC was great fun to do. The script was accepted and made in fairly short order. On the strength of this experience, I later applied to the London School of Film and TV and was eventually offered a place. The trouble was that I had also successfully applied for a writer-in-residence position at Her Majesty's Prison in Nottingham, and I had to choose. None of my friends understood this, but I chose learning about life over learning about art, rented the Norwich house out, and set off for Nottingham. This did eventually pay off in terms of my novel *Alphabet* (2004).

.

What follows is a previously written account of that very formative prison residency.

THE BUTTERFLY

"This way," the taller man says, and I follow the squeak of two pairs of shoes along a dim corridor punctuated with pairs of locked doors and metal grilles. One officer opens while the other watches, and then locks. At the fourth set of doors, we emerge into still outside air, cross a silent courtyard where weedless beds are blotched with tulip rows, and then re-enter the main building through a door marked Administration.

"Here you are, Miss."

The room, which has windows set well above head height, smells of fresh paint. There's a table covered with a white cloth surrounded by eight chairs upholstered in blue. Seated are a birdlike woman with lashings of glossy chestnut hair and a large man in a baggy sweatshirt and jeans who heaves out of one of the chairs and offers a hand to shake.

"We must be mad!" he says, and he has a point: Writer in Residence, in Her Majesty's Prison, Nottingham, for a term of one year. Not just any old prison, but one that specializes in Lifers and difficult men, uncooperative, violent offenders, otherwise known as basket cases. Who would apply for such a job? Writers, it seems, are nearly always broke and will do anything, though right now, I do have options: a hard-won place at the London School of Film and TV. So, I tell myself, I've just come to look.

The last candidate to turn up, almost ten minutes late, is an ex-inmate, wearing a Victorian style pinstriped suit and silver fob watch, who arrives slightly drunk. We set off on a tour that begins in the accommodation wing with its smells of stale food, body odour, and drains. We see an eight by four cell, complete with the bump on the wall where once the treadmill was set; a tiny library; a huge, well- equipped gym; the Education Department humming in its fluorescent glare. In the technology workshops, inmates, some boyish, some well into their sixties, take apart and reassemble television sets in slow motion, the babble of the radio filling the spaces between them. They look up at the group of strangers staring in at them, take note, but don't react;

it is if our two worlds are running in parallel. In the laundry, men sweat rivers as they load machines and push huge carts of wet laundry or folded sheets from one station to another.

Back in Administration, a dainty buffet of vol-au-vents, quiche, celery sticks, and radish flowers has appeared. We fill our paper plates and do our best to talk informally.

The Governor, a man with a tight collar and a fleshy, lost-seeming face leans in and asks me:

"Why would a woman want to spend her working week in a high-security men's prison?"

"To find out what it is like," I reply. "Curiosity, I think."

"Would you write about it?"

"I don't know."

Later, on the train home, I think about curiosity and frighten myself with stories: Eve's thirst for the knowledge of good and evil; Bluebeard's wife unlocking the door of the bloody chamber and all but perishing there; Psyche yearning for a glimpse of her lover, Pandora opening that box. These stories have been elaborately analyzed by literary scholars and psychoanalysts alike, but their common message, what they are telling me, now, is that curiosity frequently brings a woman far more than she bargained for . . . Even so, and despite having options, I take the job when it's offered, and find myself three months later assigned to Ken.

Ken is close to retirement and wants to breed water spaniels in Ireland when he's free. Every day for several weeks, he accompanies me on what's called walkabouts. He's glad of the break from routine, talks constantly.

"You'll soon learn," he tells me. "Don't give an inch, don't take anything to give to anyone, and don't believe anything they tell you. That said, why not have a word with Alex here."

Alex stands too close. A tiny, wiry man. Veins writhe on his forehead and arms.

"I'll tell you one thing—" he says, his eyes level with mine, unavoidable, "to survive, you hate. You hate them," he nods at Ken; his voice tightens, "because of what they do to you and what they think of you. They hate you because of what you've done to get here, because they know you hate them and because you make them hate themselves ... because they've chosen. We haven't! If the place goes up, you—" he jabs a finger towards my chest, "you'd be one of them ... That's how it is. Sorry," he adds, "it's the fucking situation," then concludes with an abrupt handshake and a nod, before turning his back on us and striding away.

We walk on. Ken hums softly under his breath, as if nothing extraordinary has been said, unlocks another pair of doors. I follow him further in. It's too late to turn back: I've committed myself to a year, moved to the city, rented a place to live.

Natural light filters in from far above, but the accommodation wing is a dim, colourless space, sometimes eerily quiet but often, as now filled with a mind-numbing sound mix: beneath the yells, and crashes and the various kinds of music played simultaneously and loud, our footsteps reverberate on the metal staircase, each step felt, not heard.

Men are on the move from work to lunch. Everyone must watch his own back. Sharpened ballpoint pen holders and batteries in socks, Ken informs me, are the weapons of choice, and as he speaks, two men fall into a scrum on the floor. A whistle shrills, Ken shoves me against the wall, sirens blare and more officers arrive, red-faced and wild-eyed, to break things up.

"See?" Ken says.

Outside, Jason pushes his wheelbarrow wearing enormous, udder-like, red rubberized gloves: his job is to collect the excrement, mostly but not always wrapped, and then thrown from the windows of the unplumbed cells overnight. The installation of in-cell toilets and washing facilities, Ken explains, is proceeding but only very slowly because the prison is so very full and taking one cell out of use to refurbish it necessitates forcing two or more men to share while the work is done, which creates a whole other set of problems.

Meanwhile, men do not want to have a turd in their room all night and Jason is on the case. He likes the job.

"Gets me out and about," he says.

Solitary is for punishment but also for protection. Bugs, paper-pale, blurred from lack of exercise, gestures at the newly installed sanitary unit in his cell. Bolted to the floor and walls, gleaming, it dominates the small room like an altar.

"I," he says in a quiet, monotonous voice, "am one of the lucky ones."

But Harry, in the neighbouring cell, is not having that at all:

"That's what they tell us, and of course we'd rather not slop out. But look at it this way: you could be slopping out in another situation—say it was a hospital in wartime or a monastery or something—" his long face cracks into a smile as if the place has suddenly appeared to him, benevolently transformed, full of Benedictine chanting, "it wouldn't bother you that much, would it? What matters is what goes on between people—" He pauses, points at the unit, "it says, you're shit, right?"

Harry's cell also contains a cardboard table and chair, three oranges on the windowsill, a radio and a pile of library books. Ken Follett, Joanne Harris, Dostoyevsky. He might be interested in a writing class, he says, but he doesn't like people much. He prefers it down here.

"Had enough?" Ken asks. "Blot it out," he suggests. "They've done something wrong; that's why they're here. Read his file; read 'em all, that's what I advise."

In Education, where I'm based, they disagree: reading files gets in the way of relating to the person as he is, now; they want to build on the good, not hark back to the terrible past.

The Education buildings—a series of temporary structures marooned within the main courtyard—are grey and cramped and even more airless than the rest of the institution, but despite this, Education is another world entirely. There are books, posters, reams of paper, newspapers, computers, felt-tipped pens, packets of cookies.

Literacy, Numeracy, Sociology, Cooking—and now, Creative Writing—are delivered along with the tea and Jaffa Cakes. Men come here to escape the miasma of purposelessness that pervades the rest of the institution, but also, because Education is almost entirely staffed by women, they come to hear female voices, inhale perfumes; take in the carefully chosen, modest but colourful clothes and, I'm reliably informed, imagine what's beneath:

"You're just wank material," as Alex says. "Don't you forget it."

I don't, but I understand that they also come here to talk. In the wider prison, men hate words. They blot them out and read the body. They gesture: draw a line across the throat, give the finger, push their chair back so it screams on the floor, and throw out an expletive or two for emphasis. Speakers walk away from each other mid-sentence. No one can ever see any point in trying to unravel a misunderstanding; explanations are pointless and the day's talk often amounts to a series of outbursts, witnessed by another person or persons, who blocks most of it out ... But here, people use language to connect with the other person rather than push them away, and you can see jaws and shoulders relax as the class settles itself around the rickety tables and waits for the session to begin. Attending means relegation to a minimum wage, but even so, there's a very long waiting list.

Outside the computer room, a man with a shaved head and a scar that runs from eye to mouth waits his turn.

"This place," he announces, "has improved my marriage one hundred percent! I write every day. Feelings, and so on. Never had time for stuff like that before. And I read hers too. Study them. Before, she was a stranger with a familiar face. I didn't know her at all. She was just a cartoon figure in my head, with woman written underneath ... I used to hit her. Can't now, of course."

Here, in Education, men use words more as women do. And at the end of the day, as they walk back to the main prison, they shrug them off again and do what they have to do.

"Still here?" Joe offers his hand to shake and grips mine as if to kill it. His hips are as thin as a child's, his skin pricked with fresh blue tattoos. I remember the last time we met; it was at the gate, a battered car delivering him back to the prison, his mates returning him and his suitcase in a cloud of smoke from a week's home leave. "I'm out on leave again Friday," he says now. "The old lady died. I knew her seventeen years. So they have to let me go to the funeral. So long," he says, and before I can reply, grinds his cigarette under his heel and walks away.

A week later he is wandering around with his eyes scoured red from an accident with the weed eater. He doesn't mention the funeral, but tells me several times how he is going to sue the Home Office for not providing him with safety goggles. Can I help him with the writing?

"Him?" Scoffs a fellow prisoner "I don't talk, I do. He's all talk. Mouth. Blather. Words."

The act of speaking seems to be what provides release, rather than what is said. Most of what's said is sarcasm or lies. The drive to return again and again to words, to check out that they say what was intended, to listen to the music they make, to want the best, and re-arrange them—here, in the prison, that is tantamount to madness. Sentences don't rate finishing. Details are immaterial. One stupid cunt is much like another.

'See?' a man will ask, but he won't believe me if I say yes. Stories are left unfinished: 'End of Story' stands in for the crisis point of an account; the rest—the culminating violence and its aftermath, feeling, meaning—these are passed right over. Inevitable, perhaps, or simply uninteresting: "So then he came up to me and I got out my blade. End of." As if all stories were the same and ended that way. But they don't! I want to yell. Here you are. What happens next?

The officers' equivalent is a shrug. Except one day:

"How are you?" I ask the Key Man on my way out.

"What can you expect?" he replies. "Years since I did any-thing constructive." He holds my gaze as he unlocks the outer gate. "Don't," he adds quietly, "Don't tell me I can always leave. I need money." Another officer emerges from the gatehouse, virtually dancing on the spot. His face glows, his eyes glitter with aggressive jocularity:

"He's having you on! He loves it here, really! It's the uniforms, see! Turn him on, they do!" Their laughter is like machine-gun fire; the door slams shut.

To want language to connect me to another person is to want myself and the other person to matter. To admit hope, which leaves you open...forget it! End of.

Even so, six men, including Harry from Solitary, turn up for the first writing workshop, and one of them asks:

"Would you read this out for me?"

Two paragraphs, written on lined paper in minute, hard-pressed script describe an eight-year-old's terror, trapped in the over-furnished front room of a terraced house, hearing the carriage clock tick and watching his father slowly unbuckle his belt, extract it from the loops of his waistband and ready himself to strike.

I fit my mouth carefully around the words.

"Thanks," he says, swallowing.

"You've got bottle, mate," Harry tells him and everyone agrees on that.

"I might do some more," he says and then another man has something too and reads, for himself, an account of being woken in the middle of the night by his alcoholic mother, made to complete the day's unfinished chores, and then sent to sleep in the bathtub.

I don't know what I expected, but it wasn't this. I have no training to draw on, just my own instincts, and Ken's well-meant but questionable advice. I have no idea what is the best way to handle what is beginning to happen in my class. But at least we're talking. And listening—and the words definitely matter, almost as if we were somewhere else.

Soon the class is full and we are discussing a story about triplets in the womb which the writer calls *that dark, loving place*:

"It wasn't a battle of wills, but of needs and wants," he writes. The female fetus takes more than her share of sustenance and when the narrator's brother dies before term, "she no longer needed to steal it; she simply claimed it as her own."

One of the teachers is pregnant and brings in the printout of a recent ultrasound; another inmate makes an ink drawing of the three fetuses, floating in black. We decide to publish an anthology.

No one calls the prison a family because, despite the awful experiences of most inmates, a family is still considered to be a good thing. Nonetheless, one group of people here is charged with the care of another and, in that way at least, the institution does have the shape of a family. It is the kind of family where the men set the rules and the women, doing their best to be kind, sometimes break them but sometimes threaten, when desperate: "You wait until your father gets home!" It is the kind of family where the children fight each other for what scraps of attention and affection are available, where real communication is minimal and self-expression oblique. People cry secretly at night; everyone suffers.

I'm part of it too. I leave every night, but I think about little else and despite the pious hope that the experience will in some way be inspiring, I'm not writing, not at all, except for taking these notes.

When I try the family idea out on Ken, he shakes his head and tells me all over again how, eventually, I will learn. "You'll see the truth," he says, and I think of some exotic butterfly fluttering in the immense dim space of B wing, appearing, then disappearing, me running hopelessly after it with a net.

Files must be read in the Records Office; I spend days there, alone with the physical agonies, mental torture and broken lives—the intricate trails of suffering which the men I've come to know as thoughtful, helpful types, and in some cases also as neglected or abused children, have left behind them. What have I learned? This at least: I can be at the same time overwhelmed with pity for and repelled by the very same person; that a man can be both kind and cruel, heroic and savage. Both, and.

I have been given my own keys, attached to a long chain which must be worn fixed to a belt. I can open almost every door; can wander, without Ken, through the prison at will, and at any time of day or night.

In the recreation room, light flickers over the taut, pale faces of the group of men watching a documentary about a massacre in Vietnam. Roll-ups are passed from hand to hand, grabbed, fought over—the smoke of these thin cigarettes made from butt ends smells like death itself. Just outside the TV room, a man with congealed blood on his forehead leans against the wall, hands in pockets, ignored by passers-by; further along the wall stand other men with tiny pupils and frozen faces.

Alan from the writing group is passing on the landing above. "Watcha doing in here?" he yells down at me.

What to say? I came here out of curiosity, but I know nothing, have no answers. I'm groping my way, perhaps, towards some kind of understanding, but meanwhile all I can do is to insist that the words and stories that pass between us here bear meaning and have consequences, even if we do not yet know what they are.

.

I returned to London after the prison residency, and focused mainly on short fiction along with a little writing for TV and film. I continued to be fascinated by the fantastic and mythical, and by how they could be blended together, something I'm still very interested in. Very disappointed and disillusioned, as well as increasingly cynical about an industry that seemed to be becoming ever more focused on numbers and bottom lines, I didn't really see a place for my kind of writing and felt I might never write another novel.

At the same time, I was going through a painful and protracted relationship breakup and so, over a year or so, things got to the point where I had to force myself to get up in the morning. A doctor suggested anti-depressants, but I felt this would be a mistake; I sensed that I needed to get to grips with what was not working in my life and make what changes I could, rather than take a pill to feel better about it. I looked for something useful and meaningful to do, and volunteered weekly at night on a homeless crisis line with the UK housing charity Shelter; along with this, I took up jogging (still a habit) and began to see a psychotherapist (very helpful indeed).

Eventually, I signed up for a training course in Gestalt therapy—an approach which seems like a natural fit for creative types, since you get to do things like speak in the first person from the point of view of all the elements in a dream (including inanimate objects). In the middle of all this exploration, I came up with the idea that I would take a post-graduate qualification in housing management that was being offered at the London School of Economics, and then be qualified for a Proper Job Doing Something Useful. Despite my CV consisting mainly of having written novels and stories and being part-way through a training in Gestalt therapy, I talked my way into a sought-after place on the course, along with a generous grant for fees and living expenses. Clutching my new briefcase, I duly turned up for class, only to realize within hours that I and the LSE had made a ghastly mistake. Fortunately, I had not cashed the grant cheque and someone else was able to take my place.

This sounds like, and was, a bit of a fiasco, but I do feel it was an important step in the process of coming to understand what I was and am: a writer with a strong interest in difficult, quirky characters and unanswerable questions and also one who really cares about form. It takes a long time to wrestle a project into shape and do something very different with each book. I want to connect, and I am glad to have my work read and appreciated by as many readers as possible, but I don't expect everyone to like it and I don't find it helpful to chase after commercial success. Some books do better than others in that respect. All in all, it's more sustainable for me artistically, emotionally, and financially to have some other kind of part-time work and allow the writing to do its own thing. Mostly this works out well for both art and life.

Other residences have also been productive in the same rather slow way. In the early 1990s, the British Council sent me to Finland to the Lahti International Writers' Reunion and then, twice, to speak about contemporary British women's writing and run some creative writing workshops at a conference for teachers of English from Finland and the Baltics. Other writers got sent to the Caribbean.

These first visits were in the summer (my dates are hazy here but let's say 1990–92), with long days and "white nights." I became quite fascinated by the country and its landscape, which seemed initially very low on drama (most of it is rather flat, with lakes and birch trees), but which both insisted on and rewarded study. What had seemed initially almost monochrome and indeed monotonous revealed itself in time as a blend of subtly varied tones. The more I looked the more I saw, and small variations grew in significance. It was a landscape that demanded careful attention and I came to enjoy giving it.

I became interested in one of the other groups accommodated on the fringes of the conference site—a religious camp of some kind—and talked to several people about the tradition of Christian summer camps in Finland and some of the activities participants engaged in, such as carrying backpacks of stones to symbolize their sins. I'm agnostic, but find religious beliefs and behaviour very interesting.

I formed a friendship with Tuija Talvitie, then director of the British Council in Finland, and travelled with her and her family on a short holiday to the Åland Islands in the Gulf of Bothnia. I subsequently wrote about the experience in "The Pike's Heart," which won the Traveller Writing Award and so sent me and my boyfriend on a rather surreal prize-winner's flight on the Concorde to New York and back. The luxury of the journeys to and from the city stood in stark contrast to the intervening week of budget accommodation in a rather spartan guesthouse run by Lutherans (or was it Jesuits?). I found it both strange and exciting to walk through the familiar, almost mythical sights of the city as well as to discover new places such as the Isamu Noguchi Garden Museum in Queens.

Another consequence of the Finnish summer schools was a 1994 residency in Tallin in nearby Estonia, which at that time had only recently gained its independence from the Soviet Union. I returned to Tallin in 2009 to teach a summer school course and speak about my novel *Alphabet*; by then the ancient city centre was full of the kind of shopfronts, cafés, and roaming tourist crowds you might find in any European city. It was very different when I first visited in 1994. Back then, the restoration of Soviet-neglected historical buildings was underway, but capitalism had barely taken root. There were some shops and restaurants, but with the exception of one particular pub, they were hard to detect because of the lack of advertising or signage. New, strange goods were just beginning to flow in. An unaffordable pineapple sat in disintegrating glory on a platter in the grocery section of a department store that was still under construction.

As part of the Tallin residency I taught compressed contemporary literature courses and a writing course to a group of extremely serious and thoughtful students who spoke and wrote excellent English. Many of them were fluent in other languages, too. They wasted no time and were utterly devoted to their literary studies. Two short stories were inspired by my stay there: "My Beautiful Wife," also titled "The Second Spring After Liberation" and "It Is July, Now." Two chapbooks of short fiction were translated by Anne Allpere (her name then; she has remarried since and is Anne Lange) appeared after this first visit. Visiting Tallin in 2009 I was happy to see Anne again and meet her new husband and child.

When I returned to Finland in 1998 I was in the early throes of working on my first novel for some time, *The Story of My Face*. I'd decided that the Protestant sect my protagonist Natalie encounters had its origins in Finland, and I was delighted to travel with my daughter, who was then coming up to two years old, to the University of Vaasa. This was north of where I had been before, on the coast of the Gulf of Bothnia. It was the first time I had been somewhere so wintry and seen sea-ice—the ethereal turquoise glow of it. I was there for the end of winter, when people were still driving across the bay on the ice, and I stayed until the beginning of spring, by which time they had stopped. On May 1, I watched the first boats push their way through ice that had become soft and almost slushy and soon would vanish into the sea.

My daughter attended daycare and I taught, part-time, a mixture of writing and literature. Aided by Pat Poussa, who had organized the residency, and other academics at the university, I used my free time to research the nineteenth-century history of

Protestant "awakenings" and to visit various churches, vicarages, villages, and museums. All this gave me lots of interesting detail that fed directly into the nineteenth-century plot strand. I finished the second draft of the *The Story of My Face* not long after, and had a publishing contract for it by the time my husband and I had decided to move to Salt Spring Island.

Over a period of several years in the late 1990s, I continued with my explorations of Gestalt and other therapies, alongside various part-time teaching jobs, and eventually emerged from my lengthy breakup into a new relationship with Richard Steel, who soon became the father of my first child and then my husband.

I put my therapy training to practical use for a year or so in a job doing groupwork in a residential rehab for drug users—and, at the same time, bit by bit, despite myself, and almost secretly, I found myself writing the novel that became *The Story of My Face*. The book was interrupted when I had our first baby, but it turned out that my daughter was a great afternoon napper, and Richard a very involved, nappy-changing father who also shared the housework and encouraged me to put aside time to write, so I did resume work on the book fairly soon. I found I could do far more than before in a limited time. Should it be a surprise that being loved, loving, and happy really helped me as a writer?

The Story of My Face marked a huge step forwards for me in terms of storytelling. My first two novels were apprentice-pieces, remarkable only for dealing with subject matter not much dealt with at the time. In writing them I had learned the basics of telling a longer realistic story. In the next two novels, *Island Paradise* and *Frankie Styne and the Silver Man*, I had been able to expand my range and play with more speculative and imaginative elements. I had a lot of fun with *Frankie Styne* and was delighted to see it connect well with a Canadian audience when Biblioasis reissued it not long ago.

The Story of My Face was a different animal from these first four books. Wrestling it into shape was major work. From draft to draft, it went through many shifts in perspective and structure, though the heart of it remained the same: the story of a neglected teenage girl, Natalie, and her relationship with Barbara, a middle-aged woman, member of a strict Protestant sect that bans all representative imagery, who becomes a kind of surrogate mother to Natalie. Their relationship exposes a secret Barbara has kept from her husband, and, as a consequence, both the family and the sect implode, in the course of which Natalie suffers a horrible injury.

There are three narrative strands: the core of the story, which takes place in 1969 in England when Natalie is a teenager, another strand taking place in Finland in the late-nineteenth century, and the third part, a frame story that links the other two together, and is roughly contemporary to the time of writing (late 1990s), also set in Finland. The three strands are braided together, though it's an irregular braid, dictated by a kind of emotional logic, rather than a strict 1,2,3. The most exciting aspect of writing this novel, though, was experimenting with point of view. I ended up using a first-person narration that also manages to get inside the heads of the other characters. This transformed the story and is something I'm still proud of. All in all, *The Story of My Face*, written when I thought I had given up long-form fiction, turned out to be more sophisticated, intricately plotted, and successful (both artistically and commercially) than my previous novels. It also made use of my interest in the mythical in terms of story structure and imagery.

At the same time as I was drafting and re-drafting *The Story of My Face*, Richard and I started to consider a move to Canada, specifically to the West Coast, a place where he (Canadian by birth, though British by upbringing) had spent summers in his youth and where he still had a clutch of aunts and cousins whom we had visited.

We felt we had to leave London; it was incredibly expensive, the air was polluted, and neither of us had lucrative work. Living in a metropolis on a budget was far less pleasant a prospect for a young family than it had been for each of us before. Of course, we did not need to move so very far away as we did, but once we entertained the idea and discovered the Gulf Islands, the dream of it took hold of us and we acted quickly, not wanting the two children to be disrupted by a move once they had friends and schools. I would say now that we made the move impulsively and without exhaustive due diligence: I certainly did not know very much about Canada's politics or colonial and pre-colonial history, or about the education system in BC, or even about the publishing and literary scene in Canada. Also, I did not know that after my years of not-being-a-novelist, *The Story of My Face* would be long-listed for the Orange Prize and sell well in the UK, or that my next title, *Alphabet*, already begun after the Nottingham residency and then abandoned, would follow in fairly short order.

·

The Nottingham prison residency had been a decisive, exhausting, and in some ways deeply rewarding experience. I shall always be grateful to it for a very visceral understanding, gained from talking to inmates and reading their records, of something I had only known more theoretically before: that the same person could be both kind and cruel, a bully and a victim, and that I could feel pity, horror, and outrage, all at the same time.

In terms of writing, the experience did not bear fruit for many years, but this is a bit of a pattern with me. I knew, in its immediate aftermath, that I wanted to explore in fiction the many feelings and questions it had thrown up for me, such as: Was it possible to change as much as some of the men I had met needed to change in order not to be a threat to others? If you changed that much would you still be the same person? Could anyone thrive in such an environment as I had seen? And if deep change was possible, what would it feel like to undergo such a metamorphosis? Having witnessed a prison wedding, I was also fascinated by the desires and motives of those women attracted by prisoners and in particular serious offenders.

Fairly soon after the residency, I had the idea of following a man through a life sentence, a kind of opposite to the usual crime story which ends with the incarceration of the villain. I developed a character, Simon Austen—a deeply damaged young man serving Life for the murder of his girlfriend. She had disobeyed him in a trivial matter, which he found intolerable, and the crime was horrific. I had a very strong sense of his voice, and began to work on the story, initially in first person. I ground to a standstill after reading some of it aloud to my writing group. One member of the group (now a very well-known writer) interrupted the reading and told me to stop as it was upsetting her too much. She did not enjoy the feeling of menace. Part of me was furious (why did she not pop outside for a moment?), and another part of me knew that her feeling of being threatened might be evidence of the power of the writing, but even so, I was anxious about what I was doing and found it hard to continue after this. As I realized later, there were other problems with the early form of the story, so I can't blame the interruption entirely, and indeed, it was ultimately useful. In any case, I put the book aside and did not look at it again until we were packing to move to Canada. At that point, I sat on my office floor and read it through. I could see immediately that it had some real strengths, and I could also see what was wrong with it: I had become too interested in some of the women Simon corresponds with at the beginning, and so the story had become diffuse and lost momentum. I could see, too, that the best way to tell this story would be to use what I call a "close third person"—filtered through his eyes and often in his voice, so almost but not actually first—this would give both me and the reader just a touch more distance from Simon. I began work on *Alphabet* as soon as *The Story of My Face* was complete and it came out in 2004/5. Research had to be done by correspondence and interlibrary loan, but apart from that, the structure of the story was clear to me and the writing, when I finally settled down to it, went relatively smoothly and quickly.

I'm still pleased with *Alphabet*. I'm delighted that most readers have complex and contradictory feelings about Simon (often a mixture of empathy and mistrust), but end up rooting for him to some degree. It's a novel that connects with my core interests and preoccupations as a person and as a writer. These boil down to "character" and, in particular, *difficult* characters who create strong reactions in others, including the reader; people who both attract and repel. I'm fascinated by how such people come to be as they are, their motivations, and the way they struggle with the possibilities for change and transformation that life throws in their path. A lot went into *Alphabet*: not just my experience of the prison residency and the stories shared with me there, but also my previous thinking about men and masculinity and about the way men and women are supposed to be and to behave towards each other—and, of course, the training I did (after the prison residency) as a psychotherapist. That said, all this had been thoroughly digested, so I don't think it is in any way an instructive or preachy book.

My then agent and the UK publisher Weidenfeld and Nicolson were of the opinion that *Alphabet* was a harder book to sell because it did not appeal to women readers in the same way that

The Story of My Face did; in theory it would appeal more to male readers, I was told, but the problem there was that they were less likely to read it because it was written by a woman. There may have been a grain of truth in this; however, the novel garnered some great reviews written by men, and when they *do* read it, both genders certainly connect with the story. I was delighted when it made the Governor General's Award shortlist in 2005, just a few years after our arrival in Canada.

Prior to our emigration, I did not conduct a thorough review of my writing so far. Neither did I weigh the move up in terms of literary costs and benefits, but I would say in retrospect that there have probably been both, and that they are inseparable. For example, it has taken me a while to get to the point of tackling Canadian settings and characters (I have done so in *The Find* and in my short fiction and current WIP) and much of my work is still set elsewhere, which may be something of a disadvantage in publishing terms over here; on the other hand, writing about a new place as a bit of an outsider is a strong and interesting perspective to take, and, like many other writers no longer living where they were born, I find that writing about home from away also works well, though it does make research very cumbersome. Google maps only provides the basics. You can't just take a train and go and see what somewhere really looks like, hear the soundscape, inhale the smells, understand the streetlife.

I've certainly been seen by some as a newbie and "not Canadian," but even so I feel my work has been well-received and respected, and this feeling solidified for me last year (2018) when *Dear Evelyn* won the Writers' Trust Prize for Fiction. Perhaps, being a newcomer, I've made more effort to connect with other writers here than I did in the UK, and perhaps because BC and Salt

Spring are home to so many of Canada's writers and naturally I run into them (and perhaps simply because many years and more books have accumulated), I have ended up feeling much more a part of the literary community here than I did in the UK. I was especially aware of this and very touched when Barbara Gowdy, whose wonderful story collection *We So Seldom Look on Love* I had reviewed in 1993 when it came out in the UK, gave my 2014 collection *Paradise and Elsewhere* a truly heartfelt blurb. Something seemed to have slotted into place over those two decades.

In any case, knowing none of this, we sold our terraced house in London and moved to ten acres on Salt Spring Island off the coast of BC. Richard set up shop as a furniture maker and then a gallery manager and curator and I have continued to write, at the same time as teaching part-time at Vancouver Island University. We both also work hard in the vegetable-growing, firewood chopping, and yard-work departments. Our children have grown up here.

The island, we eventually learned, has other names, including ĆUÁN, and is part of the traditional and unceded territories of first peoples from the Hul'q'umi'num' and SENĆOŦEN language groups.

It may seem paradoxical, but in some ways leaving the UK brought out the best in my complicated relationships with my family, as well as the opportunity to become part of the Canadian side of Richard's family. At the same time, the move did represent, for both me and Richard, a separation from our pasts and a new start. That said, I underestimated how hard it would be to leave. All those goodbyes were very difficult, even though we knew they were not permanent. Friends and family you know you will visit and have come to stay. And while losing easy access to each other is difficult, longer visits can be in some ways better than more frequent but briefer ones. One thing I had not bargained for, though, was realizing, in the run up to our departure, that I would likely never see again most of the local shopkeepers and many of our neighbours, my daughter's kindergarten teachers, or any of the locals we met and greeted on our walks hither and thither every day. Along with the big relationships that have to be sustained in a new way are a multitude of smaller ones that you just lose. I remember bursting into tears all over again when this hit me. At the same time, though, once you arrive in the new place, you are busy making new connections.

The difficult years were of course those in the middle of our time here, when my parents began to decline, and I found myself flying back to the UK every three months and feeling torn and guilty; now that time has passed there is much less of a pull. I still miss friends, as well as many landscapes and voices, along with cultural things such as the galleries and theatre in London. But the country we left no longer exists; I live here now.

When we arrived in Canada in June 2001. Our youngest was by then eighteen months old, very sociable, and a keen walker. He had spent the entire flight trailed by one or the other parent as he walked up and down the aisles greeting anyone awake, and then, as the plane began to descend, he vomited copiously, covering the entire front of my shirt. It did not seem auspicious. Our encounter with the immigration officer was mercifully brief, though we still had hours to go before arriving in Sidney in British Columbia to stay with Richard's aunt and visit with other family.

Within twenty-four hours, my daughter was pulling on the mermaid outfit we had made together at home in England. Soon, she sat on a float with a burly Neptune as part of the town's annual sea-themed parade, and was warmly applauded by a crowd of very elderly people she did not know. She has, thank goodness, always been very adaptable. Jet lag and exhaustion doubtless played a part, but the beginning of our time in Canada felt surreal to me.

I remember feeling much better once we were just the four of us and on the half-empty ferry to Salt Spring—a forty-minute journey that is always lovely in summer and one with which Richard and I were both familiar from our previous visits.

The Story of My Face came out in Canada in the summer of 2002. One of the first reviews, in the *Globe and Mail*, commented on the "tightly-written, wonderful structure" and summed the book up as "a compelling and unpredictable journey." This seemed like a good start, and by that time, we had settled in somewhat. A year or two later, I found part-time work teaching fiction-writing at Vancouver Island University, where I eventually become a half-time professor. Of course, it's always hard to balance a day-job with writing, but working at the university has helped me to understand the place where I now live, and to articulate my ideas about the writing of fiction and how it can be taught. And it has connected me to students of all ages and writer-colleagues such as Marilyn Bowering, Susan Juby, Jay Ruzesky, Sonnet L'Abbé, and Robert Wiersema. It has helped me to belong here.

Soon after our arrival on Salt Spring I became part of a women's writing group that met alternately on Salt Spring and in Victoria, and through that I encountered others still, including Lynne Van Luven, who I remember introduced me to Jack Hodgins, among others, at a garden party of hers. Lynne had to leave the writing group due to the demands of her academic and administrative work, but soon became a friend, mentor, and collaborator. The group eventually folded, but for a few years was a very valuable sounding board for work in progress.

I read at a few festivals when *The Story of My Face* came out, and certainly felt that I, hitherto a complete unknown, was in some small way being introduced to and accepted in the literary world over here. Of course, this was and is an ongoing, two-way process. I went through an intense and continuing period of "reading

Canadian," beginning with *Island*, a collection of short fiction by Alistair MacLeod that I purchased the summer of our arrival in my local bookstore, the owner of which has become a dear friend. I loved MacLeod's writing and was particularly struck by "The Boat."

Other discoveries in those early years were Eden Robinson, Madeleine Thien (her stories, *Simple Recipes*), Lisa Moore, Russell Smith, Caroline Adderson, Miriam Toews, and Bill Gaston. New work came out from Barbara Gowdy, whom I'd already read and admired. I caught up on Alice Munro, began on Mavis Gallant. It seemed that the short story was very much alive and well in Canada, and it still feels that way despite its perceived lack of commercial potential.

An independent film company, True West, showed an interest in *The Story of My Face* and eventually took out the first of many options, though to this date no script has been written, let alone a film made. A couple of years later, I was invited to be one of the jurors for the Governor General's Awards, and the year after that, *Alphabet* was a finalist for the same award ... I'm not sure what I had expected, but recall feeling pleasantly surprised by all this, and I have found Canadian writers, even those very well-known and busy, to be open and friendly. As the years here accumulate, I do chafe at having my British origins stressed and restressed by reviewers, but then perhaps I have not helped matters by only occasionally writing stories set in Canada.

The acute outsider's eye has its benefits, but it is a challenge to write with confidence fiction set in a country you did not grow up in and absorb through your pores. It took me about five years to complete *The Find*, set in Alberta and British Columbia, and the novel came out in 2010 with a Canadian publisher, though it was deemed "too Canadian" for the UK market. Perhaps researching and writing this novel was an attempt to learn and to situate myself?

I first met Caroline Adderson at a literary festival in Sidney around 2004—the same one, I think, where I met Alistair MacLeod. I much admire her work, and we've become friends over the years. On a visit of hers to Salt Spring we hiked Mount Erskine, and as we toiled up what's known as "the assault course" I spoke about my short fiction—I had enough for two books by this point—and explained that I was between agents and given that in any case none of them want short fiction, I would have to send it out myself. The prospect was rather daunting. Caroline recommended John Metcalf and Biblioasis to me, and vice versa. Before long I had two collections of short fiction in the pipeline, as well as a brilliant, acute editor devoted to the short story and the sentences that it is made from, a man who will, tactfully but obstinately, fight you to the death over a comma, and blithely suggest that you trash the two weakest stories in the book and quickly come up with a couple of new and better ones instead.

John's original response to what I had sent him was to acquire the more conventional of the two collections, *The Two of Us*, and we quickly started work on it. After some weeks, I asked him about the other, shorter MS, *Paradise and Elsewhere*—a set of fabulist and speculative fictions written over many years. He told me he had not yet got to it. A little later, when I asked again, John told me that he had not read it because he tended to dislike "things of that kind"— fables, myths, science fiction, and so on— and did not want to upset me by rejecting it. I was disappointed, since of the two books I thought it by far the more original and distinctive, but accepted his position and said I would send it elsewhere; John then got back to me fairly shortly saying he had read *Paradise and Elsewhere*, loved it, and wanted to put it out first. We stopped editing the *Two of Us* and set to on the shorter book.

I've always been particularly proud of *Paradise and Elsewhere* for managing to pass the "things of that kind" barrier, and much appreciate John overcoming his resistance. I still feel the book is one of my best.

Critical response to P&E was wonderful to the point of overwhelming. Amy Bloom baptized the book with a sprinkle of adjectives that included compelling, moody, and shape-shifting; Barbara Gowdy added vibrant, startlingly imaginative, wise, smart, very funny, and very humane. I was amazed at the lengths reviewers went to in order to find the right combination of descriptors.

I did very much want these stories to take the reader to somewhere new. I remain very grateful to all those who so far have taken the risk of reading *Paradise & Elsewhere* and for all the clever, passionate, and dedicated people who work at Biblioasis, the super-indie publisher who took the book on.

P&E was nominated for the Giller Prize (as later was *The Two of Us*), and all in all this felt like an excellent start to my relationship with a new publisher, one who also wanted to reissue some of my backlist, including *Alphabet* and *Frankie Styne and the Silver Man*. None of this was going to make any of us rich, but there was a deep pleasure in having these books brought to their best form, valued, presented to the public, and all available under one imprint. Despite (or because of) its tiny size, Biblioasis seemed very effective in terms of getting critical attention for them and finding new readers for the backlist titles. I felt seen for what I was. This was very welcome after a period of feeling what I did was deemed too quirky and somehow not commercial enough. Four books came out in as many years, and meanwhile I worked in fits and starts on what eventually became my eighth novel, *Dear Evelyn*.

Dear Evelyn went through many changes (and titles). Its deeply personal nature was a large part of the challenge. I visited the

UK very frequently in the last years of my parents' lives. They had always been argumentative but as old age eroded them, they became embattled. It was hard to watch. My father had a fall, and following his recovery from that, my mother refused to have him come back to the house. He moved into a care home, even though he would have preferred to stay at home, and could have been comfortable there with a small amount of reorganization and help. We were all shocked, but Mum was adamant. At the same time, she unearthed the letters he had written to her during the Second World War and gave them to my oldest sister. We all read them. The contrast between a passionate beginning and seemingly bitter and desolate ending was stark. I knew I wanted to explore it in fiction, but it took me years to find out how.

I began with some short stories. I became interested in the poetry that had been important to my father all his life, and knew I wanted to somehow include that, and the poet Edward Thomas (who had lived in the same South London area as my parents in the run up to the First World War), and so I did, but eventually the poetry and the Thomas got badly out of hand and I had to weed a lot of it out. My mother died suddenly. I asked my father for his permission to somehow use his letters in a project I did not know the shape of; he gave it and I spent months typing them out. Then about a year after my mother, my father died. I remained committed to a work of fiction about a long marriage like my parents'. Progress was very slow, though I knew some of it was good. Then, when I had speeded up a bit and had about half of a book written, I became increasingly inhibited by anxieties as to what my sisters might feel about the project, which was fiction, but very lifelike and deliberately so. There was no way through this but to ask them to read it and see how they felt—an extraordinarily risky move to take given my sensitivity to others' judgements of early work.

I was lucky that there were no powerful objections or ultimatums, and I continued much less inhibited. When I submitted a possibly complete MS to John, he encouraged me to cut several entire chapters, and pushed me to streamline, intensify, and make the most of the raw emotional potential of the rest. My UK editor had concerns about the then too-brief middle of the book, which I was now seeing as a novel (or novel-in-stories). I spent a summer building it up and was excited by the process. After years of crawling, I wrote quickly at the end. To my amazement, it was finally done, bar all the line edits and proofing. It took at least eight years, all in all.

I was delighted when *Dear Evelyn* was shortlisted for the Rogers' Writers' Trust Prize in 2018. I had no hope that it would win. Based on previous experience, I felt that I might turn out to be a writer "much listed," and that there could be worse things to be…As a result, I was unprepared and found myself in tears as I improvised a brief speech in front of the huge gala audience. My publisher, Dan Wells, and his wife, Alexis, were there and they too were on the brink of tears.

One result of the prize has been a much wider audience for this book than the previous titles. Despite or because of its lifelike quality, Englishness, literary allusions, time-jumps, and peculiar intensity, it's a work readers and other writers here in Canada (and abroad) have connected with very strongly; it is deeply satisfying to me to have made the book how I wanted to be, and to feel this ongoing connection. I feel I'm lucky to do what I do, and to do it here. As for what comes next, experience has taught me that it is best not to say too much about that.

LOW TIDE

KATHY PAGE

t was hot, the sky a bowl of blue; waves slapped against the rock. I remember still the astounding sensation of the air on my face, stomach, shoulders, back and limbs—all over, like invisible hands. How it was to stand upright on new legs and feet: utterly strange, yet easy, and then, a moment later, such a feeling of weight! The land's pull made each step an intentional thing and turned mere standing into an act of resistance. In-tensely aware of my new flesh, I waded ashore and walked along the beach, leaving my prints in damp, newly exposed sand: my heels, the balls of my feet, my ten toes.

At the far end of the bay was a small island and a white and red lighthouse. A rowboat had been dragged up on the beach and by the boat stood a man, watching me through binoculars. Did his watching change me that first time? Or did I, wet-dreaming until I caught fire, invent him, then split my pelt with longing and climb out of it? Maybe it was both of these things; in any case, at the beginning neither of us cared. When I drew closer, I noticed his clothes: long pants, a shirt, a jacket, all of them faded by the sun and ruffled by the breeze. Thinking that I might yet need my old sleek skin I looked back then to the rocks, but the tide had turned and they were all but submerged. For a moment then I felt the sharpness of the sand blown in the breeze, and knew that the sun could burn me. And I missed my kind, the underwater sounds, all the old freedoms, but I told myself: *No matter, you must go on now*, and walked towards the man, who let the binoculars hang about his neck and strode, then ran to meet me.

His beard and hair were a mid brown, wiry, trimmed, if roughly so. I liked his face. It broke open and contradicted itself: he smiled, yet his cheeks were wet, his eyes, sea-green, wide with astonishment.

"I knew you must come back!" He gasped for breath, his hands heavy on my shoulders. "But not like this! Where the hell are your clothes?" He laughed, sloughed his jacket, held it out for me, though I did not feel embarrassed, despite the way his gaze exposed me even as I covered myself. I noticed his skin glistened with sweat. Would mine do the same?

"I've come from the sea," I told him, "I left my coat on the rock." My voice emerged rough-edged, sore. He raised the binoculars again. "I think I see something dark in the water. We'll take the boat and look."

So we pushed out. He took the oars and I the glasses, and I quickly learned how to use them to bring the distance close. At times I too thought I could see a dark thing floating just below the surface of the water, but once we drew close I understood that it was nothing but a reflection of the rock, and despite him saying that whatever I had left there would likely wash up on the shore, I knew that I must act as if my old skin was gone, and that now I must live on land.

He said he was my *husband*. He kept the lighthouse, and as well as that, he was a kind of artist, one who used science in the service of beauty, he said. Surely I remembered that? And the bed he had built for us on the third floor of the tower? Our wedding day, the drunken priest? The night of the storm?

"I remember none of it," I told him. I was sitting on a pile of sacks in the stern of the boat. The ocean was flat and glossy, as the tide flowed in and bit by bit filled up the bay it rippled gently as if there were muscles beneath its skin. Reflected light flickered on our faces. The man who claimed to have married me looked away a moment, then back.

"That may be for the best," he said. "Everything will be better this time, Marina, I promise you. I'm very sorry. I think I had every right to be angry, but I never meant to hurt you."

Naturally, I marked the word, *hurt*. And yet I knew that it was not me that he spoke of, and he seemed sincere. I liked his smoothness, the lean, muscular look of him, his strong-fingered hands, the intensity of his gaze. And that first time, constrained as we were by oars shelved to each side of us and by the struts and seats but most of all by being in a small vessel floating on the roof of my former world, can only be called exquisite: sex so gentle in its beginnings, so constrained and restrained—yet only seeming so, for within those limits our bodies' sensations were amplified like voices trapped in a cave, and at the end, shuddering, we broke free of all bounds, left the world and returned to it as if new. I saw, afterwards, that his hand bled from where he had slipped it between me and the floor of the boat.

.

Marina, he called me, yet he never thought to introduce himself and I discovered his name only after he had taught me to read. From the start, he taught me a great deal. That first day he showed me how to manage the oars and it was I who pulled us back to the lighthouse island, along the narrow cove to the one place where it was possible, at certain times of day, to land. Together we hauled the boat beyond the tide mark and secured it with rocks. "You can walk around the island in an hour," he told me. By then, he had stopped saying that surely I remembered, and simply explained how things were and would be, though he frequently grasped my hand, as if to be sure that I was real.

He showed me a vegetable garden, a garden shed, a chicken coop, a smoke hut. The keeper's cottage, low with thick walls and small windows, was built right up against the tower. A smaller dwelling closer to the garden stood empty: out of parsimony, he said, the Lighthouse Board had not yet replaced the deputy keeper. His face darkened and he added that it was all the same to him, and likely they never would ... "In any case," he told me, gesturing at the tower, "the deputy is an unnecessary position now that my gearing system has so much improved the efficiency of the clockwork. The winding schedule is very manageable. You'll see."

In the future, he told me, all lighthouses would be powered by electricity, a thing like lightning, controlled. And they would be connected by another system of wires that carried voices from place to place and even from one continent to another ... But the very remotest of them, such as East Point, would likely wait until last. "And so until then," he said, pushing open the door into the kitchen, which was shady now but still warm from the range on the far wall, "we'll live here and be the world to each other." He pulled me close and reached under the jacket to feel the slippery heat between my legs. His hands shook as he unfastened the horn buttons, and soon we made good use of the table.

How willing I was! He liked that. Likewise, I told him, and he liked that too. Both of us were greedy for pleasure. But more than that, I craved the deep forgetting at the heart of the act of love, that shedding of the trivial particulars that separate one being, one species, from another. Our desires were attuned, our bodies spoke. He fitted me. I liked him well, from the length and firmness of what he called his member to the gleam of his body hair in the firelight and the long muscles of his arms and legs. He seemed a good mate, even though after the act he must ask, whispering, his lips to my ear, his hands restless on my skin,

"Did you open yourself like this to *him*? Even if you did so, I do forgive you, because you have returned. But tell me, please."

"I don't understand," I said and pulled away.

.

Afterwards I was always raging hungry, but I knew nothing of cooking and kitchens. This too I learned, though only to a degree: I kept my taste for raw things, and ours was a poor diet apart from the fish, mussels, and eggs. We had carrots, potatoes, cabbage, and dill. Flour-and-water biscuits. Bitter coffee. Dried beans to be soaked in the pot. Ham. Salted butter and even saltier meats in cans. We frequently needed some brandy to wash down our meal.

And neither could I sew, and I saw no reason to. The machinery of the light interested me more. Above us, burning always, was the enormous light, reached by a long spiral climb that felt to me as if I was ascending inside a giant shell. The four oil lamps at the top of the tower were set inside a first order Fresnel lens taller than a man, a glass beehive, he called it, though also, I thought, it could be a gigantic insect eye. In daytime, the lens glittered and took on the colours of the sea and sky; at night its many planes glowed, so that it appeared to hover in the room: a hallucinatory vessel, a ship that might have travelled from beyond the moon. There were eight bullseyes to magnify the light. Above and below each of these were the panels set with many glass pieces. Each of these nine hundred and forty-four curved sections had been individually cut and ground and then set exact in its curved brass mount. Light, like the sea, was made of waves, he said, and these glass prisms caught and focussed waves into a narrow, concentrated beam that could be seen twenty miles out to sea. Floating on mercury and driven by elaborate clockwork, the lamps revolved inside the lens, giving the beam its characteristic pulse.

Despite the ceiling ventilation it was unbearably hot near the light. Below, in the watch room it was cooler, and there, at five in the morning and five in the afternoon, without fail, we re-filled the kerosene, and wound the clockwork tight. It was a circular room, with strong oak floors to support all our supplies and equipment, and generous windows all around to let in light. There was a desk, where the lighthouse records were written, and shelves where they were kept; a narrow door led out to the observation platform. The platform was also used to support the ladder when the light room windows were cleaned after heavy storms, and in any case, according to regulation, no less than four times a year. Also in the watch room was a bed built out from the wall: Why, he said, add in a journey up and down the spiral stairs when night observations needed to be taken? And why be separated? Why stay down in the gloom of the cottage, when there was so much light to be had and we could see each other so very well?

"I shouldn't believe in you," he said, looking up into my face while I knelt astride him on that bed, rocking, squeezing just enough to keep us both on the brink of our double descent, "but I must."

.

I always believed in him. But at night my underwater dreams seemed just as true: the dives and twists, the impossible grace and freedom of a lost world. More than once I woke in tears and the feeling lasted for days: a terrible grief and longing to be where I could no longer survive. All I could do then was gaze out to sea, or walk the shore cursing myself for being careless; I yearned for that dense, oily fur, the fat-sheathed musculature beneath. There was no remedy. But if he was gentle, he could ease me back to the pleasures of our life on the island off East Point, where gulls and terns and albatrosses soared and wheeled and plummeted into the water, and the wind blew clean and constant, bending the low grasses and the wildflowers and the few small trees back towards the mainland, and bringing with it the smells of ozone and kelp and emptiness, while all the time the clouds it pushed across the sky stretched and grew and shrank and grew again.

Still surrounded by the sea, I lived on land, a wife of sorts. I practised my letters. I learned how to keep the record. In a single sentence that ran across the width of the book, I must include the weather, any passing vessels, any incidents, and the state of the equipment and supplies. I learned about the winds and Mr Howard's names for the clouds: the veils of cirrostratus, the ominous mounds of cumulonimbus, heavy with rain. I learned how to trim the lamps and clean the parts of lens, how to use the telescope, how to calculate distance, read a chart and judge the course of a ship.

He did explain the camera, yet would not teach me to use it: the apparatus and the process were still in development, he said, the chemicals noxious … More than that, I think, its power was new and excited him to a point that he could not bear to share it. He believed the camera would eventually be able to capture even the subtlest effects of the weather on the sea, and motion itself, but for now, the subject must remain still for minutes on end while the light worked its transformation on the plate. He could not have enough portraits: I posed both with and without clothes, standing, sitting and lolling on the rocks, in the water, walking the beach, on the bed; I posed even while I slept, and was later able to see how soft and peaceful my face appeared when my eyes were closed.

He had a chest of clothing which he said was mine. *All right!* A woman's, at least, he said. Though why? I was comfortable enough in his shirts.

"Just try them," he said. "I want to see." We rifled through and I marvelled at the vast skirts, a boned bodice, at the tiny mother-of-pearl buttons on the placket and sleeves of elaborate shirts patterned with tiny flowers and needle-fine stripes. Everything but the skirts and bloomers looked too small. But the rustle of it all! Such stuff! I tied the corset around my head with a shirt, pulled a pair of drawers over his.

"Like this?"

"Though of course," he said once our laughter subsided, "this is what you will have to wear when Mr Davis visits to make the inspection at the end of the month."

"Really?" I told him, wiping my eyes. "You'll have to show me how."

He reached into the chest and pulled out two small shapeless pieces of fabric.

"For your legs," he explained. "Would you please just try them?"

The material, I later learned, was made from moth cocoons and the finest water-repellent wool of a special breed of sheep; all clothes then were made from beasts and plants. And the stockings did settle lightly on my skin, almost but not quite as if they were part of me. Serious, then, he fetched his camera, set up the stand, then posed me on the bed all but nude, propped up on my elbows, legs akimbo, in such a way that any viewer's gaze would follow the dark lines of my stockinged legs to where my sex, part anemone, part oyster, stretched between the two white strips of upper thigh.

"Don't blink. Stay still," he warned me, the watch ticking in his hand.

And after that, there were yet more photographs. These light pictures, he told me, made by and of the real body, were no mere daubs or imitations or interpretations, but a physical print of sex itself—that raw thing which joined humankind to the beasts, the irrational heart in the thinking machine, the greedy void that hid beneath the skirts of romance, the thing that lodged not just between our legs but also somewhere deep in the brain, hidden in a place which would some day be found and understood ... The century to come, he told me, would be all about seeing the invisible, the interiors of our bodies and minds, the atoms of matter, the surfaces of the moon and stars. Open your legs wider, he said. Touch yourself.

And after all, he decided, it was far better that the inspector did not see me. Let alone the challenge of dressing—her things, whoever she was, did not fit me, a woman still part wild—his neglect in reporting my return would involve too much explanation. The smokehouse was the obvious place for me to hide during the inspection. But it was always possible that just this once Mr Davis would decide to glance in there, or that I might grow restless, peer out of the window as they passed and give us both away ... Did I understand how important discretion was?

Not really, no. Not yet. Any suspicions I had floated too deep to see or really feel; I knew only that something new burned inside him and I did not like it.

Suppose I waited the visit out in the bay at the north end? The inspector would never go there, would not even know such a private spot existed. Or better still, leave me on the mainland—I'd shelter in a cave or bush until it was safe to return ... I do believe the keeper saw the sense of these stratagems, and even wanted to enact them. But he could not. He could not allow me to be beyond his sight and reach.

"Why ask," I said, "if you will not hear what I say?" He caught me by the arm as I turned away; I bit him, drew blood. We fought hard, breathed in grunts as we yanked and twisted, gasping at what the other could inflict, though either we were perfectly matched or neither of us was quite prepared to deliver defeat; our struggle took us to the ground, and there turned blow by blow into its opposite, or else love became a battle; it's hard to say which, and when we woke, bruised and aching in the half-light of a new morning we were shocked at ourselves, terrified, when we realized that we had slept, fucked or fought through changing of the lamps. A strong wind buffeted the tower and though there was no sign of any harm done, we might never know if someone had been misled by the darkness, whether we had done any harm.

We were both overwrought, he said, and offered a tonic: another of his inventions. Just a few drops on the tongue—a sweetness, which soon became metallic. Then a vast, dense fog surrounded and infiltrated me, overwhelmed all my senses; sight, then hearing, touch and smell. I slept so soundly that I could neither move nor cough, but for good measure he tied me and fit me inside a box: I know this only because of the photograph. And shortly after I came to in the watch room, weak, hungry and at the same time nauseated, the birth pangs began to roll through my lower belly and up the insides of my thighs.

He would not seek help. There *was* none, he said.

Limbless, covered in thick fur, her small face arranged around dark, deep eyes like mine, our child was stillborn. I wrapped her and held her close, knew I must return her to the sea and begged him to let me go down to the rocks. "I'll take you," he said, and though his voice was gentle, he was rightly fearful that I might swim away or drown myself. He grasped my hand tight and would not let go as we clambered back from the water's edge.

And perhaps it was to the good, he said, adding syrup and a measure of brandy into hot tea: the same for each of us, and I watched him drink first. The island was no place for a child, he said. Mere breeding was not what free thinkers such as he and I were for.

Free?

He said that he understood that I was sad, that words failed me, but he knew it would pass. And luckily, we had our work for the light, the routine around which all else must be fitted … Winter would come soon, bringing storms. We must eat well, gather back our strength, and put everything in order.

Now he wore the keys at his waist and locked doors behind him. When he was away, I was bound to the bed. And yet I also worked my share, cleaning the panels of the lens, and, when permitted on the windy platform outside the watch room, I scanned the sea for ships. I explored my prison too; I found, folded and tucked into the back of the Bible an article headlined *Tragic Death at East Point*: Two days after the storm of November 3rd, the battered body of the deputy lightkeeper at East Point had been washed up some three miles south of the island, following a failed attempt to launch the lightship craft in order to aid a whaler in distress. The fate of the whaler was still unknown.

A small key at the back of the desk drawer led me to a box containing a single photographic print of a woman who could only be my namesake: she wore the clothes I had handled, and stood against the whitewashed cottage wall, her blonde hair blurring in the breeze. Beneath the photograph was a lock of red-gold hair, and a copy of the signed statement the keeper had submitted the day following the discovery of his colleague's body. *I was sadly mistaken*, he wrote, *in thinking my poor wife cured of an infirmity for which she had in the past been treated. Acting impulsively during a fit of hysterical mania brought on by the storm and feelings of guilt concerning the loss of the deputy, she cast herself into the water while I slept.*

And now the days shortened; flocks of birds passed, returning north across the vastness of the ocean. I said nothing to the keeper, but thought often of Marina, whose body had never been found. Had she loved the deputy keeper, or simply been the object of his affections? I did not like to think of her as drowned, let alone murdered. Did she go into the sea? Perhaps she was like me, but able to return? Had she found her skin? Or did she swim in the awkward human way to the mainland, and make some kind of escape ... Who knew, I told myself, but that she might be living with natives in the bush, or have got so far as the town and have booked her passage out under a new name. Out there on the platform, buffeted by the winds, I breathed in the cold salt air and watched the seabirds, marvelling at the way they stayed together, and at the steady beating of their wings, mile on mile. The largest birds, the mollymawks, pass without apparent movement or effort through the air; their wings fixed, just barely tilting from side to side to ride the currents like waves, they simply turn their heads the way they wish to go ... Such huge birds, the mollies, yet it was as if they had no weight. I watched them slip and soar and it lifted my heart. I longed for the bird-feeling and imagined it: the ocean and the land spread out beneath in intricate detail, but also in depth and with extraordinary focus. In my mind's eye I saw as if from very far above the rocks the island and the tower where I myself stood looking out. The wind blew steadily to the east and the air seemed to offer itself to me. And I would not go back inside, would not endure another night with Clarence Morgan, the clockwork beneath us unwinding itself cog by cog until the next time it must be set, and the next, and the next. Ignoring his call, I climbed onto the rails, balanced for one terror-stricken moment then gave myself to the wind.

Immediately I felt the new strength in my chest and back, the structural dominance of two great limbs.

The water below was almost pink. Just two wing-beats, and I was rising fast. I could no longer hear his call, and did not look back, for the air is a kind of ecstasy, a far freer thing than even a swimmer could believe.

Yet I'll admit that come spring, on my way to the grounds, I did return, and landed on a low cliff to watch my former keeper, on the beach below, set up a new version of his camera. The apparatus was directed at the seals sunning themselves on the rocks. He was thinner and older than I recalled. He had broken his promise not to hurt me, and there was a gun slung over his shoulder which I knew he might use. Yet even so, watching him, I felt for the first time the need to open my wings wide and stretch my neck to its utmost, then tuck my head deep down this way, then that, to stretch and bow and tread out the steps of our dance. A sound came out of me, part shriek, part moan: oh, look at me! For looking is the beginning of the dance. He must see me exactly as I am and what I do, the exact way of it, and I, likewise. And by scrupulous imitation, turn on turn, we come to see better and prove to each other that we see, and what we see. We must show that each can and will exactly follow the other, or, failing, try again…

Hearing me, the keeper turns and reaches for his binoculars. He faces me, but gives no sign of recognition or sympathy. My call dies in my throat; I put myself into the wind, run, and scull hard until the updraft bears me and I ride suddenly without effort and free of the earth's jealous pull; I soar above vast ocean into the even vaster air. I must fly on to the place where I will meet my kind, and find the one with whom I can perfect the dance.

ACKNOWLEDGEMENTS

"The Procedure" by Caroline Adderson was originally published in *The Walrus*, March/April 2022. Reprinted by permission of the author.

"Last Call at the Dogwater Inn" by Kristyn Dunnion was first published in *The New Guard Volume V*, 2016, after winning the Machigonne Fiction Prize, and later appeared in *Stoop City* (Biblioasis, 2020). Reprinted by permission of the publisher.

"Calm" by Cynthia Flood first appeared in *What Can You Do* (Biblioasis, 2017). Reprinted by permission of the publisher.

"The Wolf Expert" by Shaena Lambert first appeared in CNQ 97 and was reprinted in *Best Canadian Stories 2016*. Reprinted by permission of the author.

"Armada" by Elise Levine was first published in *Best Canadian Stories 2016* (Oberon Press) and later appeared in *This Wicked Tongue* (Biblioasis, 2019). Reprinted by permission of the publisher.

"Low Tide" by Kathy Page first appeared in *Paradise & Elsewhere* (Biblioasis, 2014). Reprinted by permission of the publisher.

NOTE ON THE EDITOR

I worked with Tim and Elke Inkster as general editor of The Porcupine's Quill for seventeen years and I'm now entering my twentieth year as a fiction editor for Dan Wells at Biblioasis. I have edited books by all the writers represented in *Off the Record* and all have been a delight to work with.

I can no longer pretend I am middle-aged and so, in my dotage, I have returned to my own fiction and am happily deeply engaged in a novella called *Lekythoi* which will be the final story in the saga of Forde, misunderstood writer of near-genius, a fiction figure some claim to be my alter ego. I would dispute this claim as verging on slander.

One of my favourite writers is Kyril Bonfiglioli. *His* "Note on the Author" in his novel *Don't Point that Thing at Me* reads:

> By an odd coincidence Kyril Bonfiglioli is about the same height and weight as Charlie Mortdecai, [the novel's protagonist] is also an art dealer and has similar tastes and talents but there the resemblance ends, for he has never killed anyone in his life. On the other hand, he is still only 43.
>
> He is a Balliol man, of course, lives in the country, is more or less unmarried and has not recently counted his children…
>
> He is loved and respected by all who know him slightly.

Now *there's* an author for you!

JOHN METCALF
Ottawa, September 2023